Mark Forsyth

A SINGLE
Voice

$\mathscr{A}$ SINGLE *Voice*

The Unexpected Life Is No Less a Life

KRISTEN M. OAKS

DESERET
BOOK

SALT LAKE CITY, UTAH

Library of Congress Cataloging-in-Publication Data

Oaks, Kristen McMain.
  A single voice / Kristen McMain Oaks.
    p. cm.
  ISBN-13: 978-1-59038-859-4 (pbk.)
  1. Single people—Religious life. 2. Single people—Conduct of life.
3. Christian life—Mormon authors. 4. The Church of Jesus Christ of
Latter-day Saints—Doctrines. 5. Mormon Church—Doctrines. I. Title.
  BX8643.S55O25 2007
  248.8'4—dc22   2007045765

Printed in the United States of America
Worzalla Publishing Co., Stevens Point, WI

10   9   8   7   6   5   4   3   2   1

CONTENTS

CONTENTS

PREFACE

This is not simply a book about being single. It is a book about being alone and walking by faith. It is a book about discovery and developing inner strength and courage and deciding what we really cherish and believe. It is not a book about being discounted and discouraged.

At some time in our lives, single or married, we will all be alone and dependent on only ourselves and our Heavenly Father. We will experience emotions and feelings and challenges and joys that only come individually. How we choose to respond is up to us.

The spectrum of single members in The Church of Jesus Christ of Latter-day Saints is immense. What does a giddy and eager twenty-year-old have in common with a forty-five-year-old widowed sister with three children? How does a young divorcee relate to a never-married sixty-five-year-old sister? The common link among single members—among all members of this Church—is a devoted and growing belief in our Lord and Savior, Jesus Christ and His promises to us.

I wrote this book at the urging of my husband. In addition to his service in a wide range of employment and Church callings, he is a son, a father, and a grandfather. He was reared by a widowed mother, and he has experienced the loss of a loving wife and the ensuing loneliness. Since our marriage, he has watched me make the transition from single woman to wife. His personal and Church experiences have given him unusual insights into the lives of single people. He felt a need for a book focusing on this subject.

I believe that single individuals need the Church and that the Church needs the testimonies and talents of its single members. The mission of The Church of Jesus Christ of Latter-day Saints is better fulfilled when all of its members are working to build the kingdom of God. My life and the lives of other single individuals have been greatly blessed as a result of active involvement in Church service. The gospel is "good news" and "glad tidings" for all of us, regardless of age, language, nationality, or marital status.

In addition to my own experiences, I have drawn on the adventures (both happy and challenging) of many of my single friends. This book presents slices from the lives of single persons of varying levels of maturity who face very different challenges. The only consistent factor is faith in Jesus Christ and a willingness to make and keep covenants. This book is about the acquisition of that faith—and ultimately how that faith provides meaning, security, and joy—in giving voice and purpose to a single life.

ACKNOWLEDGMENTS

*T*his book took a lifetime to live and six years to put on paper. I wish to thank the many people who inspired and contributed to its contents. Only a few are named here.

For stories, wisdom, and quotations I am grateful to Brittany H. Anderson, Julie B. Beck, Donna Lee Bowen Barnes, Laurie Beardall, Ed Borrell, Emily Brooks, Linda Charney, Debbie J. Christensen, Carol Clark, Linda Doyle, Elizabeth Duran, Marjorie Gerratt, Jan Hemming, Marjorie P. Hinckley (deceased), Ann G. Hyde, Vicky Javids, Jill Jones (deceased), Kathy Kinney, Suzan Lake, Cathryn Manning, Bonnie Parkin, Allyn Rogers, Christine Skelton, Susan Sterzer, Kris Stone, Stephanie Tanner, Shari Taylor, Patrice Tew, Wendy Ulrich, and Annie Vernon. Their words of wisdom provided depth and clarity to the principles taught.

To all those who worked with the Young Single Adults and guided me: Marcia Bean, Daryl and Hank Hoole, and Russell Skousen. I appreciate your insights and understanding.

To the many young women who gathered around my table and shared their feelings and experience I give special thanks: Linda

Marie Beitler, Britni Brewer Bigelow, Jennifer Elggren Van Orden, Renée Greenburg, Tali May, Nicole Parker, Angela Shields, Jocelyn Sparks, and Rebecca Whitney.

I am also grateful for the noble and valiant influence of sisters: Veronica Bertone, Margot Butler, Jenny Cuthbert, Dini Hansma, Diane Higginson, Susan Jensen, Barbara Lockhart, Veronica Manantan, Cécile Pelous, Stella H. Oaks, Lennie Pilabello, Lucille Sargent, Linda Suda, Edna Suda, Abbie Telliani, and Lea Tesaluna.

To readers and editors for their opinions and help: Melissa Beck, Jan Liad, Kristen Olsen, Emily Snyder, Sidni Taylor, and Ann Marie Toone.

To my visiting teachers, who encouraged me: Lia Davis and JoAnn Nelson.

To my family, whose input and ideas and support were of great help: TruAnn Boulter, Margot Dixon, Jean Ekins, Amanda M. Holbrook, Sarah Thompson Johnson, Portia Mandel, Linda Lundgren, Margaret P. McMain, William A. McMain, Evelyn O. Moody, Dallin D. Oaks, Kristie Oaks, Lucy R. Park, Kate M. Park, Heather P. Ward, Sharmon O. Ward, and Stephani Ward Steelman.

To Margie McKnight for her choice additions and constant making of copies.

To Jim McKean and Dave Madsen, who kept our computer functioning.

To dear Jana Erickson, who helped me keep going, and to Suzanne Brady for her understanding heart, meticulous editing abilities, and spiritual vision. To Richard Erickson, art director, for a beautiful cover and layout, and to Tonya-Rae Facemyer and Rachael Ward for their professional typography.

I give extra special thanks to Sharon Pritchett and Mary Kay Stout for the many hours of editing and shared ideas and to my husband, who was my cheerleader, editor, support, and best friend.

INTRODUCTION

I have a vested interest in single adults because I spent so much of my life as a single woman. My name is Kristen Meredith McMain Oaks. I married Elder Dallin H. Oaks when I was almost fifty-three years old, long after everyone in my family had given up hope I would ever marry anyone. My sisters told me after our marriage that they had believed all marriage opportunities had passed me by. What did not pass me by, however, were the wonderful years I spent as a single woman and an active member of The Church of Jesus Christ of Latter-day Saints. I rejoiced during these years, and I suffered through them, too, while I was discovering what Heavenly Father wanted for me—He was blessing me with adequate time and experience to build a solid and sure testimony.

Being alone is never easy, but being single in The Church of Jesus Christ of Latter-day Saints is a unique challenge because our Church is a family-centered Church. We live to be with our families eternally.

"The message of the Restoration of the gospel of Jesus Christ blesses families. Because of the Restoration we understand God's

1

purpose for families: 'The divine plan of happiness enables family relationships to be perpetuated beyond the grave. Sacred ordinances and covenants available in holy temples make it possible for individuals to return to the presence of God and for families to be united eternally' ('The Family: A Proclamation to the World,' *Ensign,* Nov. 1995, 102)."[1]

When you know your eternal purpose, nothing is more frustrating or disheartening than being unable to achieve it. I prayed and wished and begged the Lord for an eternal family. I wept and wasted time and mourned for such a family. I ultimately realized that I had to begin to live to have such a family, that everything I did as a single woman would dramatically influence the blessings I hoped so deeply to receive. The Lord was always there for me. He supplied direction and comfort and revelation, and He protected me. For that I am eternally thankful. Every one of us, married or single, must prepare individually to return to our Heavenly Father.

I am writing this book for those who are currently making their life's journey alone—single, divorced, or widowed. I did not learn everything about single life, but I learned enough to share. I sometimes learned more than I wished to about being alone, about waiting for blessings, about using time, and about trusting in my Heavenly Father. I discovered that the journey could be just as hard or as easy as we determine it to be. In retrospect, I see that the purpose of my journey was to cultivate faith and to develop personal testimony.

Faith is trust. Faith in God is trust in God, and that includes trust in His timing. My favorite teaching on that subject was given by my husband a year after our marriage. The setting was a meeting with missionaries in Manaus, in the rubber-rich jungles of northern Brazil. Pushing aside his prepared notes, Elder Oaks followed the Spirit in teaching the missionaries that they could not plan their lives. Afterward, he sat down beside me, surprised even at himself, and whispered, "I wonder why I said that." We came to understand all too well the following week, on September 11, 2001, as we ate our breakfast bowls of cornflakes and watched the destruction of the World Trade Center towers and the attack on the Pentagon. Our world would never again be as certain or secure. It became a world where, to keep composure and direction, we needed to trust even more completely in our Heavenly Father.

Elder Oaks refined and repeated his talk on timing in a Brigham Young University devotional six months later. Key paragraphs from that talk are quoted here:

"In all the important decisions in our lives, what is most important is to *do the right thing.* Of almost equal importance is to *do the right thing at the right time.* People who do the right thing at the wrong time can be frustrated and ineffective. They can even be confused about whether they made the right choice when what was wrong was not their choice but their timing.

"My first point on the subject of timing is that the Lord has His own timetable. 'My words are sure and shall not fail,' the Lord taught the early elders of this dispensation. 'But,' He continued, 'all things must come to pass in their time' (D&C 64:31–32).

"The first principle of the gospel is faith in the Lord Jesus Christ. Faith means trust—trust in God's will, trust in His way of doing things, and trust in His timetable. We should not try to impose our timetable on Him. As Elder Neal A. Maxwell has said:

"'The issue for us is trusting God enough to trust also His timing. If we can truly believe He has our welfare at heart, may we not let His plans unfold as He thinks best? The same is true with the second coming and with all those matters wherein our faith needs to include faith in the Lord's timing for us personally, not just in His overall plans and purposes.'

"Elder Maxwell later added, 'Since faith in the timing of the Lord may be tried, let us learn to say not only, "Thy will be done," but patiently also, "Thy timing be done."' Indeed, we cannot have true faith in the Lord without also having complete trust in His will and in His timing.

"... In our service in the Lord's church we should remember that *when* is just as important as *who, what, where,* and *how....*

"We prepare in the way the Lord has directed. We hold ourselves in readiness to act on the Lord's timing. He will tell us when the time is right to take the next step. For now, we simply concentrate on our own assignments and on what we have been asked to do today. In this we are also mindful of the Lord's assurance: 'I will hasten my work in its time' (D&C 88:73)....

"The achievement of some important goals in our lives is subject to more than the timing of the Lord. Some personal achievements are also subject to the agency of others. This is particularly evident in two matters of special importance to young people—missionary baptisms and marriage....

"For example, we cannot be sure that we will marry as soon as we desire. A marriage that is timely in our view may be our blessing or it may not. My wife, Kristen, is an example. She did not marry until many years after her mission and her graduation.

"The timing of marriage is perhaps the best example of an extremely important event in our lives that is almost impossible to plan. Like other important mortal events that depend on the agency of others or the will and timing of the Lord, marriage cannot be anticipated or planned with certainty. Latter-day Saints can and should work for and pray for their righteous desires, but despite their efforts, many will remain single well beyond their desired time for marriage.

"So what should be done in the meantime? Faith in the Lord Jesus Christ prepares us for whatever life brings. Faith in Christ prepares us to deal with life's opportunities—to take advantage of those we receive and to persist through the disappointment of those we lose. In the exercise of that faith we should commit ourselves to the priorities and standards we will follow on matters we do not control, and we should persist faithfully in those commitments whatever happens to us because of the agency of others or the timing of the Lord. When we do this, we will have constancy in our lives that will give us direction and peace. Whatever the circumstances beyond our control, our commitments and standards can be constant. . . .

"Wise are those who make this commitment: *I will put the Lord first in my life, and I will keep His commandments.* The performance of that commitment is within everyone's control. We can fulfill that commitment without regard to what others decide to do, and that commitment will anchor us no matter what timing the Lord directs for the most important events in our lives.

"Do you see the difference between committing to what *you will do,* in contrast to trying to plan that you will be married by the time you graduate from college or that you will earn at least X amount of dollars on your first job?

"If we have faith in God and if we are committed to the fundamentals of keeping His commandments and putting Him first in our lives, we do not need to plan every single event—even every important event—and we should not feel rejected or depressed if some things—even some very important things—do not happen at the time we had planned or hoped or prayed for them to happen.

"Commit yourself to put the Lord first in your life, keep His commandments, and do what the Lord's servants ask you to do. Then your feet are on the pathway to eternal life. Then it does not matter whether you are called to be a bishop or a Relief Society president, whether you are married or single, or whether you die tomorrow. You do not know what will happen. Do your best and then trust in the Lord and His timing.

"Life has some strange turns. Some of my personal experiences illustrate this. . . .

" . . . after I had completed my service as president of Brigham Young University . . . the governor of the state of Utah appointed me to a ten-year term on the state supreme court. I was then forty-eight years old. My wife, June, and I tried to plan the rest of our lives. We wanted to serve the full-time mission neither of us had been privileged to serve. We planned that I would serve twenty years on the state supreme court. Then, at the end of two ten-year terms, when I would be nearly sixty-nine years old, I would retire from the supreme court and we would submit our missionary papers and serve a mission as a couple.

"I had my sixty-ninth birthday in the summer of 2001 and was vividly reminded of that important plan. If things had gone as we had planned, I would now be submitting papers to serve a mission with my wife June.

"Four years after we made that plan I was called to the Quorum of the Twelve Apostles—something we never dreamed would happen. Realizing then that the Lord had different plans and different timing than we had assumed, I resigned as a justice of the supreme court. But this was not the end of the important differences. When I was sixty-six, June died of cancer. Two years later, I married Kristen McMain, the eternal companion who now stands at my side.

"How fundamentally different my life is than I had sought to plan! My professional life has changed. My personal life has changed. But the commitment I made to the Lord—to put Him first in my life and to be ready for whatever He would have me do—has carried me through these changes of eternal importance. . . .

"Do not rely on planning every event of your life—even every important event. Stand ready to accept the Lord's planning and the agency of others in matters that inevitably affect you. Plan, of course, but fix your planning on personal commitments that will carry you through no matter what happens. Anchor your life to eternal principles, and act upon those principles whatever the circumstances and whatever the actions of others. Then you can await the Lord's timing and be sure of the outcome in eternity."[2]

PART ONE

The Single Dilemma

CHAPTER 1

MY SINGLE YEARS

*I remember feeling many times that I was just marking time,
waiting for my life to happen.*

I belong to The Church of Jesus Christ of Latter-day Saints in the
final days before the Savior returns to this earth to rule and reign.
There could be no better and more eventful time in which to live. It
is a time when all the great and terrible events foretold in the scriptures will come to pass. It is a time of great adventure, a time to be
valiant, a time to rejoice, a time to testify, a time to join in the battle
for goodness and right. So much was taking place around me, and
yet I was struggling just to get started—I was a single sister in the
Lord's army, and I was still seeking to find my place. On occasion
my experience was similar to sitting around waiting to receive my
uniform before I could enter the war.

Elder Jeffrey R. Holland has written of living our lives in these
last days. His words rang especially true to me because I often waited
in uncertainty about the direction my life would take, not realizing
how much control I held over that direction and over my own personal happiness.

"We must not be paralyzed just because [the Second Coming]
and the events surrounding it are ahead of us somewhere. We

cannot stop living life. Indeed, we should live life more fully than we have ever lived it. After all, this is the dispensation of the *fulness* of times."[1]

Although, as Elder Holland suggests, we are living in the "greatest of all dispensations," as a single woman I remember feeling many times that I was just marking time, waiting for my life to happen. I had to learn to make it happen. In my early twenties my life was not progressing confidently in the direction I had envisioned for myself. In fact, it seemed not to be progressing at all. I did graduate from college. I did teach school. I did buy a car. But I was waiting for my life to happen. I was afraid to develop myself too much because somehow I mistakenly believed that I might make myself unattractive to a prospective husband. In reality, maintaining the status quo was making me unhappy. President James E. Faust cautioned single members, "Being single does not mean you have to put off being happy."[2]

I wanted to be happy. I wanted to be content. I looked to examples in my life, to the scriptures, to literature, and to the words of the living prophets to help me. Looking at sisters around me, those who were happy and fulfilled, I began to notice that their happiness had nothing to do with their marital status. It is so important for singles to integrate themselves in a married community at church and with family to maintain an eternal and balanced perspective.

In her novel *The Face of a Stranger,* Anne Perry, herself a single, faithful Latter-day Saint woman, writes words that had significance to me. She writes of Hester, who is fast approaching age thirty, and the advice given her: " 'Do I detect a note of self-pity, Hester? . . . You will have to learn to conquer that. . . . Too many women waste their lives grieving because they do not have something other people tell them they should want. Nearly all married women will tell you it is a blessed state, and you are to be pitied for not being in it. That is arrant nonsense. Whether you are happy or not depends to some degree upon outward circumstances, but mostly it depends on how you choose to look at things yourself, whether you measure what you have or what you have not.'"[3]

President Harold B. Lee gave similar advice: "Happiness does not depend on what happens outside of you but on what happens inside of you; it is measured by the spirit with which you meet the problems of life."[4]

I realized that I had to go forward with my life. In my late twenties, I began a major identity check. My dreams of having a husband and family were not coming true and looked as if they would never come true. After a crushing breakup with a longtime high school boyfriend, I realized the identity I expected for myself as a stay-at-home mother was not going to be: no children and no one to support me financially, emotionally, or physically. This was an incredibly heart-wrenching time for me. It was heart-wrenching because I had not prepared for it or even anticipated it. This was not the life I had expected, and I had no plan of action to accommodate it.

Many can relate to this who have had their plan for life shattered by a divorce, by a death, by a disappointment, or by a major betrayal. We need a period of time to heal and to regroup. In my case, I was given help in the form of a dear friend, Donna Lee Bowen. She is a tenacious visionary and has great determination to get things done. She was merciless. She told me to get on with my life and make something of it. She saw more potential in me than I saw in myself, and she helped me have the courage to try new things.

The reality hit me that I had no real skills to support myself. My studies in English literature had fed my soul, but now I needed to feed my pocketbook. I attended graduate school to learn a skill so I could support myself, and then I just kept going to school because no one stopped me by marrying me. More than that, I loved every minute of learning and discovered not only new ideas but also my own capabilities. Where I had felt shy and somewhat incapable, I now felt I could function. The fear that I could not support myself left me, and I became excited and even intoxicated with my occupation. I earned a master's degree and ultimately a doctorate in education. The great blessings from all this experience were the things I learned that would help me so much as a mother. (See chapter 3, "Single Switch Points.")

I continued to pray and ask for direction from Heavenly Father. Spiritually, I am a late bloomer. Slowly, ever so slowly, spiritual things unfolded in my life and came to serve as the foundation of my life. I came to know revelation is real. At age twenty-six, I went on a mission and learned Japanese. I also learned a new depth of commitment to Heavenly Father. I learned to persist—by going door to door in monsoon weather, by eating chicken skin and seaweed, and by being told by people looking me directly in the face that no one was home. The truths of the gospel became truer to me as I declared them to others. Truths do distill upon us, a drop at a time. To this day, whenever I walk down a busy street, I look at the people passing by, think how the gospel could bless their lives, and want to tell everyone of its truth. That mission laid the groundwork for my life.

Life was not perfect, but I was going forward. Work became a blessing to me. I moved from the classroom to consulting. Heavenly Father provided so many opportunities for me. The Lord kept directing me to opportunities where I could grow and contribute and find happiness.

There were also many hours alone. At times I felt quite content and occupied; at other times I felt actual physical pain. In fact, at times the pain was debilitating. Being alone was not fun for me. Everyone is different; we all have differing needs and desires.

My great love is children. My sisters were generous in allowing me to take care of my nieces and nephews. I felt my time with them was more than just a travel opportunity or time to play. It was the "sacred, noble stewardship" Elder M. Russell Ballard described to teachers and leaders of children because "we are the ones . . . to encircle today's children with love and the fire of faith and an understanding of who they are."[5]

We prayed together, visited Temple Square, and had walks and talks. I attended their baptisms, Primary programs, and sacrament meeting talks. We also had sleepovers and went to plays, museums, carnivals, car washes, libraries, and bookstores. We cooked and we swam and we played. We did school projects together. We visited Nauvoo, Illinois; Gettysburg, Pennsylvania; and Park City, Utah. I was available for every school project and activity. Homework became my specialty; I fear I sometimes gave too much help. The Lord blessed me with a wonderful family, and I stayed close to them and had the privilege of nurturing them.

This time with the children in my family brought me great joy and contentment, and it also provided me with experience—experience that would later benefit me as a wife, a mother of six, and a grandmother of twenty-nine.

The more I devoted myself to the gospel, the richer my life became. I believe that is Heavenly Father's plan. Service and activity in this Church enrich our lives. All those years of cooking for Young Women parties, planning Primary activities, and making Christmas wreaths at Relief Society Enrichment meetings began paying unexpected dividends. I learned domestic skills and, more important, the Lord put me in contact with noble Church members of varying ages. The Church community provided me with experiences that would bless me for my future family life. It was like practicing in a flight simulator. I learned how to calm screaming babies, to instruct children, to interact with priesthood holders, to support the priesthood, to conduct meetings, to counsel, to cooperate, and to be part of a group—skills that are integral to family life.

Many times living a happy and contented life was a day-to-day challenge. Daily small acts of faith strengthened my relationship with

Heavenly Father. I was more valiant some days than others, but I persisted because I so much desired His Spirit to be with me. I prayed and He answered. I read the scriptures and came to understand His doctrine. I attended the temple to serve and to receive revelation. I was protected by these small acts. Just as Elder L. Tom Perry promised, "The discipline contained in daily obedience and clean living and wholesome lives builds an armor around you of protection and safety from the temptations that beset you as you proceed through mortality."[6]

By age fifty-two I lived alone, had my own condominium, had a terrific job working for a prestigious publishing house, and had just purchased a new SUV. My employment as a national and international educational consultant who trained teachers to teach reading was purposeful and rewarding. For me, teaching reading and doing missionary work are on a similar plane because they unlock a beautiful world of possibilities and understanding for those we teach. This work also provided me with all the perks of travel—from free tickets to Marriott points. I worked hard, and when I played, a world of possibilities opened to me: Boston for a visit with a friend or Disneyworld with my nephews. I loved my Church callings. I was the Gospel Doctrine teacher in a home ward I dearly loved, surrounded by great friends and leaders. My parents were still living, and my sisters were my best friends. Life was good.

As the years went by, I began to believe less and less that I would marry in this life. I never doubted the Lord and my patriarchal blessing that I would have my husband and family but maybe not while I lived on this earth and on my timetable. I remember friends saying, "If you just give up hope and turn it over to the Lord, it will happen." This caused me to wonder if I had given up enough hope.

In fact, I trusted the Lord. I had complete faith that He knew who was best for me and that He also knew the time that was best for me. That trust helped me avoid much pain and anguish. Many older singles will identify with me when I say I accepted my situation, and it was fine with me. The Lord had blessed me with a full and happy single life. But I never gave up the desire to marry or the hope that it would happen.

I never had the goal to marry an Apostle. My goal was to draw close to Heavenly Father and make my life as meaningful and happy as I could. Because I value and believe in the plan of salvation, I wanted all the blessings associated with it. That included someday, in this life or the next, finding a companion that I loved and respected, a man I could trust and depend on, who would be loyal to me and active in the Church. I wanted to marry a man who loved the Lord more than he loved me, whose allegiance was to His eternal covenants. It would simply follow that such a man would be true to me and our future family.

Pivotal Experiences

The Blessing

I look back on small pivotal choices (though as I experienced them, they did not seem pivotal) that were to have great effect on my future marriage. Every one of these decisions was based on my adherence to gospel principles and my obedience to promptings of the Spirit. Over years of time and with repeated efforts, I learned to listen to the promptings of the still, small voice, and those promptings blessed my life.

A time came in my life at age fifty-two when I had to make a major life decision. As a consultant who traveled constantly, I earned a generous salary. I had many travel perks but few time perks. In fact, I often left late Sunday evening and returned home Friday night. My only social life occurred in this narrow weekend window of time. I spent my spare moments almost exclusively with my family and in church. Each weekend when I returned from assignments, I drove directly from the airport to pick up my nieces and nephews, and they stayed with me. Saturday I prepared my Gospel Doctrine lesson late into the night and taught it the next morning. Then on Sunday evening I would depart again for work.

It was a difficult time in my life because I wore "golden hand-cuffs." Whenever I wished to quit my job, it became more lucrative. Most of my life, energy, and time were going to my employment. Concerned and feeling unable to change my life, I asked my bishop for a blessing. He blessed me. What he said was specific to me, and I do not advise you to do what I did unless you are likewise counseled in a blessing. I only advise you to be obedient to the promptings you feel for yourself. In that blessing my bishop told me, "If you do not quit your job, you will have your blessings in the eternities but not in this life." When I heard his words, I felt the truth of them. I had to stop traveling and find employment at home. For a single sister, giving up financial security is no easy thing. I had no new job to go to. I had to go on faith to resign from my job.

After this blessing I went home and prayed for guidance and strength. It was a very fearful and uncertain time for me. I believed the bishop's words, but I had to believe them enough to act on them. "If you believe all these things see that ye do them" (Mosiah 4:10). If I had not had more than thirty adult years of trying to obey my priesthood leaders, to trust in their advice, and to believe that the counsel they offered was inspired, I would not have had enough personal strength to resign from my job. Anyone who supports herself and has house and car payments can understand. Anyone who has left longtime employment and security to serve the Lord can empathize. Considering resigning from a career into which I had invested nearly twenty years was no small thing for me. I had seldom applied for employment; I had nearly always been approached by others. This time no one was calling with a job offer. I had the prospect of living off my savings while working for minimum wage.

Looking back, I realize it was pivotal that I trusted in and acted on the blessing given me. I decided I had to stop relying on "the arm of flesh" (2 Nephi 4:34) and on my own wisdom. I determined to do what the Lord had told me to do in the blessing. In January 2000 I began writing letters of resignation; I had a wastebasket full. I wrote and rewrote the letter to Human Resources multiple times. Finally I wrote a letter clear enough that no one could doubt my intention to resign. I gave notice and planned to leave on July 1, 2000. It was not until six months later that I learned that my future husband, at the prodding of his eldest daughter, Sharmon, was to commence his search for a wife in that very month.

The Trial

Friends and family questioned my actions. After I wrote my letter of resignation, I jokingly told friends, "I want to stay home and fold socks and clean the house." One man at church said to me, "Oh, Kristen, with all your skills, you want to do more than be a nanny!" He did not share my vision of a future husband and family, but his evaluation of my new job activities would prove partially accurate.

After I gave notice of my resignation, the company increased my workload and responsibilities. I have never traveled farther nor worked longer hours. I felt frail and began to worry about my health. When I returned home, I stayed up and studied into the early morning hours to prepare for my Gospel Doctrine class. Travel and work plus Church responsibilities began to seem almost overwhelming. My workload became so heavy I questioned if I could do it all. I also knew that teaching the Sunday School class, especially preparing for it, was blessing my life and feeding my spirit. I remember exerting every bit of physical effort I had to keep teaching my class. I needed the Spirit more than I needed sleep. I would not give up my calling. I persisted. Only later was I to learn why this calling was so pivotal to me, because through it one class member would eternally bless my association with my future husband (see chapter 5).

I felt tested, not only by circumstances but also by Heavenly Father. My demanding workload and dismal dating life were taking a toll, even though I had always had a strong conviction that everything would turn out well in the end. During that time in my life I remember flying in airplanes and weeping from tiredness. I would turn to my scriptures and find solace. It was a time to help me cement my faith. To complicate matters, at the end of June a competing corporation called to offer me my dream job, which would mean living in New York. I began to wonder which path to follow.

An Answered Prayer

I conferred with a close relative and shared my plans to resign my job. My aunties, hearing at a family luncheon that I was about to become unemployed, arranged an appointment in June with a General Authority who had connections with the publishing business, the field I was just leaving.

This meeting with a General Authority was extremely unusual for me. My exposure to General Authorities had been minimal, and I liked it that way. I had the utmost respect for them. I revered them, but I also understood the line of priesthood jurisdiction and felt confident that my home teachers and my bishop were sufficient to bless my life.

Shortly after my meeting with this General Authority (I do not use his name lest my account brand him as a particularly effective matchmaker), Elder Oaks phoned him and asked if he knew someone he should get to know as part of his search for a wife. I was promptly lined up to meet him. Elder Oaks's immediate phone call to me created a few daunting circumstances: he wanted to bring his daughter Sharmon to meet me before she left town the next day. I did not tell him I had just had a permanent and needed to cover my head. We decided on a walk in Liberty Park. When I met my future husband and his daughter, I was wearing Levi's and a baseball cap (to hide my curls) for our walk.

Looking back, I would never have planned to meet an Apostle of the Lord and his daughter dressed so casually. But that baseball cap allowed me to just be myself.

Our initial meeting and the conversation that ensued seemed like that of three longtime friends. Elder Oaks told me that he had often taken walks with his wife, June, who had died two years earlier. I asked him to tell me about her. From the beginning we felt calm and relaxed with each other. Sharmon shared much about their family and her mother. We laughed and talked, and our courtship began.

Because Elder Oaks felt that in our dating we should not attend public events together, we began from that day to visit family members, eat with them, take walks, go on picnics, and have ice cream on backyard patios. These activities provided an in-depth opportunity to really learn about each other. It was very sweet, romantic, and low-key. I suggest that if you desire to really get to know someone, spend a good many dates in the company of that person's siblings, parents, or children.

What distinguished my courtship with Elder Oaks was the total peace and assurance I felt that all would be well, whether we married or not. We developed a wonderful friendship, and I came to love his family. Now, much to my delight, they are my family as well.

Looking back on my single years, I am so very thankful for the time I had to learn the gospel, to live the gospel, and to make Heavenly Father my best friend. Time is a dear friend also—it mellows us and matures us. My wish for other singles is that they enjoy each and every day of their life. Now that I am married, I do not feel that I have graduated to a higher plane. I do know that I feel more complete. I know that all we do in life contributes to our future happiness. When I look back on my single life, my only regrets are that I spent too much time worrying about my future and too little time in the kitchen. I would do anything to be able to make better dinner rolls.

CHAPTER 2

THE WORTH OF A SINGLE SOUL

Remember the worth of souls is great in the sight of God.
—Doctrine & Covenants 18:10

*W*e live in challenging times. Sister Patricia Holland said, "Surely there has not been another time in history when women have questioned their self-worth so harshly and critically as in the second half of the twentieth century [and into the twenty-first]. Many women are searching, almost frantically, as never before, for a sense of personal purpose and meaning; and many LDS women are searching too, for eternal insight and meaning in their femaleness."[1]

As we search for personal purpose, the gospel is the solution to our problems and not the cause of our sorrow. As Church members we have specific expectations about what will bring us happiness: marriage, home, and family. When these goals have not been met or even approached, we sometimes lose our eternal perspective and begin to doubt ourselves. Not being married can translate into a feeling of low self-esteem in which many single Latter-day Saints begin to question their own self-worth.

I have observed that feelings of inadequacy can begin at an early age. In our culture, where marriage and family are so highly valued, single people begin to question where they belong and how they can contribute. One of our darling granddaughters at Brigham Young University shared with me, "In the Church culture a man is still considered young at twenty-one, but a woman is considered on her way to being an old maid at age twenty-two." She was starting to feel the pressure of being a potential old maid in her sophomore year of college. That standard seems very young to me.

Our granddaughter is not alone in her observation and feelings. Many single members of the Church feel tormented by their inability to be blessed with marriage and family on what they consider a typical timetable. I know this because the first questions I am asked by singles relate to my fifty-two years alone. "How were you single and happy? What did you do to endure life as a single woman? How did you make it through as a single person? What did you do to make your single life fulfilling?"

My answer is always the same: "Just live the gospel."

How do we deal with a circumstance we never bargained for—and worse, that we never prepared for—that seems to affect all the members of our family and even our standing in society? The answer is simple and yet so often so very hard to achieve: By applying the principles of the gospel and knowing we are precious in the eyes of God, we can attain peace and happiness.

Family Influence

Older single persons often find themselves the center of great attention and affection as loving and caring relatives seek to cajole, humor, goad, and provoke them toward marital union, not realizing the lack of available compatible mates. These efforts are made out of genuine love and concern, but often they only increase our sensitivity to our single condition.

Monica, my neighbor, noted that when her darling older brother turned thirty-five and was not married, her family became nervous. Among Latter-day Saints, not being married becomes a family affair. It isn't enough that singles agonize for themselves, but every relative seems affected by their single state. Mothers are concerned for their daughters and cry for their unborn grandbabies. Fathers become anxious for their daughters with no one to care for them. Men who are single are often interrogated about whom they are dating and how the relationship is going. When someone in a family does not marry, the entire family can become apprehensive for the future of that person. There is a general uneasiness that something is not quite right.

Parents play such an integral part in their children's lives. Their influence and opinion are paramount in the lives of their offspring. The very first sentence of the Book of Mormon testifies of their impact: "I, Nephi, having been born of goodly parents, therefore I was taught somewhat in all the learning of my father" (1 Nephi 1:1).

Nephi had knowledge of the goodness and the mysteries of God because he was taught by goodly parents. Because of his obedience to them and to the knowledge they taught him, he was highly blessed. He sought to honor his parents by living in the manner they taught him, and that included marrying in the covenant. His and other examples of noble and righteous servants continue to influence us.

Perhaps the greatest influence in our lives is that of our own mother and father. Whether our parents' marriages were happy or unhappy, I believe that a sincere desire of their hearts is for their children to achieve happy marriages themselves.

I know from personal experience as a daughter who deeply loves her parents how frustrated and inadequate I felt I was in their eyes because I did not marry in the time that they expected. All my three younger sisters had been married for years before I was. My singleness was only one fact about me, but in my family it seemed to have become the dominant fact. My parents felt my pain and mirrored it back to me and even intensified it—which was never their intention.

Nothing was ever said about my singleness. Quite the opposite, in fact. My parents loved me, included me, gave me gifts, and invited me to dinners and to accompany them on vacations. They would laud my accomplishments and compliment my achievements and notice my clothes. Yet, I sensed an unspoken distress over my future happiness and security. This, in fact, was confirmed when I met my husband. My parents shed tears of relief. They were so comforted by my marriage and not just because my husband is an Apostle. I could have married any righteous man. They just desired for me to have a companion and friend who would watch over me.

Though I was caught up in the delirium of happiness every bride experiences, I was also more than a bit dismayed by their relief because I thought my single life had been quite wonderful. I had supported myself well, I had worked worldwide, I had a life rich in adventure and goodness. There was a part of me that wished they had celebrated and respected my single life as much as I did myself. I did not want them to discount how significant and important that part of my life had been to me.

It was only natural for my parents to have concern for me. Parents in The Church of Jesus Christ of Latter-day Saints are commanded by their Father in Heaven to watch over and instruct their children: "For this shall be a law unto the inhabitants of Zion. . . . And they [parents] shall also teach their children to pray, and to walk uprightly before the Lord" (D&C 68:26–28).

Parents are commanded to teach their children the ways of the Lord so they can govern themselves. The fruits of such faith and living are celestial marriage and family, but sometimes those fruits seem late in coming. They may not come in this life. I would never wish for parents to mourn or worry because a child is not married. I believe parents are not primarily responsible for the marriage of their children, for parenting is done in conjunction with Heavenly Father. Remember how much He loves us and that He is there to help parents with their children.

Sometimes only by letting go of our children do they grow. Sarah, a neighbor, said her older, unmarried son was struggling. She felt that marrying a good young woman was the answer for him. She went to the temple to fast and pray about his struggle. The Spirit whispered to her, "Don't save your son from the consequences of his choices. Let him experience them fully, and it will be all right." She learned the lesson that her adult son was responsible for himself. He is not yet back in the Church, but he is back in reality and paying his credit card bills—a first step toward responsibility.

My father recently passed away, and I think of his influence on my life. When I remember him, I remember that his greatest desire for me was not simply that I marry. He and my mother wished a full, happy, productive life for me, regardless of my circumstances. He taught me about books and travel and respect for those around me. He wanted me to get an education and give back to the community around me. My parents also taught me to enjoy caramel corn, to love my sisters, to laugh often, to work hard, to tell the truth, to serve and love others, and to treat everyone equally. I had wonderful parents.

Many are not so lucky; they grow up in situations where demonstrable love and trust are not part of their childhood. But our experiences, positive or negative, do not have to keep us from building a happy marriage.

The greatest expectation of our Heavenly Father is that parents teach their children to love and honor Him. The Lord is pleased with our devotion to Him, no matter what our marital status. That belief is confirmed to me by the following scripture: "For my soul delighteth in the song of the heart; yea, the song of the righteous is a prayer unto me, and it shall be answered with a blessing upon their heads" (D&C 25:12). The Lord doesn't say only good singers or opera performers please Him; He gives His promise to "the righteous." The quality of our faith and the condition of our hearts are what is important, whether we are married or not. Our real worth is as children of a Heavenly Father who loves us.

Even if we are converts to the Church and came to know these doctrines as single adults later in life, that is fine. The important thing is that we embrace the knowledge that we are children of a God who knows us and loves us.

With a knowledge of the fullness of the gospel, we can have complete confidence that our Heavenly Father and Jesus Christ will watch over us. They offer the ultimate in care and protection. Following the commandments ensures our safety beyond any protection offered by the arm of flesh. As members of the Church we have to remember that and make it a reality in our lives, especially as we move into a turbulent future. Alone or married, we can make it with the help of our loving Heavenly Father.

A mother who watched her daughter, a never-married young woman of thirty, becoming discouraged and bitter over her single state, asked me for counsel. The mother confided, "I have been telling her she will receive her blessings if she is just patient. I want to counsel her with truth, and I am just not ready to tell her she may not marry."

I told the mother, "Listen to your daughter and try to understand her feelings. Tell her that all will be well and to never give up hope. Our responsibility is just to do our part. The Lord is going to give us the life that is best for us. One way or the other, it is not going to be easy."

During a seminar I met another concerned mother and her lovely single daughter in her mid-thirties. The mother shared with me that male relatives in the family were almost insistent that this young woman was denying herself marriage because she was simply too picky about a prospective husband. The mother told me privately, "I would worry about her too except she is so devout and steady and righteous. She reads her scriptures, prays, does service, attends the temple, and is active in the Church. She is just the perfect daughter. I believe she is close to the Spirit and is making correct decisions."

The mother asked me, "What do you think? Did other opportunities present themselves to you? How did you wait? How did you know whom to marry?"

My reply to her is the reply I would make to every single person: Follow the Spirit. Marriage is the most important covenant you will ever make. When I seriously considered others before I met my husband, something always obstructed the relationship; it somehow wouldn't work. When I prayed and fasted in other situations, sometimes I felt nothing, sometimes I felt confused, and sometimes I felt overcome with sadness. With those other dating opportunities, I always felt I would be settling for someone not completely right for me—even if he was a wonderful individual. When I met and began dating Elder Oaks, it was a most peaceful and pleasant experience. It was not hard or traumatic. I loved him and respected him. You should only consider marriage with someone that you love and respect with all your heart. Anything less will be inadequate eternally.

Never let the opinions and pressure put on you by others unduly influence your choice of a marriage partner. The most important choice we make in eternity is whom we marry. Elder Bruce R. McConkie said it so memorably: "I believe that the most important single thing that any Latter-day Saint ever does in this world is to marry the right person, in the right place, by the right authority; and that then—when they have been so sealed by the power and authority which Elijah the prophet restored—the most important remaining thing that any Latter-day Saint can ever do is so to live that the terms and conditions of the covenant thus made will be binding and efficacious now and forever."[2] That choice is personal and sacred.

External and Internal
Pressure to Marry

The reality exists that we live in a time when it is the norm to be unmarried. According to the United States Census Bureau, 95.7 million Americans are single or unmarried. Of females in that group, 63 percent are women who have never been married. Another 23 percent are divorced, and 14 percent are widowed.[3]

As the population of unmarried people grows, their commercial worth increases, and they become a target for worldly enterprises. We are told as women that we can have it all. The expectations go far beyond a husband and family. Women today are told that to be truly of worth they should pursue a graduate degree and a professional career and undergo liposuction. Advertisements beckon us to become sleeker, softer, and more seductive. The call of many voices can become confusing. The standard only goes higher on how we should look, act, and enjoy our lives. There is a pervasive idea that what we have makes us important.

Scott C. Marsh, part-time faculty member at the BYU Marriott School of Management, points out that we live in a materialistic society where we gauge our happiness by what we have. In a survey on happiness in the United States, participants stated they were happiest when they had more than their closest family members or nearest neighbors. The more things they owned that could be seen or observed by others, the better they felt they were doing, and that made them happy.[4]

I contend that this way of measuring also seems to apply to our marital status: somehow marriage is seen by others as making it to adulthood and having more. Those who are not married seem somehow deprived. We will never be happy if we buy into a worldly idea that our worth is dependent on external achievements or possessions.

The result of this perception is that women begin to question everything about themselves. Instead of gratitude, there is a mentality of scarcity. I found that my sense of loneliness increased when I didn't concentrate on my many blessings. We can develop a profound sense of gratitude.

Unsolicited Advice

Single members need to exert faith and a strong sense of self to withstand comments made to them. We need to depend on our divine knowledge of who we are to get us through.

Someone told me of a friend who joined the Church at age twenty-eight. She is successful, outgoing, and attractive. She loves the Church and believes its teachings with all her heart. During a discussion over lunch she and our mutual friend spoke of the future. The new convert said that in five years if she is not married, she might become less active. My friend was stunned and asked, "If you have a firm testimony of this gospel and believe it with all your heart, how can you say that?"

The convert's reply was that when she joined the Church, she felt she was a fully functioning, capable adult. She was only twenty-eight, and the years ahead seemed full of potential and happiness. As Church members fellowshipped her and learned of her single status, they would comment, "Don't worry, you're still young. You'll be okay." Their continual comments made her worry. She had come into the Church feeling okay about herself, but now she was beginning to doubt her worth and her future. She wondered if she really had a place or could make a contribution as a single member.

She is not alone. Often the problem of singleness is compounded by well-meaning friends and family members who offer unsolicited advice. (I refer to this advice often because so much is given so abundantly and generously to singles.) The range of suggestions varies from wearing more mascara to losing weight to attending more multistake activities to looking into good retirement plans. Suggestions meant to soothe often cause hurt feelings to fester.

One letter I received from a single sister laments the unwanted advice given her: "Every Sunday while at church I am bombarded with advice, comments, and chats and am reminded of how, until I am married, I am a handicap to the Lord's plan. This incessant bombardment of 'good intentions' leads nonmarried individuals to believe they are without value within the Church, the gospel, and the plan."

I too received much advice, and many times this attention made me doubt myself. I began to wonder what was wrong with me because I was not finding my celestial companion, no matter how much I dated, read my scriptures, lost weight, or prayed. I felt that something must be incredibly wrong with me. This thought was often verified by others around me who asked why I was single. In fact, one counselor in a bishopric of my ward often assured me that I would have my blessings in the next life. I wanted my blessings, and I wanted them now. His words were so disturbing to me that I sometimes imagined myself grabbing him by the necktie and commanding him never to say them again. His words were meant to comfort me but instead only reminded me of how far away my blessings seemed.

One divorced friend, Kathy, described what the wait for a new husband meant to her: "I said to you that I do not believe that men love women because that is easier for me to believe than the other conclusion I can draw—that men do not love me. I suspect you can see how a generalization is less devastating. I have considered why marriage matters so much (besides the commandment and having children). I have come to the conclusion that women believe marriage is proof that they have worth. It is the ultimate game of choosing sides for teams. It is hard to be picked last, but not to be chosen at all is unbearable—especially if you know you are a good player and can help the team. Not only are you excluded but you also have to stay around and watch the game. The members who were chosen wonder why you were not chosen. A multitude of reasons is invented, whether voiced or not. What answer do you give when someone dares to ask why you are not playing in the game or why you were not chosen to play? The answer is that you do not know why you were not chosen, and it hurts because you would like to play."

Kathy's words went straight to my heart. She felt as I had felt, but she had the perfect words to express her feelings. "I have come to the conclusion that women believe marriage is proof that they have worth" rang true to me. I realized that as women of God, if our only proof of feminine worth is marriage, we have forgotten our true identity as daughters of God. Who we are and why we are here is so much more encompassing.

Kathy spoke of an enduring sadness, a sense of loss. "Though the loss *feels* very real, it's never clear if it actually *is* real" because it is "the slipping away of a dream."[5] If we compare our milestones in life to those of married couples, we will always come up short. Kathy's statement "you also have to stay around and watch the game" reminded me that one never gets used to being single because just as one rite of passage in life goes by, another comes. You watch your friends marry, then have children, then prepare their children for missions, then have grandchildren, and then finally go on missions with their spouses. This seemingly unremitting experience seems to have no end.

"Rather than the continuous loss experienced after a death, the hurt of singleness may ebb and flow over time and be triggered by circumstances like weddings, births, weekends, holidays, or family celebrations. Because of this noncontinuous process, it never feels quite legitimate to grieve. Confusion, loneliness, sadness, hurt, and hopelessness are grief feelings, however. And with each passing year, the loss feels more potent and painful."[6]

When I was single, I would evaluate my life against that of my married friends and always feel many steps behind. It took many years for me to accurately begin to evaluate the life Heavenly Father had given me. I realized I had not been evaluating myself by any celestial standard because I had an eternity to accomplish those things.

My friend surmised that if we are not married, it must follow that we are not lovable. A woman without a man is still of infinite worth. Often as a single woman I had to remind myself that I was lovable, that "the worth of souls is great in the sight of God" (D&C 18:10), and that I was one of those souls. It was only through weekly (sometimes semiweekly) temple attendance, scripture reading, and prayer that I could keep my focus and maintain my faith in myself and in the Lord's love for me. The Holy Ghost became a great friend and comfort.

Becoming "Anxiously Engaged"

For me, waiting was a divine challenge. The desire of my heart was to be married. Before I turned to Heavenly Father and developed faith adequate enough to cope with my circumstance, I searched for possible reasons I was not married. Something had to be wrong with me. I felt I must lack some personal quality or have committed some sin of omission or commission that I wasn't even aware of. I kept looking for answers outside and inside myself. I wanted relief from my pain, and I came to realize it was only possible through faith in Jesus Christ.

Because of Jesus Christ, the plan of salvation is in full effect for everyone. I knew, as Sister Julie Beck has said, speaking for unmarried sisters, "We did not fight a war in heaven to be single eternally. We did not sign up for only part of the program. We signed up for the whole plan—to make covenants, to be sealed eternally and have posterity in the eternities. We do not abandon true principles while we are waiting for our blessings."[7] I wanted to live to receive my promised blessings.

The deep-seated faith necessary to do this does not come automatically, instantaneously, or even easily as we turn our lives over to our Savior, Jesus Christ. It requires patience. It is the Lord's way for us to develop in a slow and consistent manner. In the scriptures we are told that truth will be unveiled to us a bit at a time. The Lord teaches us, "I will give unto the children of men line upon line, precept upon precept, here a little and there a little; and blessed are those who hearken unto my precepts, and lend an ear unto my counsel, for they shall learn wisdom" (2 Nephi 28:30).

As we draw close to the Lord and our testimonies increase, our ability to endure happily increases. A personal testimony comes through the Holy Ghost with power and much assurance. "For our gospel came not unto you in word only, but also in power, and in the Holy Ghost, and in much assurance" (1 Thessalonians 1:5). Our personal testimonies are the binding power that makes us equal in the sight of God, regardless of our race or nationality or married state. These testimonies provide us with the power to endure with cheerfulness and dignity.

Being unmarried becomes a blessing when it provides an impetus for us to examine our lives, purpose, and values. Hopefully, in such an examination we can discover the magnitude and depth of our own true worth and that of others. If we look to Christ for answers, He will give them. We should always maintain our celestial goals of marriage, but having additional time and increased desire to know the Lord allows us to concentrate on our personal spirituality. The best and most holy resolution we can ever make is to become a more devoted and committed disciple of Jesus Christ. The more we know of Him, His doctrine, and His teachings, and partake of the ordinances, the more significance His Atonement has in our lives. It also follows that with our increased devotion and understanding of Him, the happier and more complete we become. That doesn't mean there will be no more bad days but rather a lot more happy and contented ones.

There also comes a time in the life of single sisters when they realize they must become *players* in the game of life and make their own happiness. The time comes sooner or later (each of us is different)—and possibly after a few unsuccessful trials—that we decide it is time to progress. Sitting around waiting for someone to make a marriage proposal is a very passive position to take in life. I had somehow deluded myself that if I did not get chosen for marriage, I could not choose a life for myself. I came to the realization that I had not been deprived of a choice; my choice would just come in a different time. Because of varying circumstances at different times, all of us, married or single, will face challenges.

The choice for devoted Latter-day Saint women is not just to simply go forward and try to be happy and create a fulfilling life. As women of covenant our goal is to go forward and develop strong testimonies and nurturing and caring hearts that will prepare us for our roles as mothers in eternity. With that end in mind, I determined to go on happily, to become "anxiously engaged in a good cause" (D&C 58:27), and to believe that the rest would take care of itself.

Heavenly Father increases our faith in ourselves as our faith in Him increases. He blesses us with a confidence that all will be well. We know if we keep the commandments and do what is right, we will be happy. In fact, the Lord promises that if we are faithful, "Ye shall always rejoice, and be filled with the love of God, and always retain a remission of your sins; and ye shall grow in the knowledge of the glory of him that created you, or in the knowledge of that which is just and true" (Mosiah 4:12).

Time is short, and our salvation is on the line. In the great plan of eternity we have such a small moment on this earth. As members of The Church of Jesus Christ of Latter-day Saints we have a responsibility to make our moment bright and to live to our full potential, married or not.

Our testimonies, our closeness to our Father in Heaven, and our ability to serve and love and laugh and enjoy life do not depend on whether we are married or single. If we look to Christ for answers, He will give them. It also follows that with our increased devotion and understanding of Him, the happier and more complete we will become and the more we will comprehend our true worth in the sight of God.

CHAPTER 3

SINGLE SWITCH POINTS

*If one advances confidently in the direction of his dreams
and endeavors to live the life that he has imagined, he will meet
with a success unexpected in common hours.*
—Henry David Thoreau

The advantage of being single is having great autonomy in choices, such as how to spend time. Along a railroad track are switch points, locations where a train can be switched from one track to another. Singles have many switch points, all determining the course and direction their lives will take. Very small and seemingly insignificant choices—when we get up and go to bed (we can stay up all night and watch videos), whom we associate with (hang out with), where we work, where we vacation (we can take off on a moment's notice), what we study, even what we choose to eat or not eat (popcorn or pizza for weeks at a time)—affect our futures.

Many people have asked me, "How do you make a single life a happy one? " My answer is, "Create the best life possible. The decisions you make determine where life takes you. I would make every effort, married or single, to get closer to Heavenly Father, to get the most education possible, to make my home a heaven on earth, and to learn how to manage my time and finances." I sought for and still seek for any experience I can have to make my life happier and more fulfilling; being single or married has nothing to do with it.

As then-Elder Gordon B. Hinckley taught many years ago: "The course of our lives is not determined by great, awesome decisions. Our direction is set by the little day-to-day choices which chart the track on which we run."

He spoke of an experience he had while working in the private sector. "Many years ago I worked in the head office of one of our railroads. One day I received a telephone call from my counterpart in Newark, New Jersey, who said that a passenger train had arrived without its baggage car. The patrons were angry.

"We discovered that the train had been properly made up in Oakland, California, and properly delivered to St. Louis. . . . But in the St. Louis yards, a thoughtless switchman had moved a piece of steel just three inches.

"That piece of steel was a switch point, and the car that should have been in Newark, New Jersey, was in New Orleans, Louisiana, thirteen hundred miles away."[1]

Does it surprise you that such a seemingly small modification could have such a momentous effect on the destination of the train? Can you relate that to the seemingly minor choices we all make that can have a profound effect on our lives? You have the capacity and the power within you to achieve almost anything if you ask the Lord to guide your decisions.

Having the Lord involved in the switch points, the incremental decisions we make every day, is so important because we can seldom see the eternal consequences. Elder Richard G. Scott describes how this is done: "When we seek inspiration to help make decisions, the Lord gives gentle promptings. These require us to think, to exercise faith, to work, to struggle at times, and to act. Seldom does the whole answer to a decisively important matter or complex problem come all at once. More often, it comes a piece at a time, without the end in sight."[2]

Without the end in sight, it is possible to drift aimlessly in a post-adolescent state, waiting to become a responsible and contributing adult, never committing to a course of action, never deciding to go forward, and trying to maintain a youthful persona that has long outlived its usefulness and appropriateness. Small switch points and subtle promptings can help us set a course to maturity.

Some readers may be struggling or may have struggled to achieve their goals and set their switch points. While he was president of Brigham Young University, my husband advised students well about their efforts to go forward: "The strengths you develop by this means will be with you in the eternities to come. Feel no envy for those whose financial or intellectual resources make it easy. The stuff of growth was never made of ease, and the persons who have it easy will need to experience their growth with other sacrifices, or forego the advancement that is the purpose of life."[3]

Follow heavenly promptings; they will point us in the direction we wish to go. We will be saved countless hours, months, and even years in wasted time on needless detours. In addition, we will have a much greater probability of meeting with unexpected success.

Spiritual Switch Points

So many influences can deter us from listening to the Spirit and selecting the switch points that would lead us to develop our spirituality and faith.

The world is constantly tugging at each of us to be less than we should be. Sometimes the disparity between spiritual and worldly forces is evident. Sister Elaine Dalton, first counselor in the Young Women General Presidency, told me that when she first landed in Africa, "My senses were assaulted by the stench of foreign smells and I felt overpowered by a new culture, but on my return to America my spirit was assaulted by the worldliness around me."

Often the differences between good and evil are not so distinct.

Many times we are not even conscious that our lives may be deviating in a direction away from our eternal salvation. In a campus devotional talk, a General Authority promised the students they would be blessed if they did not study on Sunday. He testified that as a student in a rigorous graduate program in a great university, he had not studied on Sunday and had been given clarity of thought, inspiration, greater ability to retain information, and other gifts of the Spirit because he honored the Sabbath. As I left the chapel following this devotional, I heard a young male student behind me say, "That guy is so out of touch, he must be in dreamland. School is so much harder now. How could he say that?" I looked at this young man, attending a university with a much less rigorous curriculum, and thought sadly of the wrong choice he was making.

I felt great sympathy for this student, who rejected advice from his Church leader about the blessings that come from keeping the commandments of our Heavenly Father. He had lost his vision and direction. He was stuck in just trying to get by day to day. The question wasn't simply about studying on the Sabbath. His switch point was leading him to disregard sacred truths. It could have been any principle, from the Word of Wisdom to pornography to more subtle temptations like love of luxury or lack of awareness of the limitations and sufferings of others. The reality of gospel principles had somehow come to be commonplace, of no value, and therefore not significant. Unknowingly, by first not valuing his own religion and then going contrary to its teachings, this young man had set a switch point that could lead to a series of tragic events in his life that he could not foresee.

We will all have questions or doubts, and how we respond to them will make a great difference in our lives. President James E. Faust said: "In my lifetime, there have been very few occasions when I questioned the wisdom and inspiration given by key priesthood leaders. I have always tried to follow their counsel, whether I agreed with it or not. I have come to know that most of the time they were in tune with the Spirit and I was not. The safe course is to sustain our priesthood leaders and let God judge their actions. . . .

"I do not speak of blind obedience, but rather the obedience of faith, which supports and sustains decisions with confidence that they are inspired."[4]

To proceed confidently and set correct switch points in our lives, we need to seek the help of our loving Heavenly Father. During my graduate studies at Brigham Young University, the college thrust was to learn with the Spirit because the Spirit could direct, intensify, and magnify the things we learned. The more we sought the help of the Spirit, the better and more quickly we assimilated information. Learning with the Spirit is not just confined to classrooms or preparation for school examinations. It applies to everything we do in life and every place we do it—our homes or our offices or our wards.

Understanding this great principle when staffing her office, a member of an auxiliary general board wanted to create a climate where the Spirit was strong and revelation would thrive. She searched to hire people who had set their spiritual switch points in order—by reading the scriptures, praying, and attending the temple. This sister knew that if she surrounded herself with people like this, the Spirit would flourish around her. After she had selected such help, one day as she struggled with a problem she called in her assistant and asked, "We need a miracle, and you are invited to participate. Would you like to join us in prayer in asking Heavenly Father to help us?" The faith of that single sister added to the circle of faith of others in her office and made a contribution that helped sisters around the world.

The Spirit provides not only direction but also protection in our lives. Our grandson Brent Ward shared an experience about heeding such spiritual promptings. Immediately after the funeral of his wife June, my husband asked this grandson to join him in a road trip through southern Utah. Brent was a perfect traveling companion for his grieving grandfather: quiet, caring, and at home in the outdoors. Twice on this road trip his grandfather, face buried deep in a newspaper, called out, "Slow down, Brent!" The first time, Brent touched the brakes just as a deer leaped across the road. The second time, in a small Utah town, Brent hit the brakes just in time to avoid hitting a small child who had darted into the road.

Often in our lives the promptings do not come so immediately, and the resulting blessings are not so obvious. Keep looking to your Heavenly Father. When the time is right He will direct you. He has told us, "Behold, this life is the time for men to prepare to meet God; yea, behold the day of this life is the day for men to perform their labors" (Alma 34:32).

The Lord knows how difficult it is for many of us to make the right decisions at our spiritual switch points. He is mindful of us. He will help us experience the great power of His Atonement almost instantaneously. In Alma 34:31, He promises us, "For behold, now is the time and the day of your salvation; and therefore, if ye will repent and harden not your hearts, *immediately* shall the great plan of redemption be brought about unto you" (emphasis added).

As our knowledge of the gospel increases, so does our desire to make commitments and draw closer to Heavenly Father. Setting spiritual switch points results in making covenants. Many confused single sisters think of going to the temple as a reward for getting married. Sisters in their late twenties and early thirties often desperately need the added blessings provided by attending the temple, but they have apprehensions about making covenants alone. One single sister in her early thirties confided in me, "I long to receive my endowments but I worry that I am sending out a signal that I've given up on the idea that anyone might ever marry me." Going to the temple alone is not a consolation prize; it is the consummate gift from our Heavenly Father. When we go to the temple we go to make covenants with our Father in Heaven. These covenants reward our lives by broadening our understanding, enriching our spirituality, protecting us, and providing us with peace and revelation. Set a spiritual switch point to make and keep covenants.

Married or single, we are all making decisions that will lead us closer or farther away from our Father in Heaven. Start now to be strong; the decisions you make will have eternal consequences. For example, I know a young married woman in her late twenties who has six children and has the eternal perspective of the importance of children and of being a mother. Many of her LDS friends, for reasons of their own, have only two or three children, and they tell her she is crazy for having so many children. She said to her friends, "Don't tell me I am crazy for trying to be obedient to my Heavenly Father and living His plan to its fullest. If I had my eye only on the world, I would probably have many fewer children but many fewer blessings, too."

Elder Henry B. Eyring has taught: "Your life is carefully watched over, as was mine. The Lord knows both what He will need you to do and what you will need to know. He is kind and He is all-knowing. So you can with confidence expect that He has prepared opportunities for you to learn in preparation for the service you will give. You will not recognize those opportunities perfectly, as I did not. But when you put the spiritual things first in your life, you will be blessed to feel directed toward certain learning, and you will be motivated to work harder. You will recognize later that your power to serve was increased, and you will be grateful."[5]

Educational Switch Points

Education is our gift to ourselves and to the world around us. It provides us with the means and skills to use our unique capabilities.

Education affects us and everyone we come in contact with. It carries the sacred obligation to serve others and provides us with an enriched world and eternal perspective. "President Hinckley has repeatedly said in various situations and places that we, both men and women, should get all the education we can. He has not been prescriptive about the discipline, but he has been clear about both the need for and the value of education."[6]

A fundamental precept of the gospel is "The glory of God is intelligence, or, in other words, light and truth" (D&C 93:36). Learning has an eternal shelf life, and whatever useful knowledge or understanding or wisdom or "principle of intelligence we [acquire] in this life, it will rise with us in the resurrection" (D&C 130:18).

It isn't easy for a woman, in the years of eligibility for marriage, when no offers come her way. She must face the obvious reality that she may have to support herself financially.

I grew up in a very different time, when women seemed to have only two options to support themselves—teaching and nursing. These are still excellent options today. My problem was that I never considered either one of them. Supporting myself was something I had not considered possible; I loved to learn and did so with no thought of needing to provide for myself. My father had taken wonderful care of me financially, and mystically I somehow assumed this care would always continue.

I knew how to work; in fact, I loved to work. I had many summer jobs, and I did well in school, but knowing that I could actually get a job and fully support myself was a completely different matter. When I fully awoke to the need for this, I was afraid, almost paralyzed, by the unforeseen challenges that seemed to loom ahead for me.

You may be at this crossroads. Nothing is more perplexing than not knowing what to do with your future, and nothing is more personally rewarding than discovering your own abilities. Read your patriarchal blessing, consider your natural aptitudes and talents, and go forward. Take the first step, and doors will open. When I set out in English literature, I never dreamed it would take me to a publishing house in Boston. My husband studied accounting and then went to law school and on to the Utah Supreme Court. With the Lord, "all things work together for [our] good" (Romans 8:28), and the information we receive may come in incremental steps as our lives unfold before us.

We are given moral agency, revelation, and inspiration, but our Heavenly Father expects us to examine our abilities and ourselves and then decide for ourselves the educational course we should follow. "A young woman told her father she was praying to know what God wanted her to study in college. He asked, 'If you came to me and asked me what to study in college, what do you think I would say?' She supposed he wouldn't really care, as long as she pursued something she enjoyed that would use her strengths, bless others, and provide for her needs. He asked, 'Why would God be different?'"[7]

Prepare to support yourself. Education is not just a preoccupation. We live in a time when it is necessary that we have a marketable skill. Education is mandatory for personal security and well-being. It is not optional, although never in the history of the world have so many options been available. Whether you are single or married, young or old, train yourself with skills and knowledge that will help you provide for yourself and your family and live in dignity.

It is disturbing that so many—especially women—have self-doubts and question their ability to succeed. Addressing Brigham Young University women students in math, science, and engineering in March 2005, President Cecil O. Samuelson said: "One of your professors has commented to me that . . . some of you have less confidence in your abilities and prospects than do your male peers, even when the evidence may suggest that this is not justified. You do need to recognize your talents, skills, aptitudes and strengths and not be confused about the gifts that God has given you."[8]

Women, especially, may receive negative feedback when they aspire to professional occupations. A young sister in her late twenties faced with supporting herself wrote for advice. She confided that she had approached an ecclesiastical authority about studying law and he had discouraged her. I do not know her abilities or her limitations; the negative counsel she received may have been based on them or on inspiration peculiar to her circumstances. But her determination could be felt through the pages of her letter, and it was clear that she should be advised to reach the full level of her potential.

As part of his message during the general Relief Society meeting held September 29, 2007, President Thomas S. Monson told the sisters: "Do not pray for tasks equal to your abilities, but pray for abilities equal to your tasks. Then the performance of your tasks will be no miracle, but you will be the miracle."[9]

The future may seem quite ominous, but with heavenly assistance we can have great hope. Elder Jeffrey R. Holland said: "*Faith* in the Lord Jesus Christ—that is the first principle of the gospel. We must go forward. God expects you to have enough faith, determination, and trust in Him to keep moving, keep living, and keep rejoicing. He expects you not simply to face the future; He expects you to embrace and shape the future—to love it, rejoice in it, and delight in your opportunities."[10]

Educate yourself in every way you can. There is nothing more fulfilling and fun than learning something new. Great happiness, satisfaction, and financial rewards come from educating ourselves. An education does not have to be simply a college education. It can be learning any meaningful skills that allow us to employ ourselves and enrich our lives. Study painting or travel or cooking or flying—whatever you have an affinity for—and do well in it.

"Formal education may be designed for the young, but the young at heart can enjoy a lifetime of learning. Learning is found not just in books. People and places are great sources of new information and experience. We can ask questions and enjoy discussions with friends and family members, learning from their points of view. We can visit a local museum to hear the story of a historic landmark or inquire at a public library about any topic we choose. Or we can visit the Internet, where a world of information is right at our fingertips."[11]

At the April 2001 general conference, President Gordon B. Hinckley announced the Perpetual Education Fund. He spoke of returned missionaries and other ambitious young men and women who have great capacity but meager opportunities. He declared, "Education is the key to opportunity."[12]

My friend Dr. Donna Lee Bowen, a professor of political science and Middle East studies at BYU loves learning. She said: "President Hinckley's injunction to get an education points to the joys and responsibilities we possess today. We have no time to fear or hold back. There is too much to be done. We have the means to learn how to make the world better, to find cures for disease, to teach children correct principles, to write good laws, to comfort the weary, to follow fair business practices, to stop war, and to foster peace. Think of it. The world has opened up opportunities never before imagined for women; less than a hundred years ago none of this would have been possible. All we need to do is to open our hearts and minds and energies to take on new challenges with a 'perfect brightness of hope and a love of God and of all men'" (2 Nephi 31:20).[13]

With these many opportunities there is an added responsibility with specific importance for the Latter-day Saint woman. Here is what President Samuelson of BYU said about this responsibility: "Suppose that in addition to graduate school you also have an interest in getting married or are already married. You are all aware that the Prophet also has spoken in favor of that proposition as well. What do you do? You think you may know the answer, but it isn't any easier. Nevertheless, you can't afford to make the mistake that Oliver Cowdery made when he 'took no thought save it was to ask. . . . ' (D&C 9:7). You 'must study it out in your mind; then you must ask [Heavenly Father] if it be right, and if it is right [He] will cause that your bosom shall burn within you; therefore, you shall feel that it is right' (D&C 9:8). . . . If it is not right, then you . . . will have a 'stupor of thought' (D&C 9:9) that should send you back . . . to re-think and to re-consider."[14]

Another friend, Jessica, identified one important caution about graduate education for LDS women. She accompanied her daughter to look at graduate schools in the eastern United States. Her daughter, highly motivated and talented, knew that by attending the number one school of her choice she could amass educational debts in excess of one hundred thousand dollars. Often it is worth it to pay for the best education, but in this case, her daughter prayed and felt that though this level of debt might not prevent her from marrying, it might eventually prevent her from stopping work so that she could stay home with her children. She felt that paying off such a large education debt might even require that the family postpone purchasing a future home. Be wise. Each of us is different. The Lord will let you know what is best for you.

I know many women fear that if they become too highly educated, they may intimidate men. It is true that a highly educated, articulate, and successful woman might scare away some men, but conversely, she will attract a confident man who will respect her for her accomplishments. A grandmother approached me about her granddaughter, who is working on her doctoral degree. She said, "I think she is intimidating men with her education. She is beautiful and devout, works in the temple, and is very active in the Church but has no men in her life."

I identified so much with this young woman, who is gaining great satisfaction from learning and progressing. We cannot stop becoming or sit and wait for our lives to unfold in a way that may never be. I would advise everyone to be the best that they can be. I would also caution them to maintain balance in their lives. I know that sometimes, because learning fed my soul, I submerged myself in my studies and became almost a workaholic. I did this not only because I thoroughly enjoyed learning and my vocation but also because it was a very productive way to make my life full and satisfying.

Finally, we have the obligation to educate ourselves spiritually by reading the scriptures, Church magazines, and Relief Society manuals. We should feast upon the words of life to enhance our present, increase our ability to teach those given to us to teach, and prepare for our eternal families.

The ultimate goal of an education is to make us better servants in the kingdom. As my husband, when he was president of Brigham Young University, said so well: "I yield to none in my assessment of the importance of our achieving in our educational pursuits, but in the long run it is the growth, knowledge, and wisdom we achieve that enlarges our souls and prepares us for eternity, not the marks on our transcripts. The things of the Spirit are the things that are eternal, and our family relationships, sealed by the power of the priesthood, are the ultimate fruits of the Spirit."[15]

Education is a gift from God; it is a cornerstone of our religion when we use it to benefit others. Whenever I drive by BYU, I read the inscription at the western entrance: "Enter to Learn, Go Forth to Serve." This always inspires me to be sure that my internal switch points are set in a celestial direction.

Financial Switch Points

If you are just beginning your journey toward financial security, read "One for the Money," by Elder Marvin J. Ashton. It was reprinted in the September 2007 *Ensign*, pages 36–39. It offers solid direction to use in setting your financial switch points.

For many years my financial plan as a single woman was pretty straightforward. Savings were automatically deducted from my pay-check, I paid tithing, I paid my bills, and then I went to Nordstrom (an upscale department store). I was mostly living for myself. Jill, a dear shopping friend, laughingly counseled me, "If we run out of money at the end of the month, we can always eat bread, water, and M&M's." That is not practical advice for anyone and is an especially dangerous switch point for a single woman.

We all need to get a financial life. Greater earning power does not necessarily correlate with greater wisdom about money. I have little financial aptitude, but I know it is wise to live on less than I earn. I worked in my father's office during the summers, and every evening we would drop off his earnings at the bank. He would say to me, "Kristen, it is not what you earn; it is what you save." My little sister Margot was always much better at saving than I.

We may have jobs and skills that earn us good salaries, yet it is a fact that many people, when they earn more money, don't become more financially secure. They just spend more and more. We live in a time when consumerism is rampant and exploited. Interest-only loans on homes and no payments for a year on consumer purchases are common. We will pay for what we buy but not for a while. There are even seven-year car loans. When you buy the car of your dreams, remember that a car is a depreciating asset, not an investment.

Having enough money is often a major concern of many single women, especially those who are supporting families. I remember when I used to receive my annual bonus and think of all the frills I could buy. One single mother I worked with told me, "Now I can get new sheets for my girls' beds and towels for the bathrooms." It can be very fearful to be without sufficient financial resources. Make sure you have adequate insurance. After the loss of her husband, one friend, an articulate and talented writer who had a lucrative editorial job prior to her marriage, found herself having to work as a waitress to support her family. For her, nothing could have been more emotionally debilitating or devastating. Make provisions for your future to avoid such problems.

Avoid debt. For a single person this may prove challenging. Often when we feel empty inside, we use our money to buy material objects to fill that void. For women, especially, there is truly such a thing as retail therapy. Shopping may be soothing to the female psyche—but not to the pocketbook. My sister and I get around this by allowing ourselves a ten-dollar spree at the dollar store.

Beautiful things also signal success to the world. Flashy cars or expensive recreational and technological toys are alluring because they suggest financial abundance. They say to the world, "I may not be married, but I can afford great toys, so I must be of worth." Take care not to fall into this trap.

Individual financial practices will greatly affect any future marriage. A recent article in *USA Today* states: "With later marriages, many people bring more assets and debt into a relationship. A result is 'two very strong opinions' about managing money, with each partner having managed his or her own money for years. If you wait until 30 to get married, you've been in a series of jobs, accumulated benefits, maybe 401(K) assets; you might even have a house. It makes things more complicated." This increased earning power also carries with it certain responsibilities. "The greater a woman's education level and earning potential, the more bargaining power she tends to have in household decisions—including financial ones."[16]

Save some of your discretionary money for the future. Plan for your retirement. Start now. Set a switch point to save a little every month, and you will reap a great dividend. Work can be a joy and a blessing, but almost every single woman I know as she nears age fifty begins to anticipate retirement or at least a change of employment. One friend who is approaching retirement age said to me, "You've forgotten how hard it is to support yourself and to make a car payment and a house payment." I can never forget the pressure of making those payments or the stress of doing taxes and paying bills by myself. I also remember that when I set aside a cushion in case of emergency—for anyone struggling and surviving paycheck to paycheck to make ends meet, this is no easy thing—I felt much calmer, less pressured to survive, and more susceptible to the influence of the Spirit.

Remember that the Lord's great blessings to His people come through tithing. Paying tithing and necessary living expenses first will also provide peace of mind. My husband often draws this equation on the board when he is teaching tithing: "Ninety percent [of income] plus blessings is greater than 100 percent [of income] without blessings." He tells how at age ten he asked his widowed mother, "Why do you give all that money to the bishop when we need it more than he does?" She instructed him, "There may be people so rich they don't need to pay tithing, Dallin, but we are not among them. We must pay tithing because we are not rich, and we must depend on Heavenly Father for all the blessings we can receive." Her advice can bless all our lives. One additional financial obligation for all of us as specified by our religion is that we give back to others less fortunate than ourselves. Under the Lord's plan we are responsible to care for more than just ourselves.

A Switch Point to Home

Due to health and emotional concerns, some will always need to live with their parents. Living with a family can be a blessing. For many others, however, there comes a time to move out of the basement and create their own independent home environment. The transition from the parents' home to their own home may be a bit late in coming for singles because they are often waiting for someone (a husband or wife) with whom to leave home. One father whose daughter had just graduated from college and returned home to live with him asked her, "Do you know 100 percent how much I love you?" His daughter replied, "Yes, Daddy, I know." He asked again, "Are you 1,000 percent positive how much I love you?" The daughter again replied, "Of course, Daddy." He said, "Good, because it is time you moved out on your own."

Be wise enough to leave. Having wise parents who make us leave is a blessing because leaving forces us to grow up on one level and find a place of our own. The initial move may seem somewhat traumatic. You may lose some of the comforts of home and access to your parents' food supply, but you gain a newfound sense of adventure and confidence. I remember that my first apartment had a cord from the refrigerator running across the kitchen floor. I kept mentioning that it might be dangerous, but my roommate kept reassuring me, "It's charming." We were happy to be living independently with our secondhand furniture and borrowed silverware.

Later, in my thirties, having my own home made me feel independent and self-sufficient. I remember signing the mortgage agreement, suddenly aware that I had signed myself into bondage for fifteen years. Eventually that feeling became one of pride in my home ownership. My home was my space, and I loved being there. I set a switch point to improve the environment I lived in. An entirely new world opened up for me. Financially I had to set my house in order to get the funds to fix up my home. I learned about color and hue and furniture. I contacted painters and builders. I had a vision of what I wanted my surroundings to look and feel like. It was so much fun. I attacked my home room by room—everything from molding and painting to new carpet, and I loved every minute of it. I created a new "red room" and loved just sitting in it. The result of my effort was that I felt a stronger sense of personal worth because I had created a beautiful place for myself to live. By doing mundane things that might seem insignificant to others, I became a happier and more satisfied woman. My plans improved my life.

One story I especially love concerns a sister who was not going to wait for marriage to get rid of her ugly secondhand orange plates. "At age twenty-eight, Jean concluded she did not need to be married to buy 'real' dishes. She chose a pattern she liked and invited friends and family to select items from her wish list for birthday and Christmas gifts. She bought herself a plate or bowl when she reached an important goal. She loved using her dishes every day, and she assumed the adult roles of entertaining family or friends with more confidence and pleasure."[17]

When you get your plates, start using them, too. Don't put off the time to do your best cooking and festive celebrations for some nebulous time in the future when you marry. Create a quality of life and the environment you desire now. The benefits will be immediate, and your experience will prove an advantage to you in the future. Many of my single friends have become gourmet chefs and gracious, inclusive hostesses.

As single sisters we have little control over when we will marry, but we do have control over the environment we create for ourselves. Look at your homes, your situations, and the way you live. We are all women of God, and our mission is to nurture and love those around us. President John Taylor instructed us, "We have been commanded of the Lord to set our households in order. . . . Have you done this with your . . . households?"[18]

Our homes can serve as spiritual sanctuaries from the evil and temptation that might envelop us. During the February 9, 2008, worldwide leadership training meeting, Sister Susan Tanner, Young Women General President, warned against "emotional homelessness" and living in places without the power of the Spirit—places that make us vulnerable "to despair, drug abuse, and immorality." President Monson has taught us that our homes should be places where there is a "pattern of prayer," "a library of learning," a place where "we enjoy a legacy of love."[19]

It is within our power to create homes that are havens of holiness when we invite the Spirit to dwell with us. By living righteous principles we can construct a refuge that will buffer us from the storms of evil that surround us. The scriptures we read there, the prayers we offer there, and the actions and language we use there will form a shield of goodness that will protect us from the world.

When we set our switch points to create homes for ourselves, we become more committed and decisive about who we are and what we want to become. We don't just wait for marriage to take on responsibilities and grow up. In addition, when we, as women of covenant, create our own sacred environments, we become more sacred too. Our earthly homes are a prototype of our homes to come.

The Switch Points of Service

The Lord commands us to love Him and to love one another. No one is exempt, married or not. We have an obligation to serve those around us in our families, wards, and communities. When we vote or volunteer or visit a rest home, we are contributing to the society around us. We should magnify our callings, help our neighbors, and really be our brother's keeper. Then, under the law of the harvest, we benefit by becoming more caring and more connected with those around us. Just as President Gordon B. Hinckley spoke of the need for new converts to have "a friend, a responsibility, and nurturing with 'the good word of God' (Moro. 6:4),"[20] everyone can benefit from these three connections.

College students and busy professionals may become so occupied with their personal struggles that they lose the perspective of service. Earlier, in addressing students about their need to reach out, then-Elder Hinckley said: "If the pressures of school are too heavy, if you complain about your housing and the food you eat, I can suggest a cure for problems. Lay your books aside for a few hours, leave your room, and go visit someone who is old and lonely. There are such right here in this valley. Or visit those who are sick and discouraged; there are hundreds of that kind here, including not a few on this campus, who need the kind of encouragement you could give. If you are complaining about life, it is because you are thinking only of yourself. There was for many years a sign on the wall of a shoe repair shop I patronized. It read, 'I complained because I had no shoes until I saw a man who had no feet.' The most effective medicine for the sickness of self-pity is to lose oneself in the service of others."

He continued: "There are some girls on this campus who are worrying themselves almost sick over the question of whether they will have opportunity for marriage. Of course marriage is desirable; of course it is hoped for and worked for and sought after. But worrying about it will never bring it. In fact, it may have the opposite effect, for there is nothing that dulls a personality so much as a negative outlook. Possibly some of you will not be married; but don't forget that there are other things in life, other pursuits to be followed."[21]

President Hinckley was speaking to all of us. He was teaching us that there is great power in positive thinking and the power of thinking of others. His optimism and positive outlook blessed our entire Church. He always looked to the future and how to make it better.

The service we render to others in our communities and through humanitarian projects makes the world a better place. On a personal level it opens doors of sweet association and friendship and places us in a position to empathize with and understand others different from ourselves. It connects us emotionally and spiritually to those around us and helps us develop kind and compassionate hearts. There is no better training ground for healthy relationships and the building of self-esteem. We are better for lifting those around us.

Our service to others prepares us for the demands placed on us in our occupations, marriages, and our own extended families. I heard a General Authority giving counsel to new Church leaders ask, "How do you want to be remembered?" We can begin today to create the legacy and memories that we want to leave with others. We will all leave a legacy of memories, so why not make them worthwhile and wonderful?

When I think of a legacy of memories, I think of one person in particular who has left a great legacy of love in my life—my husband's first wife, June. She passed away more than ten years ago. I have come to love her very much, although I never met her. I love her because her great capacity to love and teach has blessed my life. She was a wonderful teacher to her children in a thousand family home evenings, in personal one-on-one conversations, and in multiple precious moments when she shared gospel truths. She taught them all how much they were loved by their Heavenly Father. She was always extremely honest and forthcoming. I see her great influence in her children, who are now parents themselves. They love their children and keep their covenants and honor their marriage vows.

I have learned of her happy nature and humor as her children have spoken of her. June was quick-witted and spoke her mind. We often sit as a family, and her children share their stories of her. One story the children love to hear and retell was of their trip with the Baker family to Brookfield Zoo, near Chicago. June and her dear friend Marian Baker, each with four small children (eight total) proceeded on an afternoon outing. Marian remembered, "As we handed our tickets to the man at the gate before boarding the merry-go-round, he commented, 'Well, it looks like you are having a party.' June's quick comeback was, 'No, these are all our children, and it's no party.'"[22]

All the children depended on their mother for her honest feedback, wisdom, and love. Jenny, the youngest child in the family and extremely close to her mother, recalls at age fourteen still sitting on her mother's lap because she loved to be near her. She enjoyed spending time with her mother and often preferred time with her to time with her peers because her mother was so much fun.

Anticipating her death, June spoke to her children about accepting a new mother when their father remarried. She set her switch point of love to the future. She knew her husband would not do well without a companion. She was not jealous or competitive because she really had tasted of the love her Heavenly Father has for His children. She wanted her home to continue to be a place of affection and faith where His Spirit could reside. Her children have been wonderful to me because of the faith and understanding of their own mother. She truly knew she was a daughter of her Heavenly Father, and she wanted everyone to feel of His love.

President Hinckley wished all of us to look to the glorious future that lies ahead of us. He wished us to live lives that reflect our beliefs:

"We of this generation are the end harvest of all that has gone before. It is not enough to simply be known as a member of this Church. A solemn obligation rests upon us. Let us face it and work at it.

"We must live as true followers of the Christ, with charity toward all, returning good for evil, teaching by example the ways of the Lord, and accomplishing the vast service He has outlined for us."[23]

We live in a remarkable and extraordinary time, a time when worldly fears and influences tempt us to live below our privileges and opportunities. In 2004, President Thomas S. Monson advised us, "It is worthwhile to look ahead, to set a course, to be at least partly ready when the moment of decision comes."[24] The course we set will bring us to the destination—the life, the mate, and the testimony we desire and ultimately achieve. It is a time for faith, a time to confidently adjust and monitor our personal switch points toward eternal life.

PART TWO

Social Life

CHAPTER 4

EVERY SINGLE HOLIDAY

Holidays can pose unique challenges for the single sister.
With the passing years, holidays may increasingly serve as a
reminder of unfulfilled dreams.

It was the morning of our fourth Memorial Day as a married couple, and I was excited to spend time away with my husband and some dear friends. As one of them approached our front door, she looked dejected. The good time we had been anticipating seemed in jeopardy, and I was concerned for my friend. I asked, "What's wrong? You seem so sad." She answered, "My darling single sister just called. She is dreading this holiday. She will be alone and is thinking of ways she can stay busy."

Those words brought a surge of memories. I recalled the many holidays I had spent alone and how often they had been painful. I remembered seeking out friends to be with and places to go and how lonely I had been.

I love all occasions when people come together to rejoice: weddings, luncheons, reunions, and get-togethers. As my younger sisters married, I eagerly attended every shower and luncheon. At one event a guest, with sincere caring, asked, "Don't you feel bad? Isn't this making you feel sad because you're not getting married?" I realized friends were beginning to view me, in my early thirties, as an old

61

maid, "a woman forsaken and grieved in spirit" (3 Nephi 22:6). It surprised them that I was so pleased with my sister's happiness. I was totally enthralled and did not want to miss one precious moment.

As time passed, however, my feelings became more tender, and the holidays and parties took on a new significance. As a young woman I had imagined my future with a husband and family, with ideas about how I would prepare my home and how we would enjoy every moment. When friends all around were getting married and my dreams had not materialized, I felt abandoned and distraught. My life was not turning out the way I had planned. I was confused and disappointed. I had believed it would all be so different from the way it was.

With the passing years, holidays served increasingly as reminders of unfulfilled dreams. It became more painful to be alone during them, particularly because I had not adjusted my expectations. I longed for a white Christmas with little children, a Thanksgiving surrounded by friends and family, a Valentine's Day when I was someone's sweetheart, or at the very least, a Fourth of July under the splendor of exploding multicolor fireworks with a date I enjoyed. Even those who are married and have all they need to create fun holidays find out that events often transpire quite differently from what they had anticipated. I wanted every holiday to be a perfect experience. Such expectations are destined to cause disappointment. Holidays were especially precious to me because they were often the only days in the month when I, as a consultant who traveled continually, could be assured of being home.

One single sister commented to me, "I hate the thought that well-meaning married people and priesthood leaders will read your book and assume that all single women are waiting for invitations to Christmas dinner and dreading Memorial Day weekend and Mother's Day. I get inaccurately *pitied* enough."

Singles don't desire pity, because it robs them of their personal dignity. I have chosen to write about the holidays because for me they were sometimes tedious and often lonely. I believe that for others, whether married or single, this may also be the case. The holiday may not even be the day of concern; it might be any day when any of us need a friendly greeting and an uplifting hand.

President Hinckley, the most optimistic and positive of men, recognized the pain of those around him. In his December 2007 Christmas address, he acknowledged that this most holy of seasons, when our thoughts turn to our Savior, may also intensify the sorrow felt in the hearts and homes of those experiencing adversity—married or single. He said, "*Merry* might be the wrong word. More appropriately we might say, 'It is Christmas time; what can I do to help you? Are your burdens too heavy to carry? Is your sorrow too painful?' The world is full of sorrowful people. Many of them feel totally beaten down. They are sick. They are impoverished. Life seems hopeless. Even at this season they seem oppressed by these feelings."[1]

One year as we shared our best Christmas memory at a party, a neighbor whose wife had left him and filed for divorce several years earlier, told of being at work on Christmas Eve. His heart was aching, and he felt like a broken failure. He knew that by court order he would not even be able to see his only child, a little girl, until the next day. He was going through the motions of being alive and was overcome by a deep sadness when the receptionist at his office summoned him. His beloved aunt was at the front desk with a small present in hand, inviting him to join her family for Christmas dinner. He recalled the joy that flooded over him because someone cared. He remembers that Christmas as one of his happiest. I testify too how a day alone and feeling lonely can be transformed by being included and having somewhere to go. We all need to follow the Spirit to be aware of those around us. On any given day of the year any act of kindness or remembrance can make a dramatic difference.

Christmas—the Single Biggest Holiday

For me not all holidays are created equal. While preparing for Christmas can be a festive time, this season provides many single people with at least thirty full days to anticipate spending another holiday alone. Christmas involves a lot of commercialism and often a great deal of expense, and it encompasses the entire month of December. Stores begin to advertise and decorate, radio stations play Christmas tunes, Christmas trees go on sale, and preparations begin often as early as October. Married people are often unaware of the plight of singles at Christmas. Those who are married are so involved in trying to get their own holiday preparations done that they may not notice someone alone. Singles begin to feel invisible because they are often not included in the festivities going on around them. Many single sisters have described the moment when they realized they needed to make the holidays enjoyable and worthwhile for themselves. They are correct. It is up to us to use the time and agency the Lord has given us to make our lives meaningful.

I have vivid memories of doing things to make the holidays bright. In fact, I did everything and anything I could think of: decorating an elaborate Christmas tree, baking cookies—a big domestic stretch for me at that time—delivering goodies to friends, taking my nieces and nephews to Santa Claus breakfasts and Christmas plays, and visiting rest homes. I love to read scriptures relevant to the holidays, such as prophecies about Jesus. I also love to read both the Book of Mormon and the Bible, timing my reading so that I arrive at the chapters about the Savior's birth on Christmas Eve. I made more than the usual number of visits to the temple during the month of December, and I especially liked to attend the final endowment session of the year, if I could.

I used all my strength and powers of planning to make the

holidays joyous. I remember making gingerbread houses with neighborhood children (using a glue gun because my frosting never set), having sleepovers, attending every concert of the season that I could get to, and planning presents for everyone I loved. Each year I invited my family to my home to put on a Nativity play, which I wrote and directed, and we always read the story of the Savior. Singleness did not slow down my festive instincts.

Most of the month I was happy and satisfied, but I had to make the effort to be so. Being joyous at Christmas was a challenge, but I remember the Lord blessing me in those times, providing me with extra calm and peace. One evening after our family Christmas celebration, I slept on the couch beside my Christmas tree and bathed in the light emanating from it, feeling especially near to Heavenly Father and enjoying His love and the presence of the Holy Spirit.

My extended family is strong and they love to be together, so I was always included at every seasonal celebration—dinners and tree-decorating parties and caroling. I was there, loving my family but often feeling very much alone. Ironically, it was on those special days of celebration that brought my family together that I often felt most deprived.

Holidays also mean parties—the company party, ward Christmas dinner, New Year's Eve, and any event where most people arrive as couples. I sometimes considered taking an inflatable doll as a date, but that would have created more of a scene than I wanted to make. That meant if I didn't go with my niece or sister, I felt forced to think of a man I could invite. I worried that people would think we were more serious than we were or that my date would think I was pursuing him. Some single people simply don't attend events in order to avoid either the experience of showing up alone or imposing on a friend or acquaintance to fill the social role of escort.

My happiest times came when I decided simply to enjoy the invitations offered to me and not concern myself about showing up as part of a couple. When you attend parties alone, attitude becomes very important. If you are not accustomed to going alone, you may feel self-conscious as you enter a room and look for someone to sit by and converse with. That comes more naturally to some than to others. Linda, a dear associate, said she decided not to miss any more parties at the ward, so she just went by herself, looked for friends, and enjoyed herself. The ward members were delighted to see her, and she opened doors for new friendships. Another close friend makes it easier for herself by taking pictures during social events, which gives her an excuse to walk around and interact. It helps her enjoy herself and not feel alone.

We are social creatures meant to mingle and enjoy each other. With some creativity and a little spunk, you don't have to deny yourself the opportunity to socialize in good places. My Aunt Marjorie shared sound advice about enjoying the moment. She often said, "Take a cookie when they are passed," and we knew that meant participate and enjoy it when the opportunity arises.

Divorced sisters have additional challenges at Christmas. They have sweet and bittersweet memories of the past. During a trip to Washington, D.C., I spent time in the home of a loving, wise, and charismatic friend. She makes me laugh, but in every conversation we have, I have discovered more about being a better person. She is edifying and fun and would never want anyone to feel sorry for her. I remembered when her husband left her with three small children. She stood in testimony meeting and explained the situation to her ward family. She asked us to accept her children and not to gossip, and then she bore testimony of her love and devotion to Heavenly Father.

Nevertheless, this particular December morning I sensed acutely that she felt the sting of losing her beloved husband to an alternative lifestyle. Other days might have been difficult for her, but I had not noticed. She does not complain or even talk about missing him, but her home is full of lovely things he created for her during their marriage, and she still rejoices in them. I noticed her eyes and the tone of her voice as she gazed on photographs of her once-united family displayed around the room. There was a subtle sadness for blessings lost, even after so much time had passed. When we stood before her Christmas tree, a tinge of loneliness permeated the air. She had made every effort to remain a friend to her former husband. The twenty-fifth of December was fast approaching, and she had contacted him. He was now alone, broken in body and in spirit, and living in a different state. She had invited him to join the family in their Christmas celebration, and he wasn't coming.

Christmas in a divorced household can also be a time when children and grandchildren alternate opportunities to visit. Another dear and divorced friend shared with me that her son goes every year with his wife and two young children to his wife's parents' home because they have a bigger home and a more lavish place to have Christmas. In this situation two grandparents could seem better than one. The ultimate hurt came when her son packed up the electric car she had purchased for the grandchildren, so they could play with it at the large home of his wife's parents. My friend would have loved to have been included with the other family as they celebrated, but no one thought to include her. She spent much of her holiday feeling neglected.

A widowed sister faces similar challenges during the Christmas holiday. One sister recalled for me the early years of her marriage when she and her husband shopped excitedly together at Christmas. They enjoyed every minute of selecting gifts for their tiny children. It brought them so much joy to find little treasures and special treats for their new family. When her husband passed away suddenly and left her alone, she told me of other Christmases when she went alone to purchase gifts. The joy seemed gone, and she shopped with a broken heart and tender feelings. For an entire year she lived in a shadow land, anesthetized and removed from everything around her. She described it as like being submerged in water—listening to blurred speech, seeing hazy images, feeling numb and disoriented emotionally. She remembered Christmas Eve nights alone, wrapping presents by herself for her children. There were some of those early years when she received no gift from anyone. It was a struggle trying to create Christmas for everyone else. These holidays were exhausting and not joyous for her.

Since I have been married, not a Christmas season goes by that I don't remember to some degree the many sensations of single life. Recently as I left a friend who was alone for the holidays, she asked about parties my husband and I were attending and told me her sister would be at many of them. She walked me to the car and called out, "Don't worry about me. I'm going to watch *White Christmas, It's a Wonderful Life,* and *Miracle on Thirty-Fourth Street.* I'll be plenty busy."

She may have intended to put my mind at ease, but I worried about her all night, and the next morning I called to see how she was doing. Her reply took me aback. She said, "The last twenty-four hours have been so sweet. Instead of watching movies, I went through boxes of things from my mother [who had just died] and sorted them for my brothers and sisters. Seeing all the precious remembrances in those boxes made me so thankful for the home I grew up in and the memories I have. I kept thinking about the plan of salvation and how we can be together forever."

I did not expect an answer filled with such gratitude. As we spoke it became clear to me that in her loneliness she sought our Savior, the Prince of Peace, and with her seeking had come the warm and calming influence of His love.

Whether because of our high expectations or sometimes the high expectations placed on us by others to create holiday happiness, Christmas can be stressful and, married or single, we become weighed down. When the challenges of loneliness and the desire for a companion plague us during the holiday season, my friend Susan recommends focusing on our knowledge of the plan of salvation and the very intimate love and sacrifice our Savior showed for us. Doing this, I have become so thankful for Him, and Christmas has taken on a different, less frenetic dimension. In this dispensation the Lord has blessed us with great knowledge and access to His Spirit. If we reach out and ask for His help in blessing others even in a small way, He will comfort us and help us discover joy, connectedness, and peace in our little corner of Christmas.

Mother's Day

Holidays also awaken emotions that relate to our eternal roles. Mother's Day is just such a day. This precious day arouses within us an awareness of the sacred role of women. It can also serve as a reminder of the children you do not have and the blessings yet to come. As Latter-day Saint women we have such a deep and abiding conviction of family that this day causes some single women to stay away from Church and to have a day at home to reflect and regroup. I often felt on this day that my life was not where I wished it to be; it seemed a reminder of blessings I didn't have. Many mothers, married and single, have shared with me that this day is difficult for them, too. They feel regret and worry over children who struggle, are rebellious, or unhappy. I came to realize that motherhood is a great blessing, but this period of waiting for the gift proved an enormous blessing, too.

Included among my Mother's Day memories is another very tender experience when I sat in Relief Society among noble, valiant women whom I loved, and my heart melted because of their feminine tenderness. I began weeping, not because I wasn't a mother but because Heavenly Father had bestowed on me the gift of womanhood, and I felt so blessed by it.

Sister Julie Beck, Relief Society General President, in her general conference address "A Mother Heart" provided me with a reminder of our purpose on earth as women: "Female roles did not begin on earth, and they do not end here. A woman who treasures motherhood [and treasures being a woman] on earth will treasure motherhood in the world to come, and 'where [her] treasure is, there will [her] heart be also' (Matthew 6:21)."[2] Women who treasure womanliness and motherhood experience joy on this earth because of their eternal perspective. "As they keep their covenants, they are investing in a grand, prestigious future because they know that 'they who keep their second estate shall have glory added upon their heads forever and ever' (Abraham 3:26)."[3]

During our stay in the Philippines I witnessed firsthand the great power that faith and the motherly love of a single woman can exert. In one of my auxiliary training sessions in a very humble ward with few resources, I asked if any single sisters were present. A tiny, elderly sister stepped forward. She was about four feet, eight inches tall, weighed only ninety pounds, and had an enormous smile on her face. She bore her testimony about the joy of service and her opportunities to teach and serve. After the session ended, many sisters hurried up to the front of the room to help me put my materials away. These sisters were leaders in the stake as Primary, Young Women, and Relief Society presidents. They surrounded the tiny sister who had borne her testimony and began to hug her, saying, "We are her children. She never had her own children, but she was our Primary teacher, our Young Women teacher, our Relief Society teacher, and our friend. Like a mother, she helped us, loved us, and taught us our faith. We are very much thankful for her."

Valentine's Day

Young single adults in my stake call Valentine's Day "Single Awareness Day." If you and your friends do not have a current beau, this becomes an excellent day to send flowers—even to yourself. You can also send valentines to friends. One young woman I know made cookies and took roses to friends she loves or to widows in her neighborhood. If you don't have a sweetheart, become one to others.

Birthdays

When it is your birthday in the Philippines they ask, "How young are you?" That phrase always made me smile; it embarrassed no one, and everyone would laugh aloud at the question. It is a totally positive response to the reality of another year of life. It implies another year of laughter, energy, and joy. Birthdays in America, especially for older single women, do not always evoke that sort of joy. In America when we ask, "How old are you?" it is sometimes enough to make one cringe. It seems one more step to old age and spinsterhood.

When I was in my late twenties a young man at my birthday celebration said, "You have so many candles you can use a blowtorch to light them." Suddenly I felt very, very old—and at a relatively young age. I now stand each year over my birthday cake and imagine myself with a blowtorch in hand.

Long before you could actually use a blowtorch to light your candles, there may come a birthday that entails a move. Recently during a visit to a young singles ward (ages eighteen to thirty), I stood next to a stunning single young woman who was telling her Relief Society president she was turning thirty-one and had only six months to remain in the ward. She looked stricken because it meant she had only limited days to find a mate in that ward. She felt time was running out for her.

Having lost eligibility for attending a singles ward long before I was married, I can assure you that if you attend the ward you are supposed to—no matter how trying—you will be blessed. If we follow the rules the Lord has set up, we can only be blessed. Married members have single relatives and friends. You will make a wide variety of friends among others of different ages and backgrounds, and the Lord can bless you.

As we grow older, certain birthdays carry great significance; the thirtieth, fortieth, fiftieth, and sixtieth are especially significant. Who does not want her life milestones to be as important to someone else as they are to her? If others around you forget—celebrate for yourself. I have a resourceful friend who ensures that her birthdays will be happy ones by always planning a special party for herself and everyone she loves.

Other Days Off and Weekends

At some point in my singleness I started to compare myself to Cinderella, the girl who stayed home alone while all the others went to the ball. Then a friend, Suzan, a Relief Society president in California, shared stories with me about women from her student ward who would call on weekend nights in tears because they did not have dates and felt forlorn. They would complain, "I am so lonely, and I need a date." She shared with me, "These girls needed to have a relationship with themselves before they could have one with anyone else. They were sitting around next to the phone waiting for it to ring instead of choosing to live their lives, attend plays, go out with friends, or do service. They were waiting for some man who probably wouldn't call instead of creating beautiful memories." This tidbit of information may help those sitting by the telephone. It's Just Lunch, a dating service, reported: "When there is chemistry, 97% of men will call within 72 hours to arrange a second date. So, ladies, if you haven't heard from him in 3 days, he is not interested."[4]

When I read these statistics and remembered Suzan's comments, I snapped out of my self-imposed sadness. There were a lot of Cinderellas out there, and I didn't want to be one anymore. I decided nothing could be more boring. The Lord says, "Men [and women] are, that they might have joy" (2 Nephi 2:25). In other words, the purpose of our existence is to live in joy, and it was clear that I was not doing that. I wanted to have joy whether I went to the ball or not. The weekends became a time to take all my nieces and nephews out, to visit someone elderly, to go out with my girlfriends on genuinely fun adventures, and to make beautiful memories.

I believe that life alone, especially during the holidays, can be a grueling and refining test and requires more endurance than one who has not experienced it may imagine. During those times of loneliness I often felt genuine pangs in my heart. Those pangs forced me to call upon every resource I possessed and caused me to develop in ways I could not have envisioned. I began to depend more heavily on Heavenly Father. I looked for people to serve, for ways to use my time that were meaningful, for ways to be useful to the people around me. Our daughter Sharmon told me about her friend Vicki, a divorcée, who thinks about things others will need before they think of those things themselves. She asks, "Does your mom need a ride to Relief Society? Do you need me to feed your dog while you are on a trip? Do you need me to water the lawn?" Vicki is a beautiful example of service, and she is happy and productive in a way that is an example to all of us.

I remember when my spending some holidays alone seemed like torture. The time went painfully slowly, and I suffered every moment. These days were painful because I had always envisioned spending them with my eternal family. Comparing Christmas or Thanksgiving or Valentine's Day or Mother's Day to torture in a fiery furnace may seem a stretch to some, but these holidays came every year, year after year, and served as a continual painful reminder of blessings I desired. But looking back, I see that those days provided me an opportunity to exercise my faith, my knowledge of the gospel plan, and my eternal perspective.

Lonely times can be soul-searching opportunities to turn to Heavenly Father and really discover our divine nature. These solitary struggles can serve as an impetus and refiner, helping us to rise above the doldrums of everyday living. We can discover who we really are. It took me a while to figure out that gospel principles were the only way to eternal happiness. Elder Donald L. Staheli reminded us that "President Boyd K. Packer has stated on a number of occasions that 'we all have the right to inspiration and direction by the Spirit of the Holy Ghost.' And then he adds, 'We all live far below our privileges.' . . . Many of us are missing some spiritual opportunities and blessings by letting 'the things that should matter most in life be at the mercy of the things that matter least.'"[5]

In our walk of faith, which can be challenging, we develop and change. Heavenly Father provided me the gifts of life and time, but I was to choose how to use them. I tried to become more obedient and prayerful, and I discovered there were spiritual blessings connected to my efforts. President Ezra Taft Benson described these blessings: "'When obedience ceases to be an irritant and becomes our quest, in that moment God will endow us with power.'"[6]

My experience as a single woman molded me in a way I came to appreciate. I came to know that faith is total trust in Him—trust that all will be well. We can build that trust through consistent prayer, scripture reading, and temple attendance. We also need to turn our will over to Heavenly Father and sincerely accept the reality that He knows what is best for us and for our eternal progress. A friend who was a Christian Scientist tried to explain to me her belief that through her faith she could be healed. She kept saying, "I believe if we have faith enough, it is possible for the Lord to bless us if it is His will." It genuinely surprised her when I responded, "I understand that kind of faith, and it can heal." We have a Heavenly Father who loves us and who is personally aware of us and who watches over us at all times. Developing faith in His will for us can heal the unseen wounds of our loneliness.

The Blessings of Holidays

In considering all the holidays, I believe it is clear that in large part we make ourselves happy or miserable by how we respond to our circumstances and the expectations we set for ourselves. My husband told me about a place in the developing Church where an unusually high proportion of members paid tithing. He asked an Area Seventy about the blessings he saw the people receive as a result. This was his reply: "They have not been blessed with many material things, but they have been blessed to lower their expectations for material things to make them happy. They have been blessed to see the spiritual things the Lord has bestowed upon them—peace, love, and faith. They have become much happier with less."

That story leads me to consider the expectations we place on others and ourselves during the significant holidays of the year. Our Heavenly Father would have us celebrate in His way, with a happy heart and willing hands and in the service of His Beloved Son. We are meant to celebrate in the good life around us and to create many happy moments for ourselves. I have celebrated holidays single and married. The one truth I have learned is to enjoy the day the Lord has made. Each day is the only one of its kind.

Be Grateful Every Day

In large measure, our attitude and faith determine how happy we are. Gratitude always makes it a happier day. One sister who married later in life and discovered she had cancer related how gratitude transformed her life. During a Relief Society lesson she related how her perspective of happiness had evolved as she experienced trials. She showed three pictures of herself to the class: 1) slender and beautiful in the early days of her marriage, 2) with no hair while she was undergoing chemotherapy, and 3) with her husband and two adopted children playing recently in the snow. She told the class that she was thankful for every single day. She told how, in her single days, wearing a size 6 dress meant satisfaction; during her sickness, just being alive brought her peace; and now being with family and in good health, she had tasted true joy.

She encouraged everyone in the class to make a "gratitude door"—a large sheet of white paper attached to the home door—on which they were to jot down something for which they were grateful as they came and went. Those in the class who made gratitude doors reported how dramatically the small grateful thoughts they recorded every day uplifted and energized them. One sister said, "I learned I cannot be unhappy and grateful at the same time."

We can begin now to be happy. There are also some things we can do now that will help us in the future, and I know from my own experience that they will bless your life. I encourage you to learn the womanly arts, especially cooking. One of the first questions the General Authority who introduced me to my husband asked was, "Are you a good cook?" I answered, "I can do five things well." He said, "That's great."

The truth is, I was not a good cook when I married my husband. I even burned grilled cheese sandwiches consistently. I remember placing the burned side down on the plate so it would not be immediately noticeable. My husband was an awfully good sport in the early months of our marriage, but I often wished I had spent more time in the kitchen and less time lamenting.

I have come to realize that a warm plate of homemade rolls, cookies, and a yummy roast really help to make a house a home. The family I joined had had a wonderful mother who was a great cook. They loved to eat the things she prepared. Certain foods had come to represent the holidays. When they drink Christmas punch or eat cream pies, they think of all the happy memories they had with her. There are foods that hold great and wholesome memories of her for her family. The domestic arts are important because the way a home looks, feels, and smells creates an environment of love. I am still not a terrific cook, but I am great with decorations. I just let others bring the rolls.

"This is the day which the Lord hath made" (Psalm 118:24). Rejoice in it. Live true to your covenants, and make each day as vibrant as it can be. Live the life of a woman who will, in the time appointed by the Lord, be a wife and mother. Create a sweet and holy haven to live in. Be active in your ward. Serve as much as you can, as often as you can.

We have the moment. We can seek to make our lives beautiful and full of the Spirit of the Lord every day, holiday or workday, single or married. Our reward will be joy, happy memories, and no cause for regrets.

CHAPTER 5

A SINGLE DATE

We counsel you to channel your associations with the
opposite sex into dating patterns that have the potential to mature into
marriage, not hanging-out patterns that only have the prospect to
mature into team sports like touch football.
—Elder Dallin H. Oaks

*B*ecause young women ages eighteen to thirty are greatly concerned about dating or the lack of it, I've devoted most of this chapter to them. I hope, however, that women above that age and men
also will find some sections useful. Remember that when the Lord
has someone prepared for us, it may take only one date to begin to
realize it.

The Importance of Dating

Many young women and men I have spoken with say that dating
is almost unknown among their peers. A Young Women leader said
that in a recent dating panel held in her ward, youth submitted questions that revealed an almost total lack of knowledge regarding dating: "What is the purpose of dating? Why should we do it? How do
we do it? Isn't it just as good to hang out with our friends?"

The panel members, juniors and seniors in high school whom one
would think had some experience with dating, answered only, "The
prophet has asked us to date. We think that it is a commandment."

The questions and answers left the leaders bewildered. The dating they had done as teenagers was not going on or even understood in this younger group.

For all age groups, one-on-one dating gives participants a much better idea of how individuals will behave in the one-on-one relationship of marriage than they can get from group involvement alone. Group dynamics are strong and can interfere with a couple's getting to know each other and learning about each other's core values. A couple who are interested in each other but have not been able to determine how compatible they are deserve and should give themselves privacy to discover their feelings without commitment before they become more tightly linked. They should be free to date a number of people simultaneously. This way they can compare the experiences and feelings they have with different individuals, which will help them to make a better choice. It's wise not to talk about other dates with someone you are dating. Simply enjoy and learn from your time together.

Dating does not have to be elaborate or expensive. A walk in the park, a game of tennis, or a milkshake all qualify as dates. Unfortunately, for many young people a date has come to be considered a large and expensive production signifying a deep commitment instead of a casual, inexpensive opportunity to get to know someone better. This idea has crippled dating and prevented many from participating.

Especially for young people and students, low-cost and easy-to-implement ideas of fun and imagination are best: walks in the rain, hikes in autumn, water fights with a garden hose, and ice cream eaten on the back porch. These inexpensive events have become a thing of the past in the current culture. Preparing for a date has come to mean spending enormous amounts of money on limos, buying expensive prom dresses, eating lavish dinners at restaurants, and planning months in advance. It means proposing a date through elaborate means and answering in kind. It is almost too much work to prepare for, never mind pay for.

Extravagant material expectations and indulgences even keep young men and young women from growing up and accepting responsibility. This is reflected in a new generation of men. "The years from 18 until 25 and even beyond have become a distinct and separate life stage, a strange, transitional never-never land between adolescence and adulthood in which people stall for a few extra years." These individuals are "permanent adolescents, . . . twenty-something Peter Pans" who are indecisive and delay the responsibilities of marriage.[1]

In less affluent cultures or previous generations, young men would be much more self-reliant and perhaps even important bread-winners and caretakers for their families. Meeting these responsibilities generally helps people develop self-esteem and a sense of dignity. We develop confidence in ourselves by overcoming the obstacles that present themselves in life. We learn to be competent by working through challenges. A young man who has grown up with abundant material means has probably had fewer such opportunities and may not yet have developed confidence in his ability to provide for a wife and family. The additional pressure of young women who have been indulged most of their lives and who expect costly engagement rings, followed by expensive cars, houses, and other luxuries in the initial stages of marriage may scare young men and cause them to run from future responsibilities.

A Brigham Young University stake leader told me that a young man confided in her that the young woman he wished to marry wanted a ten-thousand-dollar engagement ring, and he did not have the money. When asked why the young woman wanted this ring, the young man said, "So it will be bigger than her friends' rings." He asked, "What do you think I should do?" The leader wisely answered, "Find another girl to marry."

The immaturity of this young woman so caught up in appearances is clear, but I wonder why the young man had not already figured this out. Was he so pampered and indulged that he did not realize that his girlfriend's extravagant expectations were unreasonable and indicated larger problems to follow? The real problem facing many of us is exaggerated materialism and a desire for the things of the world, rather than the things of God.

Such materialism has provoked some to avoid the responsibilities of marriage. Many eligible young men and young women with expendable income have decided to travel the world, buy expensive cars, and purchase every new electronic device. Payment of their accumulated debts then takes precedence over dating and marriage.

The world's expectation that happiness is inextricably bound to owning lots of material goods runs directly counter to prophetic admonitions to marry and live simply. This important issue is best recognized during courtship, when a potential union with a spendthrift can be called off, rather than after marriage, when the issue is likely to cause multiple sorrows, including marital strife, bankruptcy, and divorce.

In the Philippines some young couples save money all their lives and go into excessive debt to provide a glamorous wedding celebration. They prolong their engagements to accumulate money and end up paying wedding expenses for years after they marry. All this limits and prevents the creation of celestial families.

During our service in the Philippines, Elder Oaks counseled young couples and their families to abandon the practice of extravagant wedding celebrations and invite only family and a few close friends. More than one couple with limited means went into the Church distribution center in Manila to purchase a simple CTR ring before they were married in the temple. They concentrated on the eternal union, not on a one-day blowout celebration with expensive, superfluous bangles and bling. These Filipino couples will have a greater chance of happiness in marriage as they focus on each other and on their covenants rather than on trying to impress people through expensive overindulgence. In addition, they have a greater chance for financial security because they are expressing the values of the Lord in their financial dealings—staying out of debt, building Zion in their homeland, and saving money for future needs.

During dating and courtship, individuals make choices about whether to follow the prophet's counsel. If you need to bring your life into greater conformity with this counsel, now is the time to do so, even if you are not dating or courting. Think of it as worthwhile preparation for the marriage you desire. The blessings of freeing yourself from financial burdens and bad spending habits will provide you greater freedom and peace of mind.

Other issues beyond materialism currently deter dating, such as the pressure to commit prematurely. Eighteen- to thirty-year-olds for whom going out as a couple has come to mean a serious commitment, not just an opportunity to have fun and get to know each other, have trouble socializing in a way that helps them move toward marriage. Some couples in singles wards say that because of this pressure, they do not date persons in their ward, or they date secretly ("stealth dating") to avoid detection. They do not even speak the word *dating* out loud. Some singles go to extreme lengths to refer to dating as anything else because dating carries the connotation of a serious commitment, and they are not prepared for that. Dating can be emotionally exhilarating for some, but for others it may seem an exercise in futility. One friend, after years of dating and no results, described her fruitless experience as midway between undergoing a continuous root canal operation and an ongoing tedious job interview.

When you have the opportunity to date, try to be a friend. Of course we want to get married, but we want to marry someone we know and love, not just anyone who breathes and has a testimony. It should be a matter of heart and mind, not illusion and infatuation. It simply takes time and experience for people to get to know each other and establish a grounded relationship. If every date is emotionally intense, with the question of marriage ever present, people can't relax and be themselves. Not only is that counterproductive but you can't really get to know others who aren't acting like themselves. That sort of intensity is unpleasant. Many men and women who have been exposed to such intensity early in a relationship will probably decide it is too much for them and will not be willing to repeat the experience.

In the Church we are counseled to date those with similar values who would make good marriage partners. If we seldom date, a date may seem to mean more than just to learn about each other. We date to get married, it is true, but we do not have to leap on every prospect as if we were ready to marry right now and were trying to decide whom to drag along. Remember, an invitation to a date is not a proposal. The Lord expects us to take our time getting to know someone, to decide for ourselves whether the relationship would be a good union, and to let those feelings of wanting to be with each other develop incrementally.

Planning is the key to success, especially with dating. Keep things small and simple. A concerned mother of a son who has agonized and prayed and worried said, "Tell everyone that a date is not a marriage proposal. If women realize this, men won't be too inhibited to plan a good time for you. Enjoy friends, enjoy time together; you will learn from all you come in contact with, and it will make you a better mate."

Elder Oaks tells young men that to achieve success they must have a plan of action—it is sort of like a missionary who seeks to baptize a family. It might begin by 1) being a friend, 2) asking out a young woman, (3) giving her flowers, and so forth. A little planning goes a long way. "Out of small things proceedeth that which is great" (D&C 64:33).

Finally, date with a purpose. While he was serving as mission president in Brazil, Grant Bangerter occasionally learned of Brazilian sister missionaries who became attracted to the American elders they served with because the elders were such worthy men. At the time there were few worthy Brazilian men who were members of the Church, so the sisters looked to the American elders as prospects for future husbands. President Bangerter would counsel them, "Your purpose is not to marry outside your nation and culture. If you go to America, you will most probably be unhappy and have a greater chance of divorcing."

He reminded them that they were missionaries who had skills and the Spirit. He told them that when they went home from their missions, they should look for young men in the community who acted and spoke and lived like future Latter-day Saint bishops. They should teach these men the gospel, and if the relationship didn't culminate in marriage for them, it might for another sister.

President Bangerter instructed his male missionaries that when they returned home, they should date at least three times each young woman they asked out. He told them, "If the chemistry and the potential for a lasting relationship does not seem to be there for you, think of a friend, and line up that young woman with him." Many marriages and sweet friendships came from his advice.

Hanging Out

Until my husband spoke of "hanging out" in his 2005 Church Educational System talk to young adults ages eighteen to thirty, I had never heard the term. Elder Oaks credits the Lord's inspiration for his strong caution about hanging out and his direct counsel for singles to begin dating.

Since that talk I have learned more about hanging out than I ever supposed possible. Young women in my ward have shared with me that when they hang out, they just become friends with the young men. Hanging out gets a bit boring because it is like being idle in a group. The boys become such good friends to the girls that no one would think of becoming serious or wanting to get to know any one better. That would break up the group!

I remember Elder Oaks's words: "My single young friends, we counsel you to channel your associations with the opposite sex into dating patterns that have the potential to mature into marriage, not hanging-out patterns that only have the prospect to mature into team sports like touch football."[2]

"Now, the important question: What did you do following his talk? Did anything change?" asked Elder Neil L. Andersen in a subsequent fireside. "Elder Henry B. Eyring gave this warning:

"'The failure to take prophetic counsel lessens our power to take inspired counsel in the future.' . . .

" . . . Those who responded positively and promptly to Elder Oaks's counsel surely found that the blessings of heaven followed. Let me read from a letter sent to Church headquarters from a couple in Arizona more than a year after his talk:

"'Your remarks have had a lasting impact on our lives. . . .

"'Your direct and clear counsel helped us realize that dating was an opportunity to get to know one another better and not an immediate commitment to a long-term relationship or marriage.'

"The result was that they *were* married in May [2006] in the Washington D.C. Temple."[3]

Obedience does bring forth blessings. As we lunched with students during a recent visit to BYU–Idaho, they mentioned how they had tried to change their hanging-out patterns. The comments of one young man especially touched me. Previously he had just hung out with his girlfriend. Their relationship wasn't going anywhere, and they were fighting all the time. But since he had begun actually planning dates and asking her out, the level of respect in their relationship had risen and they were getting along much better, even contemplating marriage.

An article in *USA Today* states that nationally singles are experiencing these same dating problems. They are hanging out, not dating or pairing up exclusively with just one person. " 'They [college women] feel they either have too little or too much commitment.' . . .

"Neither choice contributes much to finding a future husband while in college. . . .

"While men and women may 'hang out,' spending time together, what they don't do is 'date' in the old-fashioned sense. Only about 50% of [college] senior women had been asked out on six or more dates by men in college."[4]

Another concern is that as formal dating has disappeared, so have the rituals surrounding dating. Women have told me they seldom know where they stand in a relationship, and men rarely acknowledge being part of a couple.

Our niece in her early thirties confirmed this. She felt role reversals and feminism had changed the dating field. She said, "It is so confusing who asks out, who pays, and who picks up that it really hurts relationships." She told me of a handsome and eligible young man who had asked her out when she lived in New York City. He had called and asked her to meet him multiple times, and each time she paid her own way. Finally, when he asked her out for a fifth date, she declined to go, telling him she did not appreciate being treated that way. He replied, "Oh, I'm sorry. I really like you. I would be glad to pay you back the money you spent." She stopped dating him. She said, "He didn't get it." She did not want to renegotiate gender roles and expectations from the ground up when the prophets and Church leaders have already made it clear how the Lord wants these to function for our greatest happiness. She simply wanted to have these as a foundation to the relationship and be treated accordingly.

To help facilitate a successful dating relationship, it is usually wise to allow the man to be the initiator, no matter what age you are. If he makes the effort to contact you, arranges to see you, and takes care of the details, you can be fairly certain that he wants to be with you and has some idea of the basics. In addition, it is an interesting truth that the more self-initiated and independent effort a man puts into building a relationship with a woman, the more he comes to value her. You can encourage him in this by giving him time and space to decide for himself if he wants to pursue you. If he chooses not to, it may hurt, but not as much as if you initiate the relationship and then come to realize he is not interested. Worse, you may discover he is just spending time with you until something better comes along or he figures out an acceptable time and way to end things.

During my early acquaintance with my husband, I allowed him to make all the phone calls and appointments and contacts because I felt those were his prerogative until I knew him well. That entailed more than a few nail bites as I waited for him to call me. A confident woman does not need constant reassurance.

We meet others in a variety of ways. I must add that it is perfectly appropriate for a woman to show interest by inviting a man to join her in an activity. Many permanent relationships begin this way. Three young couples in our ward who dined with us in our home said that all three of their romances began when the woman instigated the first date. The men, however, were men, and began to pursue the women, and that made all the difference. If a woman decides to initiate a first date, the men appreciated something casual and informal, where they could talk and become friends with her. They also all advised, "Leave him to decide whether to attempt a second date."

When dating, many young college-age women say they appreciate a date that is *planned* and *paid for* and in which the couple is *paired off*—the 3-P dating plan Elder Oaks counseled men to adopt.[5] These young women have learned that a date isn't a proposal and they need not feel crushed if they are not asked out again. They are learning to enjoy dating and to relax and appreciate the opportunity to be with a friend in a one-on-one situation.

Because many women find dating opportunities to be rare, men should strive to make their time together enjoyable. Many women feel reluctant to put themselves in the dating arena because it is so uncomfortable. Manners help us in dating. Men should realize the importance of treating women with courtesy. Karen, a young coed at BYU, went on what she thought would be a perfect first date with a most attractive young man. During the date, he talked only about himself and never asked about her interests. When they returned home he also let her walk herself to the door. She decided never to date him again because he showed so little concern for her. Little acts of kindness make all the difference.

Our son Dallin reminded me that it is often very difficult for a man to extend himself to ask for a date because of the chance of rejection. To avoid pain or embarrassment some men sometimes find it easier not to date. They lose the opportunity for one-on-one interaction with potential marriage partners. Always remember that when someone invites you on a date, respond with courtesy whether you accept the invitation or not.

We know from 3 Nephi that our Savior built loving relationships through personal, one-on-one experiences. He understood the great significance of seeing eye to eye, speaking voice to voice, and experiencing personal touch. He invited His followers to come to Him, not in a massive group but one by one.

"And it came to pass that the multitude went forth, and thrust their hands into his side, and did feel the prints of the nails in his hands and in his feet; and this they did do, going forth one by one until they had all gone forth, and did see with their eyes and did feel with their hands, and did know of a surety and did bear record, that it was he, of whom it was written by the prophets, that should come" (3 Nephi 11:15).

The Savior made time to greet every person in a very personal manner. In addition to proving who He was, He was establishing a more direct and personal relationship with individuals who touched Him so they knew for themselves that He had suffered in their behalf and the love He had for each person that led Him to do so. He shows us that to know and understand one another "of surety," we must do so on a personal level. As human beings we were created to connect and relate in a very personal manner. That is how we learn to know and love one another.

Clearly, dating requires some effort and exposes us to some emotional risk. Hanging out leads us to become more like the world, and though it involves no emotional risk, it does not provide the opportunity for emotional fulfillment, either. Taken to an extreme form, it prevents us from fulfilling the plan of salvation as we waste away our youthful years doing basically nothing. The fact that everyone is doing it and it feels comfortable is not a reason to do it. The Lord has better things in store for us.

Whom to Date

It is common sense that we marry those we date, so we are cautioned to date those within our own religion. No matter what age we are, from sixteen to eighty-six, we make ourselves vulnerable when we date those who do not share our faith and our values. When we do so, we run a serious risk of trouble and unhappiness as the relationship progresses, or, worse, of forgetting those truths we hold sacred. A graduate student who had such an experience wrote soberly, "I would rather have the heavy feeling of loneliness than ever to compromise myself again."

Our granddaughter told me that during the summer her roommate had met a young man who was not a Latter-day Saint, and their relationship continued into the school year. The young man is handsome, charming, humorous, and attentive but does not share the roommate's values. The roommate spends lots of time with him because no one else is asking her out. (Conversely, it may be that no one is asking her out because she is spending so much time with him.) She is finding herself more and more attracted and dependent on this young man and feels she loves him. She is also feeling more and more confused and unhappy.

One evening after a date the roommate returned in tears and asked for advice about dating this young man. Our granddaughter replied, "He doesn't hold the same moral standards you do, and he doesn't believe in abstinence before marriage. He doesn't believe in or practice the Word of Wisdom. Do you really think you can pursue eternal life with someone who won't embrace the gospel of Jesus Christ and has no interest in learning about it? He has no interest in paying tithing, and he doesn't believe in it. He isn't really interested in praying or reading the scriptures. Is this really a man you want to possibly marry some day?"

The roommate is still dating this man because she has become emotionally dependent on him and does not want to be alone. This can happen to anyone of any age. It is extremely draining to extricate yourself from a romance that is not for you. Anyone who has done so will testify to that. In this case, when the values of the two people are so different, significant tears and time could have been avoided by never entering into the relationship. There is also a great danger that your own values can be eroded to conform to those of someone on whom you have become dependent. Some people justify dating such people as being an example to them and leading them to the gospel. This is dangerous and requires discernment. You may become the target of their conversion efforts to separate you from your standards.

It is also wise to listen to friends who warn you about someone they have dated. No two experiences are alike, but others' experiences can contain valuable cautions. A woman in her late forties was told by friends that the man she was dating had a consistent pattern of dating someone for a long period of time, but when the prospect of marriage came up, he would move on. This woman refused to listen to her friends, even when she saw little evidence of sincere interest. For example, he gave her a man's extra-large sweater (obviously a gift he had received that he didn't want for himself) for Christmas. She wasted many years of her life dating him, only to be deserted when she pressed him about marriage.

Also valuable are the experiences of persons who determined to break up with the individuals they were dating when they noticed behaviors that made them doubt that they were suitable prospects for marriage.

Elizabeth was dating a returned missionary, which was extremely unusual in her small branch in Chile. He attended Church services every week but did not wear a tie. She finally asked him, "Why don't you wear a tie?" He told her it was no big deal, that he didn't feel like it, and that he dressed as he felt comfortable. This answer caused her to reconsider her feelings about him. Was he also casual in keeping his temple covenants? Would he be casual about being a support and a patriarch to his family? She decided to stop dating him. Every girl in her branch thought she was crazy. "He is so cute, and there is no one else!" they chided her. Within the next month she went to a singles dance and saw a young man across the room. She noticed him first by his tie. Their relationship matured from there, and they married. Her children call this story "The Miracle of the Tie." For Elizabeth it was something more. She wanted a husband who was obedient in every way.

Elder David A. Bednar tells of a recently returned missionary who was dating a young woman he had deep feelings for and with whom he was considering engagement and marriage. Their courtship took place at the time President Gordon B. Hinckley counseled the Relief Society sisters and young women of the Church to wear only one earring in each ear. This young woman wore extra earrings. The returned missionary patiently waited for her to remove them, but she did not. "This was a valuable piece of information for this young man, and he felt unsettled about her unresponsiveness to a prophet's pleading. For this and other reasons, he ultimately stopped dating the young woman, because he was looking for an eternal companion who had the courage to promptly and quietly obey the counsel of the prophet in all things and at all times," said Elder Bednar.

We can give a false impression of ourselves to others by very small things. Elder Bednar added, "I simply invite you to consider and ponder the power of being quick to observe and what was actually observed in the case I just described. The issue was not earrings!"[6]

Because it is human nature to judge from appearances, we can inadvertently portray ourselves in a manner that does not accurately reflect what we believe.

Elder Bednar's talk had a profound effect on one twenty-six-year-old woman. She desired to marry, but nothing was happening. She had been promised in her patriarchal blessing that "a time would come when she would have the opportunity to court and be courted." She also shared this admonition from her blessing: "If you are modest and chaste and prayerfully seek the guidance of the heavens . . . you will be guided to your companion." Tears rolled down her cheeks as she looked to me for advice. The only words that came

to me were from Elder Bednar's talk about how we should be quick
to observe ourselves. She blushed as she looked at her own apparel—
very short shorts. Nothing was said between us, but she realized that
for her the issue was also obedience. From that moment on she
dressed more modestly, and within six months she met and married
a man for whom obedience was also a priority.

The Effects of Technology

Our technology contributes to a high standard of living for the
average citizen and to a lifestyle that no previous generation attained.
For all age groups, however, technological toys can distract from the
important matters of life, and they present dangers and risks. For
your own welfare, please do not spend too much time in front of the
television, at movies, on the Internet, or with video games.

When we are plugged into media and technology, we are discon-
necting from the world of people and limiting our ability to learn
personal caring and intimacy. I am not warning against an opportunity to relax in front of the TV for a little while after a taxing day or
searching the Web to learn. I am warning against living a life so
packed with technological interactions that it leaves little time for
people. Time is what our lives are made of, and it is too precious to
waste much of it interacting with impersonal digital images.

A Young Men leader in my home ward cautioned the young men
not to go to the Internet when they have an extra hour to kill. He
said he only goes online when he has a purpose and a task to
perform—to look up information or to check his bank account.
Time is precious, and we should be "anxiously engaged in a good
cause" (D&C 58:27). When we are searching the Web without direction, we are also much more likely to come in contact with porno-
graphic or other questionable materials.

"Virtual reality is the essence of reality without the consequences of it." It is only an imitation of real life. Too much time spent in virtual reality can affect our ability to "build eternal realities."[7] We want real friendships, real relationships, and real salvation. Too much technology has the potential to distance us from that.

It is possible to spend long hours alone interacting with machines and to cripple or lose our capacity to interact well with people. When we are plugged in, we are not practicing the social skills that enable us to function successfully with others, professionally and socially. We cannot read body language from a computer terminal or respond with compassion and affection to a computer game. People are more likely to speak inappropriately in chat rooms or to use text messaging and not speak at all.

We can begin to confuse and even exaggerate our ability to function in the real world because of contacts in the virtual world of possibilities. To illustrate this, I heard one neighbor joke with another who was about to go into surgery for hip replacement. "It will cost you so much money, and you don't have to go to the hospital. I learned how to do a hip replacement on the Internet this morning, and I can do it for you." Everyone listening broke into laughter at the thought that this brief exposure on the Internet qualified him as an expert in an unknown field.

We can also become detached and somehow distanced from the consequences of our actions and words. A mother told me a young man had texted her daughter that he was out front in a car waiting for her to come out for a date. She told her daughter to text back that she was not coming out unless he came to the front door. In the olden days, well-brought-up young women were taught not to respond when a man honked but to wait for him to come to the door and then invite him in and introduce him to her parents. A little courtesy can go a long way in forming successful relationships with others.

Some college women say they consider it an insult to receive an e-mail or text asking them out because there is no personal element and face-to-face interaction. A text message is not warm and inviting, but it is a way for the invitor to minimize the pain of rejection. But the price we pay by separating ourselves from one another with technology is that we become insensitive and less caring toward one another.

One young man even received a "Dear John" letter over a fax machine. His girlfriend had asked him to feed her dog because she was late for work. He was on his way to a college exam and told her he would do it right after his exam. After taking the exam, he went instead to work. The entire office told him a special message was waiting on the fax machine for him. So everyone in his office could be aware of it, his girlfriend had sent him a fax, telling him it was all over between them because of his selfishness. She used technological means to make her announcement very public. He was mortified, and it took months before he could even discuss it.

Worse, a preoccupation with technological distractions may also prevent us from listening to the Spirit and hearing the still, small voice. Constant use of cell phones and iPods and hours sitting before the computer bombard our senses and leave us little time to meditate and learn the will of our Father in Heaven. We need quiet time to understand the things of God.

Internet Dating

"It used to be embarrassing to need the Internet to date. It smacked of geeky antisocialness—people who couldn't make it in the 'real' dating world. People with something to hide. People so desperate for a date they would seek out strangers at odd hours, from their lonely, maybe even creepy dens. . . .

"But in the last few years, online dating has switched, becoming something of a destination not of last but of first resort. . . .

"As a result, nearly 1 in 4 single Americans who are looking for a romantic partner—or about 16 million people—use the 1,000 or more dating Web sites out there. That includes almost 1 in 5 Americans in their 20s, and 1 in 10 Americans in their 30s or 40s." It is big business. In 2004 these Web sites were netting approximately $470 million yearly.[8]

Has Internet dating suddenly become more safe and reliable, or is it just more convenient so we dismiss the dangers as improbable and happening to someone else? Internet dating works for the world; why shouldn't it work for us?

I know couples who attribute their meeting to the Internet. There are occasional success stories, but they are the exception. Respect yourself enough to do online dating only with great discretion and care. Although some Latter-day Saints have found eternal companions in this manner, when you open yourself up to the Internet you enter a realm that holds limitless dangers. One single sister confided in me, "The overall feeling of the thirty-one-and-above dating venue was so desperate and uncomfortable that I decided to explore other opportunities." Online dating became her alternative choice, but because online dating sites are not Church-sponsored, it was not uncommon to run into morally compromising or volatile situations.

There have also been many incidents of grave deception. For people of any age, meeting someone electronically is no substitute for the real thing. To carry on a romance online is at best to indulge in illusion. It appeals particularly to those who want the good feelings of having someone interested in them without the risks inherent in real relationships. Not only are such involvements a waste of time and emotional energy, akin to preadolescent crushes on popular media figures, but they may also be an unwitting invitation to abuse.

No matter how engaging a person may sound on the electronic media, you have no safe way to determine who he really is and how compatible you may be with him in the real world without taking significant risk. It is clear from news reports of sting operations aimed at online predators that you do not know for sure who you are dealing with when you strike up a conversation with someone in a chat room, and computer dating services may be only marginally better. Even after you have met, you cannot be sure the person is telling the truth about himself.

One middle-aged divorced man told of meeting a woman on a dating site for Latter-day Saint singles. When he went to her home, a woman with no resemblance to the picture on the Internet invited him inside. He felt uncomfortable and duped, but what was more difficult for him was that within minutes the woman broke down in tears and announced that she knew by the Spirit that they were to be married. Their virtual expectations led them both into a very unpleasant situation.

Seeking an eternal companion, a young single mother encountered a man her age on a commercial online dating service that advertised itself for single Latter-day Saints. After meeting and getting to know him a bit, this young mother, her parents, siblings, and friends agreed that he was intelligent and kind and worthy of her interest. They dated for months before he confessed he was already married. It was a prolonged and sad lesson for her and her family.

Instead of using the Internet to meet others, you are usually safer to socialize within traditional patterns—in groups and organizations where people meet and have known each other for a long time or have mutual acquaintances. Always rely on prayer and the Spirit to guide you.

Meeting Someone at Church

When you meet someone at church, you can usually assume that you share similar values. I can directly attribute my marriage to my Church service. We had been dating and were enjoying each other's company, but before he allowed his feelings for me to develop any further, he wanted to know more about me. Unknown to me, he prayed to meet someone he knew and trusted who had also known me for a long time and who could tell him more about me.

One Sunday when he came to dinner, I asked him if we could visit an elderly couple who had missed my Sunday school class. They were dear friends of mine, and I had heard they were ill. He walked to their door with me, which was extremely unusual because until that time we had made every effort to keep our dating private. When the door opened, Elder Oaks immediately greeted the elderly gentleman with a smile and a big hug. He was well acquainted with him, having earlier attempted to hire him as a professor at BYU.

My elderly friend had been a partner in one of the most prestigious accounting firms in America and was renowned for his good judgment and honesty. I had no idea. I only knew him and his wife as dear friends who had retired to my condominium complex. We entered their home and visited, and the time flew. I looked at my watch and asked if I could excuse myself to finish cooking dinner.

In the conversation that ensued after I left, this gentleman told Elder Oaks of their long years of friendship (nearly twenty) with me. He said that he and his wife had often commented on my singleness and expressed the opinion that I must be being saved for someone very special. For Elder Oaks, who implicitly trusted and respected this man's opinion, that comment meant he would continue to court me. As for me, I was taken totally by surprise by my friend's comments when Elder Oaks later shared them with me. The elderly gentleman had seen me serve in the ward in many capacities for many years, and the Spirit directed Elder Oaks to him as a witness of my character. I can testify from this experience that service in the Church makes a great difference in our lives and that the still, small voice can direct us to great blessings.

Building Social Skills for Dating

It is possible to improve social skills that will help us in dating and courtship. A singles ward bishop, Clyde Robinson noticed the struggle for young men and young women to meet. He wrote, "I often felt students were like ships passing in the night here at BYU, not appropriately taking advantage of the presence of tens of thousands of other young single adults here in Utah County attending BYU and Utah Valley University and involved in other organizations." He listed several factors contributing to the delay in the courtship process among young single adults, including indecision about career choices, the current trend of hanging out (which does not facilitate social-intimacy skills), and a reluctance to establish trusting and self-revealing relationships because their parents did not model good relationships for them.

Many young men in singles wards who have experienced the devastation of divorce in their family seem slow to marry. They are bright, well-educated, and committed to the gospel, but they struggle with commitment in relationships. A nephew said, "My friends just do not want to repeat that experience and seem hesitant to marry. They have everything going for them, but they seem stuck."

Bishop Robinson also sensed an attitude of biological determinism—the idea that a person is born with genetic traits, such as shyness, that are difficult or impossible to overcome. He writes, "On several occasions I called such individuals on 'mini-missions' . . . to get to know several other 'shy' individuals in the ward over a couple of weeks." Likewise, in his Human Development class at BYU, Bishop Robinson gave extra credit to those who, during the course of the semester, had a one-on-one conversation with everyone of the opposite sex in their ward. He states, "Every semester several students take me up on this assignment and subsequently write that it was hard at first, but the task got easier and they are now less shy than they were before the exercise."[9]

The task of interaction didn't actually become easier; rather, students through practice became more adept at talking to people of the opposite sex. This indicates that biology may not be the strong force many people have supposed. As with many things, comfort with the opposite sex is a learned skill, largely a matter of practice. It is possible for us to develop our social skills, and we do not have to be limited by some idea of what our inherent nature is. These skills are worth developing even at the cost of numerous awkward moments because they help us interact with potential marriage partners.

Multistake Activities and Singles Conferences

The Church has devoted much time and effort to encouraging frequent multistake activities for young single adults. Everything from service projects to educational seminars to dances are held monthly. These activities are meant to appeal to a broad spectrum of single people and provide a wonderful, wholesome way for them to meet. Take advantage of such opportunities.

Multistake activities can be great fun—if you just attend. Do not let a singles activity you didn't enjoy prevent your attendance at others. Never dwell on the negative. One single sister said to me, "I just can't go out in such large groups. I put myself through it in high school, and I cannot do that again." Another told me, "When I go to a dance, I feel like I am invisible." In large groups I felt that way, too.

Don't give up. If dances aren't your thing, do not despair. Keep looking, and you will find an activity you enjoy. Best of all, others attracted to such an activity will have interests similar to yours.

Multistake opportunities can help you grow socially and spiritually. Many of the young singles in our stake have shared what fun the activities were, how many people they met, and how they were spiritually fed.

Singles conferences also provide an occasion for older singles to meet one another. Such events may require some effort because singles may have to travel long distances to attend them. Also, there is often a great range in age among the participants. But these are wonderful opportunities to be nourished by the Spirit and to socialize among others who hold your same values.

I remember a few conferences I attended where I felt overwhelmed by the large number of people and also by the disproportionate number of women. At times I went home fed by the classes, and at times I left feeling lonely and discouraged. It is easy to become discouraged, and we may feel convinced that no meaningful good can come of our involvement, but that is a mistake. It is remarkable what situations Heavenly Father can use to enlarge our hearts and minds and draw us closer to be more like Him. If we focus on serving others as our Savior did, despite our own distress, Church programs and events for singles can hold great and unexpected blessings for us.

Conclusion

Dating can be fun. It does not have to be expensive or elaborate. It can be enhanced with some creative imagination. If you desire an eternal marriage, the best people to date are those within your religion who hold similar values and have similar goals. Courtesy counts, and dating allows us to hone our social skills.

Dating also leads to marriage. As Elder Oaks said in his April 2007 general conference address: "In conclusion, I speak briefly to those contemplating marriage. The best way to avoid *divorce* from an unfaithful, abusive, or unsupportive spouse is to avoid *marriage* to such a person. If you wish to marry well, inquire well. Associations through 'hanging out' or exchanging information on the Internet are not a sufficient basis for marriage. There should be dating, followed by careful and thoughtful and thorough courtship. There should be ample opportunities to experience the prospective spouse's behavior in a variety of circumstances. Fiancés should learn everything they can about the families with whom they will soon be joined in marriage. In all of this, we should realize that a good marriage does not require a perfect man or a perfect woman. It only requires a man and a woman committed to strive together toward perfection."[10]

PART THREE

Everyday Living

CHAPTER 6

A SINGLE-MINDED WOMAN

We are daughters of a Heavenly Father who loves us.
—Young Women theme

*J*esus Christ taught the purpose of our life on earth. "When our Heavenly Father placed Adam and Eve on this earth, He did so with the purpose in mind of teaching them how to regain His presence."[1] With these truths in mind, each of us can choose to follow the Lord's counsel that we be single-minded in our words, thoughts, emotions, and actions. And we can reap the blessings:

"If your eye be single to my glory, your whole bodies shall be filled with light, and there shall be no darkness in you; and that body which is filled with light comprehendeth all things" (D&C 88:67).

It has been said that adversity can introduce us to ourselves. After twenty years of a troubled marriage and a devastating divorce, a dear friend found herself the sole support of herself and three children. She was ripped apart not only financially but also emotionally and spiritually. Her life seemed in tatters. Daily, multiple times, to maintain a modicum of calm and peace, she repeated to herself the Young Women theme: "We are daughters of a Heavenly Father who loves us and we love Him." She recently told me, "Those words, knowing them and believing them, sustained me and allowed me to function when I found myself in a very dark place in my life. Those words brought to my remembrance who I really was and where I wanted to go."

All of us at varying times may feel we have been cast into the deep, dark sea. Facing uncertainty and the unknown, some may feel as if they have been left adrift. On a very personal level we may face tragedy, death, and disappointment, but also on a public level we may face a sea of ambiguity and insecurity—global warming, terrorists, possible pandemics, economic uncertainty, and changing values.

We live in a world that rotates around popular opinion based on the trends and issues of the day. Popular talk show hosts, television psychologists, fashion magazines, and media commentators use skewed values and questionable practices to drive our opinions and influence our behavior. President Spencer W. Kimball instructed us, "There has never been a time in the world when the role of woman has been more confused."[2]

Confusion, discouragement, or self-doubt may erode our faith and cause us to turn away from the Savior and his kingdom on earth. If we focus our decisions on trends and worldly directions (popular opinion or social trends), we will be "tossed to and fro, and carried about with every wind of doctrine, by the sleight of men, and cunning craftiness, whereby they lie in wait to deceive" (Ephesians 4:14).

In contrast to popular opinion, The Church of Jesus Christ of Latter-day Saints teaches doctrines and principles. The difference is profound. Trends, fashions, and pop ideology are fleeting. Doctrines and principles serve as anchors of security, of direction, and of truth. If we, as women of God, fix our ideals and direction on doctrine and principles (for example, faith in the Lord Jesus Christ, following the prophet, repentance, serving others, and strengthening home and family), we will have a totally reliable and unchanging guide for our life's decisions.

To stay afloat in this dark world, we need to stay focused and single-minded, trusting in the Lord and believing in our futures and in our divine worth. The gospel is a shield from the harshness, pain, and evil that surround us. Waves of doubt and adversity almost certainly will wash over us. When we feel discouraged and alone, whether married or unmarried, our Heavenly Father is always there for us. I know firsthand that in the times of my adversity, the more I applied gospel principles to my life, the more Heavenly Father lightened my burdens. Just because our prayers are not answered immediately, by the means and in the way and time we desire, does not mean we are forsaken and that our Heavenly Father is not mindful of us. In the Doctrine and Covenants we read of great promises to those who are single-minded in their devotion to Heavenly Father:

"Therefore, sanctify yourselves that your minds become single to God, and the days will come that you shall see him; for he will unveil his face unto you, and it shall be in his own time, and in his own way, and according to his own will" (D&C 88:68).

This scripture is especially precious to me because I interpret it to mean that our individual needs and temperaments and situations are known to the Lord, and He ministers to our needs personally and explicitly. "He will unveil his face," wisdom, love, and protection to us in the time and way that are most beneficial to our eternal happiness and growth.

Satan knows that earthly concerns can test our mettle, and so he plants seeds of worry and doubt to corrode and impede our faith. Sometimes we ourselves can contribute to our own erosion of faith. Factors will vary from person to person. Often we don't turn completely from the things of God, but many of our choices lead us to be a bit less devoted, a bit less believing, and a bit less faithful. Just ever so slightly, our decisions may reflect a bit less obedience and a bit more influence of the world. It also follows that we will be a bit less happy and loyal to our Father in Heaven. We cannot be partial believers, partially steadfast, partially chaste, or even partial tithe payers without paying a spiritual price.

"He that wavereth is like a wave of the sea driven with the wind and tossed. For let not that man think that he shall receive any thing of the Lord. A double minded man is unstable in all his ways" (James 1:6–8). It is of special significance to Latter-day Saints that the verse that precedes this advice tells us specifically how to communicate with our Heavenly Father: "If any of you lack wisdom, let him ask of God, that giveth to all men liberally, and upbraideth not; and it shall be given him" (James 1:5).

In this estate we have control only over our own decisions and over our own desires and emotions. We have little control over anything else. We also have the hopes and pure motives that exist in our hearts. These are what matter to our Father in Heaven. If we turn our lives and hearts to Him, blessings will follow.

Single-minded women of God focus on building the kingdom of God on earth. In that single-minded focus, our efforts and our light will shine in different ways. Because we each have unique abilities, gifts, opportunities, and challenges, our individual works to build the kingdom will vary. We may have the opportunity to serve in the temple, to volunteer at a seniors' center, to help a neighbor, to comfort the ill, to draft legislation, to teach Sunbeams, to listen to a teenager, or to build bridges with those of other faiths.

Latter-day Saint poet and essayist Emma Lou Thayne shares her approach to being single-minded: "The best thing I have to offer anywhere is a happy person. Unhappy, I have nothing to give; I become part of the problem instead of part of the answer. Only by choosing from my own sources of good can I be a credible . . . woman."[3]

When we choose to be positive and develop a happy attitude, we make an enormous contribution. Our happy attitude makes us significant contributors in the world around us.

Service to Others Makes
All the Difference

As single-minded members of The Church of Jesus Christ of Latter-day Saints, we have the power to pray to our Father in Heaven and ask Him to help us become the men and women He would have us be. We can become more effective instruments in His hands by turning our desires over to Him. The Lord will bless and strengthen us as we serve others. Service to others provides the perspective that the universe doesn't simply rotate around us and our small problems.

The wards and stakes and districts and branches of the Church are filled with single men and women anxiously engaged in good works. One Southern California stake draws heavily on single and student wards to find outstanding early-morning seminary teachers. The same stake actively involves members of these same wards to serve in the Los Angeles California Temple, work as ward missionaries and high councilors, direct Scouting programs, and staff Young Women camp and youth conferences. In addition, members of these single and student wards have been called to serve in stake auxiliary presidencies.

Throughout the Church, wise priesthood leaders have learned that single members are effective leaders and teachers. In addition to sharing their talents and experience, singles serving in Church callings feel more integrated into their wards and stakes. Single members who serve—whether in the Church, family, or community—learn to balance work and other responsibilities in increasingly busy lives.

Service to others causes us to focus less on ourselves and our daily problems, petty grievances, unmet expectations, and so forth. Focusing only on ourselves causes us to be self-absorbed. It is a challenge to balance work, church, friends, and family responsibilities and still find time for personal growth and giving to others. A neighbor, Elizabeth, spoke to me about her daughter in her late twenties. "She would do anything for me and anyone else who asks. She has been involved with humanitarian projects throughout the world. She is generous—except with her time. With the demands at work and school, she has scheduled her days to the minute. Sometimes this causes her to serve others only when it is convenient and fits into her schedule." I identified so much with this story because the demands of working, supporting myself, and just getting through life often caused me to feel that I had limited time for others.

One of the great blessings of Church service is that we are called to the work—and we do not select whom, when, where, or in what capacity we serve. The Relief Society admonishes that "charity never faileth" (Moroni 7:46). I would also like to add that charity—both within the Church and outside it—is frequently demanding, occasionally exhausting, sometimes inconvenient, and inevitably unscheduled.

"Serving others is the best form of introspection," said J. Grant Davis. Grant was later killed in an accident. He left behind a young widow and family. Rather than wallow in her sadness, which would have been so easy with the death of this stellar young husband, his widow lifted herself and her family outside their sadness to serve others. My husband and I received a card from Mindy Davis, Grant's widow. She wrote:

"Grant's life was spent serving others in a myriad of ways. Tuesday, May 22nd, is Grant's 50th birthday. We have chosen to celebrate his birth by taking a plate full of warm chocolate chip cookies (his favorite) to someone who could use a lift. We invite you to join us in serving others in honor of Grant. We'd love to hear about your experience.

"You may have noticed the stamp on the envelope says, 'First Class Forever.' That's my Grant.

"Love,

"Mindy."[4]

Mindy has chosen to celebrate the life of her husband by serving and asking others to serve. She has used her grief to provide others a source of joy.

A friend shared how, when she was on her knees telling Heavenly Father that she was exhausted and tired of her single situation, she begged for assistance. The answer she received was to serve others. Her pain was not totally alleviated, but she was occupied and motivated and less concerned with her own problems.

For me loneliness was a challenge. If that is sometimes a challenge for you, make cookies for someone, visit a widow, or wash your neighbor's car. Call your Relief Society president or elders quorum president and ask who needs help. Some of my best experiences were in graduate school at Brigham Young University when I was an older single. I often spent time with the elders quorum president. Our dates were a bit unusual. We would pray and think of new members in our ward or those who were struggling. We planned our dates around them. We played games and had dinners. Those were the very best dates I can remember from my college years. In fact, they are about the only dates I can remember—because they were about helping others.

When you are married, your service project is sitting right in front of you. You don't have to look far to find opportunities to encourage, to comfort, to strengthen, and to nurture. The acts of service—helping with homework, planning family home evening, teaching the scriptures, tending a wounded heart—are all around you. A family puts automatic demands on a mother and a father.

When I was single I had to look for opportunities to serve others. I knew that I would be a happier, healthier person—more capable of loving and being loved—if I served others. To assuage my need to nurture, I spent hours with my nieces and nephews doing sleepovers, playing in the park, visiting the library, and going on picnics. This time together brought me much joy. I even drove my nephews as they did a paper route on weekends and holidays in the cold weather. Just being with them increased the love between us and made me feel needed. Small, mundane sacrifices of everyday life are what bind us in love to one another.

Single women can look for young mothers in their wards and neighborhoods to help. This provided me with the opportunity to nurture children, which I so desperately desired. Often I visited friends and played with their children. (To this day those children think I am their aunt, and they remember how we ate breakfast at McDonald's in our pajamas and walked barefoot through streams in the canyon.) A single woman or man has much to gain from helping a married couple with their family—fellowship, friends, and a view into how it feels to be a father or mother. Singles are in a unique position to nurture and serve.

Another important perk of friendship with married couples is the view it offers into marriage—examples of sacrifice, parenting styles, shared decision making, training children, planning finances, and so forth.

The Blessing and Challenge of Self-Reliance

President Marion G. Romney taught: "Self-reliance implies the individual development of skills and abilities and then their application to provide for one's own needs and wants. It further implies that one will achieve those skills through self-discipline and then, through self-restraint and charity, use those skills to bless himself and others."[5]

Self-reliance, as taught by the prophets, is a fundamental component of the gospel of Jesus Christ. Single women face a paradox: how do they develop self-reliance and at the same time prepare to be true collaborators and partners within a marriage? How does living as *I* prepare a person to become *we?* Whether in this life or the next, the opportunity to be joint decision makers with another person is a desired blessing. Yet many of us will develop finely tuned solo skills in managing careers, making financial decisions, setting educational goals, and addressing health needs. The single life requires an ongoing series of personal decisions about daily life and future plans. Collaboration may be limited to the workplace, civic involvement, and extended family.

The gospel principle of self-reliance is quickly understood by many singles. As a single woman, I never wanted anyone to pity me for being single or vulnerable; I learned that every one of us is at times needy and vulnerable. Out of necessity I learned to become strong and care for myself. I had to make house payments, enroll in insurance programs, and make investment decisions. If I didn't take care of myself, no one else would. I learned that decisions focusing on *self* are not intended to be selfish—they are necessary to ensure a productive, happy, and secure life. But gospel living also requires consideration for others, love unfeigned, an understanding heart, and becoming joint heirs with Christ. Singles often must look for specific ways to develop and retain these skills and attributes.

So Many Voices Distract Us

In my life I occasionally experienced conflicting feelings as I sought to be successful in a very competitive workplace and world. I struggled to find a balance in developing my nurturing and tender feelings, attitudes, and actions in a world that sometimes expected me to act differently. I was employed by the largest privately held publishing house in America. Strength, decisiveness, and assertiveness were valued attributes. As women of God we have multiple opportunities to define ourselves and represent these attributes, especially by example. As women of God we can be both capable and caring, tender and tenacious.

A new and unknown hire from Utah, I flew into Chicago for a sales presentation to a major inner-city school district noted for its gangs and troubled students. The sales manager watched me walk in the door that evening and suggested that I drink a shot of whiskey with her to prove my ability to secure the sale. In essence she told me, "Our most effective and powerful consultant drinks with me, and if you drink, it would demonstrate to me that you have the chutzpah to make this sale." She and all the other members of my company in the room felt that if I could drink the whiskey, it would mean I had the inner strength to present myself as a strong and capable woman. I did not see it that way. My understanding of gospel principles and the fact that personal strength is derived from obedience was too secure. Obviously I did not drink the whiskey or even apologize for not wanting to. I simply said, "I don't drink." We live in a world that on occasion presents us with inappropriate demands in school, in the workplace, or at social gatherings, and we need not apologize for declining. In fact, this incident cemented a strong friendship and respect between the manager and me, and afterward I was often invited into her territory.

As we apply holy principles in everyday stressful situations when we face negative distractions, all of us can be examples of cooperation, happiness, honesty, and hopefulness to those around us.

Voices can occasionally distract us from gospel living even in our own circle of friends. One single woman reported: "Male bashing seems to be the favorite team sport of many of my friends. I don't think they intend to be mean-spirited, but they are frustrated that their life plans have been delayed and are looking for an easy target. Male bashing has become the common denominator in their conversations. It doesn't take long before the language turns sour and bitterness seeps through."

After a few failed relationships or little positive interaction with males, some women become jaded in their opinions of men. Regardless of the success we may attain in other areas of our lives, criticizing others will not make us feel more fulfilled. Harsh words and strident voices do not prepare us to bless others' lives nor to be blessed by others.

Enduring Doctrines and Principles

Doctrines and principles are unchanging. Applications of doctrines and principles to the circumstances and timing of our lives are variable. That is why we need personal revelation. We will experience a constant conflict between eternal values and worldly pressures unless we ask Heavenly Father to direct us.

The question of whether or not to marry has special significance for the single sister. The doctrine of eternal marriage fixes our priorities on marriage but does not mean we should mourn if the time is not now. "Men are, that they might have joy" (2 Nephi 2:25). But the doctrine of eternal marriage does not mean we have to accept inappropriate marriage proposals, especially when they come from someone whom we do not respect and love.

Conversely, it is eternally shortsighted to pursue a professional course that makes us unavailable for marriage (the eternal value) to the right person because the proposal does not fit into our professional timing (the worldly value). When we apply doctrines and principles to our lives, we will make decisions that are pleasing to our Heavenly Father and bring us peace and joy, regardless of the expectations of others or the world around us.

President Spencer W. Kimball taught: "To be a righteous woman is a glorious thing in any age. To be a righteous woman during the winding up scenes on this earth, before the second coming of our

Savior, is an especially noble calling. The righteous woman's strength and influence today can be tenfold what it might be in more tranquil times."[6]

The world is hungry for goodness and people who believe in it and practice it. We have a potential to be so much and influence so much, and with that comes great responsibility. Eve, "the mother of all living" (Genesis 3:20), was a wonderful example to us. All women can give life to others even without giving birth. The life we provide may come in the form of providing validation and care to those around us so they can grow and flourish emotionally and spiritually.

Sister Julie Beck taught this truth: "In my experience I have seen that some of the truest mother hearts beat in the breasts of women who will not rear their own children in this life, but they know that 'all things must come to pass in their time' and that they 'are laying the foundation of a great work' (D&C 64:32–33)."[7]

Regardless of the present circumstances, we need to maintain our ideals and hopes about becoming wives and mothers. I would liken such effort to qualifying for a temple recommend when you do not live near a temple. We want to remain worthy and ready. That is no easy thing, but it does not have to be a painful reminder of unfulfilled blessings; rather, it is a long-term perspective that we are preparing for the eternities. The tenderness of our hearts and our love of others can manifest itself in all we do with everyone around us—from those in our families to those at work and in our neighborhoods. For each of us the love we demonstrate is different. Not only will our innate womanly affections benefit others now but our ability to cherish and encourage others will follow us into the eternities as well.

We also need to continue respecting and appreciating men. A woman who respects and loves herself and her roles in life will find it easier to respect everyone else around her. It would be foolhardy of us, in light of the blessings we are promised, to forget that we are women of God and that we value marriage and family and home above all other things. The world would have us think and act otherwise.

Every day you live on this earth, you are laying the groundwork for your eternal happiness. The communication skills, love, and attitudes you develop toward men will go with you into the eternities, and every moment of this preparation counts. The respect and concern you have for the men in your life now will reflect itself in your relationships to come. All of your work experience and service in the Church will give you experience as you work with different age groups, cooperate with others, and strive to support and sustain the priesthood. The more you take advantage of your callings and opportunities to interact, the more preparation you will bring to your marriage.

Nowhere else in the world can a corporate executive (man or woman) interact on an equal footing with a car mechanic (man or woman) while planning a youth conference or ward activity. The Lord has created an organization where we can flourish, grow, and develop deep friendships with a large spectrum of unique people.

The Priesthood of God

A single-minded woman in the Church may also have the challenge of discovering how the priesthood of God, the power of heaven on earth, affects her life. If weeks and months go by without a contact from a home teacher or priesthood leader, a sister may feel isolated and lacking benefit from priesthood direction in her life. Her lack of exposure to priesthood leaders may limit her understanding of priesthood power.

I have thought long and deeply on the subject of priesthood, especially because my own father was an Episcopalian. He was the best daddy anyone could have. He was the most honest and adorable man, always dressed in his bow tie and Hush Puppies, always my cheerleader and friend. I love and respect men because of his example. Yet he did not teach me about the gospel of the restored Church and did not have the priesthood to exercise in our home. I have had other friends who were not so fortunate as I because they had no father or felt that the one they had was distant or abusive.

Some Church members do not consider the power of the priesthood in their lives. It is a common idea that only when we have a priesthood holder in our home can we have access to the priesthood in our home. One married sister bore her testimony, saying, "I am so thankful to have the priesthood in my home." The single sister next to me whispered, "I have that same priesthood in my home. The priesthood power comes into my home because I partake of the sacrament, I attend the temple, I have made covenants with my Father in Heaven, and He is watching over me."

Where do we go for experiences with the priesthood in our lives? I recommend we go to church. Our own diligence in our callings at church, our decisions to serve and attend—not just for ourselves but also to build the community of Saints—naturally puts us in the path of the priesthood. You might be reading this thinking, *I don't have a major calling or even a calling at all in my ward. Where do I fit in?* You fit in because you are a child of God, and you have a Heavenly Father who loves you. If you go to your meetings and support ward activities, partake of the sacrament, and read your scriptures and pray, the Lord will help you, give you succor, and shelter you with the umbrella of His priesthood. What will that shelter feel like? It will be sweet, and you will be optimistic and happy and feel capable and strong. You will feel the comfort and guidance of the Holy Ghost. You will want to reach out to others and bless their lives. You will turn to priesthood holders for blessings if you are sick and in need. You will believe that the plan of salvation is truly the great plan of happiness.

One of my closest friends was called as a stake Young Women president. She had a resume of Church service—seminary and institute teacher, stake Relief Society presidencies, Gospel Doctrine teacher, and temple worker, among other callings. She related to me: "It wasn't until I planned and executed youth conferences, stake dances, and firesides with the stake Young Men presidency that I understood what it meant to truly 'sustain the priesthood.' It would have been so much easier to let them decide—or let us decide—than it was to decide together. Sometimes we would sit around the table, and I would wonder if we were the same species. But I learned to develop patience, value others' ideas, express appreciation, and bring extra hamburger buns to activities. I also learned that by working together we made better decisions than by working apart."

I am a convert to the Church. I did not realize the importance of the line of priesthood authority or supporting Church leaders until I went on a mission. As a twenty-seven-year-old sister missionary in Japan, I was considered *mukashi* (ancient). I had a master's degree and felt I knew it all, at least more than did a few of the nineteen-year-old district leaders who directed me. The Lord has a gentle way of teaching us. On my mission I learned respect for the priesthood of God and how a humble young man just out of high school could receive revelation. The best gift of my mission was learning that as I followed and supported my priesthood leaders, things would always turn out for the better. That mission experience has greatly blessed my married life. I learned that the power of the priesthood is the power of heaven on earth and that it can only function at its fullest in an atmosphere of support and love.

In Genesis 2, God said, "It is not good that the man should be alone; I will make him an help meet for him" (v. 18). "Therefore shall a man leave his father and his mother, and shall cleave unto his wife: and they shall be one flesh" (v. 24). The life you are living now is a foreshadowing of your life and blessings to come. You can start to make your life wonderful by developing respect for the men around you and relishing any challenge the Lord provides, realizing that He is offering you an opportunity to grow.

That does not mean you will always be free from pain and disappointment and that every day will be perfect. But you will be protected by Heavenly Father's servants and by His priesthood power. I can testify that every effort we make in trying to reach out to our Father in Heaven will ultimately, though perhaps not immediately or all at once, awaken within us the knowledge that we are eternal beings.

As we grow spiritually, our appreciation of our responsibilities to those around us also expands. President Kimball clearly described the responsibilities of the priesthood and women. During a Relief Society lesson, the teacher emphasized that "we had full equality as his spirit children. We have equality as recipients of God's perfected love for each of us." She continued to share the teachings of Spencer W. Kimball: "These are eternal differences—with women being given many tremendous responsibilities of motherhood and sisterhood and men being given the tremendous responsibilities of fatherhood and the priesthood." President Kimball also said, "Our righteous women have so often been instinctively sensitive to things of eternal consequence."[8] Women's intuitive and caring natures are great and powerful gifts from God.

Maintaining a Positive Outlook

Following an ugly divorce, a dear friend did not smile for four years. She was sad every day, and all of us around her felt sad too. We could feel the hurt and anger emanating from her, and she withered as a human being. Recently we crossed paths, and she was a completely different woman—laughing and full of light. She told me she had decided she wanted a happy life and had decided to be happy. She has developed a lovely personal trait that will continue with her into the eternities.

Maintaining nurturing and caring qualities in today's harsh world will continue to be a challenge but will also continue to be an opportunity to reveal who we really are and what we believe. It is sometimes difficult to maintain spiritual focus and balance under the pressures of everyday life. Work often becomes a very major focal point of our lives, and we develop an identity that centers on our success at our occupation. As a single woman, I found that being successful at work helped me feel good about myself and provided recognition and rewards. Our first obligation, however, is to learn that we are first and foremost daughters of a Heavenly Father who loves us. The talents that most benefited me from my work experience were how to work with other people. The skills of cooperation and harmony that you develop in one area will transfer to another.

We also live in a competitive society that is consumed with being number one. Hugh Nibley said, "Many of us would rather be Number One in hell than a doorkeeper in the House of the Lord."[9] This world is operating under a false assumption about what makes us happy. It is not about being thin or thinner, rich or richer, smart or smarter. As Elder Boyd K. Packer has taught, "The crucial test of life . . . does not center in the choice between fame and obscurity, nor between wealth and poverty. The greatest decision of life is between good and evil."[10]

Elder Bruce C. Hafen teaches us that our worth lies in our understanding of ourselves as children of God and that it does not depend on our talents, our heritage, our appearance, or our intelligence. It depends on our love of God, "and the completeness of our love cannot be judged by others. . . . For this is a love too private, too intimate and sacred to be seen of men."[11] We are all equal before the Lord, and we must be single-minded in our remembrance of that.

As a single woman who married in her fifties, I learned that being totally in charge of one's life can be a mixed blessing as one enters marriage. When I first married I began a learning curve in being a helpmate to my husband. From very small to large decisions that affected our home and family, we began to share ideas. I was adjusting. I had been single for so long that when we first married I prayed in the singular even during family prayers: "I thank Thee . . ." and "I ask Thee . . ." After about three months of marriage my husband gently suggested that I pray using "we." I had been alone for so long that I had not realized my ingrained habit. I was just learning how to be part of a twosome.

Learn to appreciate others and be grateful for all the people around you. This quality will pay off in all your relationships. Nothing is more destructive to a marriage than criticism of your partner. Nagging and negative thinking push people apart. We all hunger for appreciation and support in our lives.

When we are open to the needs of others, we open ourselves to the blessing of understanding the perspective of others. This allows us the opportunity to develop tolerance and acceptance for their opinions and actions. Nothing could be more beneficial to our eternal family. "Wives need to remind themselves that when their husbands do something differently from how they would do it themselves, it does not constitute a breach of sanity or a display of contempt. It is merely a *different* way to do something. Instead of immediately correcting a husband, first see if there is something you could learn (could happen, you know?), then see if the job gets done (that was the goal, wasn't it?), and then offer a compliment (you like those too, don't you?). . . .

" 'Trust your husband. Recognize that he has his own ways of doing things. They don't have to be done your way to be adequately done.' "[12]

My husband illustrated these points through an object lesson when several young couples dined with us before they were to be married. He counseled them that they could expect to have differences between themselves and their future companions and that they had to be accepting of the idiosyncrasies of their future partners. After his speech, to my chagrin, he showed them a new tube of toothpaste, which I had squeezed in the middle, to demonstrate his point. The table erupted in laughter, but his point was well taken.

Our uniqueness enhances our ability to be instruments in Heavenly Father's hands. We are on this earth to share our service as human beings and as daughters of God. The world would have us lose focus and sight of our eternal purpose. If you wish to prepare for life with another person, in this world or the next, you need to prepare now and believe in yourself.

An Example of a Single-Minded Woman

I looked to Sister Marjorie Pay Hinckley as an example to all of us of how to create a happy life. She was a unique combination of single-minded faith and works. She knew where she came from—her family and her ancestors. She gleaned from them. She also knew where she was going. She responded to the needs of her husband and family. She supported them at every move and made their lives wonderful. I can speak from only very limited exposure to her, but I wish to share some things I learned from her that can make any life happier and sweeter.

What I remember about Marjorie Pay Hinckley is her faith and uncomplaining nature. My husband and I had the opportunity to travel with the Hinckleys to the temple dedication in Uruguay. I spent the afternoons with Sister Hinckley and her daughter Jane.

I was distinctly impressed by two qualities she possessed and how they allowed her to be such an incredible helpmate to her husband.

Faith That the Lord
Answers Prayers

As we sat in the hotel lobby together during a long afternoon wait for our husbands, Sister Hinckley showed me a petite ring on her tiny hand and told me it had been her grandmother's wedding ring. The ring was especially precious to her because it reminded her of her grandmother's prayer of faith. Her grandmother had lost that very ring in the straw long ago, and she had little hope of finding it. Her grandmother knelt and asked Heavenly Father to help her, and she found it. Sister Hinckley wore the ring because it reminded her of her grandmother's faith and of Heavenly Father's ability to answer prayers. She had great faith in the past, and she applied it to her future. She knew she had a Heavenly Father who was there for her.

Uncomplaining Nature

Sister Hinckley lived a life of sacrifice and helping others. She was agreeable and supportive. When President Hinckley traveled, he wanted to leave when he was ready to leave. The schedule might read 7 A.M. departure, but a knock might come at 5:45 A.M., telling you the departure time had changed to 6 A.M. I remember standing in my pajamas and curlers, not quite packed and almost unable to breathe after such a knock the first morning of our trip. From that day on I arose early, dressed, and waited. I remember also walking out of our hotel room that first morning and seeing Sister Hinckley perfectly dressed, coiffed, and smiling. I was thinking to myself, *She is so flexible and uncomplaining. I want to be just like her.* She was ready and smiling at the side of her husband. She understood his responsibilities. She was a support and an advocate for her husband in all situations. I believe she had learned through years of practice and giving. She made her husband's schedule her schedule, and she was helping everything go well. I learned so much from her that day. I had been a single woman living alone, and she was a perfect example of a supportive wife and friend. She was about her Father's business in all she did.

Sister Hinckley's positive and amenable attitude is what I aspire to develop. In any situation when we are required to adjust and support those around us, we can be pleasant and gracious or difficult and grumbling. Her positive attitude was a great example and source of strength.

Becoming Single-Minded Women

Marriage or the lack of marriage does not make us happy, faithful, and steadfast women in Christ. There are no perfect circumstances, only perfect faith. We are all just trying. Whether we go forward with a husband and family, as a single mother, or as a never-married sister, we are meant to grow in stature and faith. My single years provided me with the opportunity to learn, grow, serve, and develop talents. I am so thankful for that time and opportunity to develop.

The more single-minded we are in relying upon our Heavenly Father, the more He can direct us and guide us to make successful decisions. We need to invite and involve the Lord in our decision making. His inspiration serves as a guide and protection so needed in all our lives. When we single-mindedly depend on our Heavenly Father, he can intensify our joy and help us create a more beautiful stash of memories and experiences that make the present beautiful and embolden us to believe in a better future.

The Lord loves us. He desires happiness for us, which comes directly from dependence on Him. He would have us be a standard to the world—strong, faithful, and independent from the influences of the world. A single-minded, nurturing, self-reliant woman with a wise and loving heart can make a very great contribution in the kingdom of God.

CHAPTER 7

A SINGLE DAY AT A TIME

*With the Lord's help we can handle any problem
one day at a time.*

In the Philippines the end of the sizzling summer season is heralded by strong winds. Their prevailing direction changes 180 degrees, bringing rain and storms across the islands and also some relief from the heat. But the winds persist. In our neighborhood in Manila, the wind signaled the change of season by sounding a rasping whine outside as it whipped through the high-rise buildings.

I would compare the seasonal whistling of the Philippine wind to the occasional intense heartache I sometimes experienced as a single woman. There were moments when I felt engulfed by extreme sadness. All of us have such moments—from the young married couple desiring the blessing of children to a family praying for the recovery of a loved one to someone suffering from depression to a widow dealing with the loss of her husband. But just as I learned that the storms and winds of the Philippines would at some point cease, so I learned that my moments of sorrow and sadness would cease as well. I learned that I could develop skills and attitudes that would help me through the strong winds that struck at my heart. I learned that I didn't have to experience pounding rain every day. Above all, I learned that the yearnings of my heart as a single woman could provide an impetus to seek after the things of God.

Waiting upon the Lord

These yearnings led me to greatly depend on Heavenly Father for guidance and help. I "wait[ed] upon the Lord" (Isaiah 40:31) for direction and blessings. Webster's dictionary defines the word *wait* in multiple ways, including the following: "to continue stationary or inactive, to stay or rest in expectation and anticipation, to be available or in readiness, to attend upon or respect (wait on: to perform the duties of a servant or attendant)." I am and likely always will be capable of executing all four of these definitions.

Stationary or Inactive

There were times when I remained stationary by indulging in self-pity and wasted tears and energy on expectations that were not coming to pass. I longed for what I did not have. A friend told me about a fellow worker who speaks of waiting to be happy. She will be happy when she receives a promotion, when she marries, or when she has a baby. All the rest of the time her life is bringing her no satisfaction, and as a result she is constantly unhappy. She wastes valuable time worrying about the future and what may or may not come to pass.

Expectation and Anticipation

Faith that Heavenly Father was mindful and caring moved me from stationary anticipation about the future to preparing for it and ultimately desiring with all my heart to rely on and respect the opportunities Heavenly Father provided for me. I could *wait* with the expectation and anticipation of promises from a loving Heavenly Father. I could *wait,* knowing that mortality offers "an opposition in all things" (2 Nephi 2:11) and an opportunity to practice gratitude and patience.

Readiness and Respect

I began to actively use moments and make them as happy and productive as I could. The storms of life seemed manageable, and I determined to dance in the rain of my adversity. I desired to enjoy the journey. The scriptures, as well as examples from our wards and neighborhoods, show a wide range of readiness and willingness to serve the Lord. From the parable of the ten virgins, I knew very clearly that having oil in my lamp is a responsibility that each of us has. The parable makes clear that should we not prepare, we will not go to meet the bridegroom, the Savior. Our time of readiness and service to the Lord is an opportunity to fill our lamps.

Time is precious. The use of time is paramount to our salvation. Under the plan of salvation we all have been given time and agency. We decide how we will allocate our time. Anne Frank, from her World War II attic hiding place, wrote: "How wonderful it is that nobody need wait a single moment before starting to improve the world."[1] The question becomes, How shall we make the best of it? What can we do to bring satisfaction to our lives and those around us?

Getting and maintaining the Spirit should be our first priority. You are a child of God. When God speaks to you, it will be spirit to spirit. Prepare to be worthy of such a conversation.

Seeking the Spirit helped me to immerse myself in the scriptures and to look for examples of people who knew God and felt of His love. I wondered how Father Abraham or Noah or Sarah or Nephi faced their challenges. These ancient heroes became like friends to me. They were people just like me—flesh and blood, bleeding from wounds of the heart, and yearning. They distinguished themselves because they believed without seeing. They exercised faith in the midst of intense struggles. I have come to think that their relationships with Heavenly Father—the confidence and closeness and trust they developed in Him—transformed them. They were quickened by their knowledge of God and His love for them. To be quickened can be defined as "to enter into an active phase of growth and development." They became more alive in Christ and His love for them.

In the Book of Mormon we learn that happiness is not contingent on circumstance when we look to the Lord. If we were to interview Nephi, who was highly favored of the Lord, and Laman and Lemuel about their journey to the new world, each would see it through very different eyes. Laman and Lemuel would recall leaving the wealth and luxury of Jerusalem to wander through the desert, sometimes starving and suffering. They were willing to murder their own father to remain in the city they loved. They might remember fleeing from Laban, sailing across tortuous seas, being jealous of Nephi, and trying constantly to slay Nephi. It was not pleasant for them.

In contrast, Nephi, who respected and loved his father and honored the Lord, might recall marvelous revelations, eternal promises, miraculous conquests, and talks with angels. He would speak with great respect of his "goodly parents" (1 Nephi 1:1). He would recall his successes—such as building a ship and carving a bow—and attribute them to the Lord. He would remember the blessings of visions, the Liahona, and being much favored by the Lord.

Instead of being crushed by adversity, we can combine our experiences and faith to make us stronger, kinder, and more devoted followers of Christ. I have come to believe that the Lord is trying to instruct us that blessings are not our ultimate objective for being on this earth. Our earthly objective is to build our relationship with Him and the qualities of character that will draw us near to Him. This life is a test. It is only a temporal opportunity on the way to a celestial reality.

I started to see my life in a new perspective. Material things became less significant. I began to understand that it was not the size of my house but the size of my heart that would bring me the most complete happiness. It was not personal achievements but my appreciation of the Atonement that would bring me peace and satisfaction. It was the quality of my contact with Him and His Spirit that became paramount in my life.

As members of the Church, we covenant when we take the sacrament to do what is required to always have His Spirit to be with us. When we have the Spirit the benefits are enormous. We can listen better to the still, small voice, feel less contention, and receive direction from the Lord. Especially for single people, who are constantly making decisions on their own, this assistance is crucial.

"Out of small things proceedeth that which is great" (D&C 64:33). One Young Women teacher brought a brown paper bag full of lemon drops to her Laurel class. She taught them how they should make time every day to draw near to their Heavenly Father. She then handed out the lemon drops, put on spiritual music, and had them suck the drops as they listened. She told them, "Take at least this much time every day to draw near to holy and sacred things, and spend time with your Heavenly Father."

Those few minutes of silence taught a profound lesson for all of us in the room. We all reexamined how much time each day we focused exclusively on our Heavenly Father, and we all left determined to consecrate more. Her lesson is for everyone: singles struggling with decisions, young mothers soothing screaming children, married couples settling a conflict, or an elderly patient doing rehabilitation exercises in the hospital. We all face monumental tests.

When we establish an inner oasis of peace within ourselves, it becomes possible to deal with the turbulence outside ourselves or between others and ourselves.

The Lord commands us, "Be still and know that I am God" (D&C 101:16). We need to provide time to be still, to rest, and to feel the Spirit. One young couple discovered how this calm time could bless their home. It came about quite accidentally when a power surge left all of the electronic equipment in their home lifeless. During the last hour in their evening, after they had put the children to bed, the father had the practice of retreating to his computer and the wife to her television, sometimes late into the night. With the computer and the television off, this couple read scriptures, prayed, and went to bed early.

The small miracle of what happened was related by the young mother as she taught Relief Society: "My husband woke up in a good mood. I was so energetic that I almost jumped out of bed. Even with my usual squirming babies, I was better tempered. I never realized how tired and exhausted I had allowed myself to become and how much it affected my inner peace. I learned a more important lesson too. Before I could take care of anyone else around me, I had to take care of myself."

Singles working responsible jobs, attending graduate school, or caring for aged parents also need to slow down, rest, and renew their connection to the Spirit to help them succeed.

Be Ready to Rewrite the Dream

When our preset expectations do not turn out as we hoped, we can begin to write what a close friend calls "a new dream." For her that means realigning her expectations and creating new and beautiful possibilities for her circumstances. My friend adds: "Some of our long-held dreams may need closer scrutiny. I have learned that I can 'rewrite my dreams' to be in better alignment with the blessings that Heavenly Father wants me to have. Blessings are better than dreams. Too many dreams are based on wishes and romantic illusions. The more I live, the more I recognize that some dreams really are foolish or unnecessary. Even righteous desires may need to be realigned into an eternal perspective and timeline. The delivery schedule may not be of my own making."

Rewriting the dream does not mean compromising standards or eliminating hope. Rather, it means developing greater flexibility, resourcefulness, and adaptability. If marriage and children don't come on the planned timeline, there may need to be a positive and productive realignment of expectations. Education and career opportunities may play a more prominent role in our lives. We may see the Lord's blessings poured out in ways we never anticipated.

From early childhood we realign our dreams. The realities of life will almost always be different from what we had previously supposed. We may be chosen for a different soccer team from the one we wished to be on, be sent to a different mission from the one we dreamed of, gain entrance unexpectedly to the college we wished to enter, or live in a city or a part of the country we had never anticipated living in. Our expectations will nearly always differ from the realities that come to us.

Our lives can deviate from the course we prepared for in small and in monumental ways. One sister who remains single is positive and happy because she finds her life purposeful in all the situations in which she is placed. She joined a choir, found new hobbies, became involved in humanitarian projects, and spent more time helping others.

Another sister discovered her child to be autistic. Her dreams of motherhood seemed shattered. Instead of the bonding experience and joy she had anticipated, she found herself confused and unable to cope. This challenge initially caused her to mourn, and that mourning gave birth to a great momentum to improve her family situation. She studied and questioned. She looked for educational opportunities and teachers and classrooms. As her search evolved, she created a school for autistic children, helped find trained professionals, and helped not only her child but also thousands of others with similar problems. Her challenge served to bless the lives of many around her and brought her peace and satisfaction in the journey.

Another friend differentiated between her own personal dreams and desires and the blessings the Lord had in store for her. She told me, "What I dream of and desire often has little to do with the blessings Heavenly Father has in store for me. Our dreams may be of our own making: how we expect our future mate to look, the homes we will live in, and the children we will have. These dreams have little root in reality; in fact, the dreams I've conjured up for myself actually have prevented me from seeing the blessings I do have, the ones the Lord has extended me."

She continued, "My entire life I wanted a Georgian brick home on a shady street in a neighborhood teeming with children. What I got is an orange stucco rambler home in Southern California at the end of a cul-de-sac. But it is perfect for me. I have a terrific ward and wonderful friends, and I even like the weather. All the things I envisioned never came to be, and I am still very satisfied and happy."

When we invite the Lord into our lives, He provides blessings that will ensure our future eternal happiness because they stimulate our personal growth. Answers to prayer and revelation can help us craft new courses and directions for ourselves. These new courses may have little or no correlation with those we dreamed would bring us happiness but everything to do with the vision the Lord has of our celestial potential. We are eternal beings having an earthly experience.

Inviting the Lord into our lives might supply some unexpected turns. One very talented sister, a documentary filmmaker, told how the Lord directed her: "I was in a creative field, and so I felt I needed to be more in tune with my Creator. I was praying for inspiration in writing a script, and the Spirit instructed me that 'If you want to have your mind enlightened to write things of consequence, do not see R-rated films.' That was no small thing in an industry when people were talking and referencing standard film works I was supposed to be an expert in, and I had never seen them." She continued, "I also knew the Lord had spoken to me, so it became a matter of obedience to what I had learned. I had to be obedient because I desired the blessings in filmmaking, and I knew if I weren't obedient, I would violate a trust."

All of us will experience difficult situations we desire to change. What the Lord may change is not our circumstance but our character. As our faith matures and our perspective broadens, our success in life can often be measured not in the outcomes we expected but in the attitudes we acquire—patience, love, caring, hope, and faith. We can measure our own progress by noting an increased capacity to be tolerant, to be spiritually in tune, to be in better control of our temper, to be more accepting and forgiving of those around us. We are meant not to mark time but to make it purposeful and make a mark on the world around us.

The Lord set an example for us. He offers us the opportunity to eternally progress. As He did, so we can design things spiritually—through inspiration—and then set about to create them temporally. The Lord instructed us, "For by the power of my Spirit created I them; yea, all things both spiritual and temporal—first spiritual, secondly temporal. . . . I say unto you that all things unto me are spiritual" (D&C 29:31–34). The Lord is explaining a pattern of living to us. If we draw closer to the Spirit, it follows that our thoughts and actions will bring us closer to His plan for us.

We can make plans to make our futures bright. Some of us may hesitate to plan. Much has already been written about not being a passive observer in life and not waiting to grow up and live until you have chosen or been chosen as a mate. Some of us, like me, may by nature be free spirits and a bit averse to planning. Time, however, will go on, regardless of whether we choose to plan. Karl G. Maeser even instructed the early students at Brigham Young University, "Man grows only with his higher goals."[2] To make the progress I desired— after more than a few wasted years waiting for Mr. Right—I learned that the best thing is to set a course for yourself that will bring you closer to Heavenly Father and give you more personal satisfaction. Many sisters who find themselves over thirty and single have confided to me that they wished they had prepared themselves much earlier in life to attend graduate school, to support themselves financially, or to buy a house.

One of our grandchildren is a devoted planner. She sits down and plans out her day, when she will read the scriptures, where she will study, when she will shop, and when she will take time for fun. When she finally sets out with her list in hand, she is a force to be reckoned with. She knows where she is going and what she wants to achieve, and she gets an enormous amount done. An even greater quality is that she can reorganize what she is doing on a moment's notice. I know this because she has so often been there to help with family concerns. She has the capacity to adjust and start over, regroup and redirect when necessary. Being flexible makes a tremendous difference in how our lives progress.

Since time is precious, use it well. The Church's missionary manual, *Preach My Gospel,* devotes an entire chapter to "How Do I Use Time Wisely?" Missionaries learn to set goals, to use planners, to evaluate their goals, and to revise them if necessary. They are taught to keep records and to monitor their own progress and that of their investigators. "Goals reflect the desires of our hearts and our vision of what we can accomplish. Through goals and plans, our hopes are transformed into action. Goal setting and planning are acts of faith."[3]

I would add that allowing for the Lord's hand to guide you, recognizing the unexpected use of agency by others, and being ready to adjust are enormous gifts, too.

Elder M. Russell Ballard said: "I am so thoroughly convinced that if we don't set goals in our life and learn how to master the techniques of living to reach our goals, we can reach a ripe old age and look back on our life only to see that we reached but a small part of our full potential. When one learns to master the principles of setting a goal, he will then be able to make a great difference in the results he attains in this life."[4]

I wanted a happy life, and I came to realize that this required redesigning where I was going and making decisions to progress. Plans and goals evolve as we do. One friend said to me, "After I checked off my two plans to go on a mission and then be sealed in the temple, I realized how boring my life would be if it stopped there." Life requires every one of us to monitor and adjust because circumstances are fluid and require us to remain flexible. I depended on my Heavenly Father to make it through the day. Most of the greatest joys in life come in serendipitous, unexpected surprises along the way.

I have a friend, Kathryn, who is the queen of planning. Her life is full, happy, and tremendously productive. She has taught me a great deal about making my life rewarding. She is always counseling me to have a contingency plan in case the first idea does not work. She always leaves multiple options open to herself. She looks to Heavenly Father for the long-term results and seeks to make every minute count. Her planning has made her extremely successful in her work, helped her to obtain a strong financial portfolio, and made her life fun and fulfilling. Because she considers her options, many doors open for her.

A major goal for all of us should be remaining flexible—readjusting attitudes and behaviors when necessary. Relish any situation that requires you to adjust expectations, redefine goals, and possibly even start over. Adversity or unexpected opportunities can prove blessings in keeping us flexible. As I look back I realize that the many years I spent single made me much more accepting and adaptable to situations that were sometimes difficult. It was much more than taking lemons and making lemonade. It was coming to understand, even in difficult circumstances, how precious every minute of this life is and wanting to make excellent use of it. While it might seem strange, in certain ways the days became more joyous for me because I had to seek to find beauty and happiness in my situation. I have become a more productive and cheerful and thankful woman because of this search.

Our adversities may clarify what is truly essential and dear to us. A young, successful, and motivated physician made it his goal to establish a large and flourishing medical practice. He devoted most of his time and energy to it, hoping to provide all the benefits and material security he could for his family. His young widow confided in me, "His professional goals changed dramatically when he was diagnosed with cancer. His life became so tentative he would just look forward to a day at a time. Even living to celebrate the next birthday of our five-year-old son became a landmark to him." The goals we set are always subject to change.

Nothing can protect us from sorrow and disappointment. The important things are what we learn and how we recover from the pain. President Spencer W. Kimball understood the enormous refining influence of pain. In his book *Faith Precedes the Miracle,* he shares a poem I love:

> *Pain stayed so long I said to him today,*
> *"I will not have you with me any more."*
> *I stamped my foot and said, "Be on your way,"*
> *And paused there, startled at the look he wore.*

"I, who have been your friend," he said to me,
"I, who have been your teacher—all you know
Of understanding love, of sympathy,
And patience, I have taught you. Shall I go?"
He spoke the truth, this strange unwelcome guest;
I watched him leave, and knew that he was wise.
He left a heart grown tender in my breast,
He left a far, clear vision in my eyes.
I dried my tears, and lifted up a song—
Even for one who'd tortured me so long.[5]

In retrospect, the many times I considered painful were a great gift to me because I felt an urgency to make things better. I learned to set goals despite disappointment and continue building a happy life.

Elder W. Craig Zwick said: "I found that when we're earnest in creating a life plan for ourselves, we need to allow the Lord to be the architect of that plan. When the Lord is the architect, long-term benefits result and connect us to additional opportunities and experiences that accelerate our capacity for growth."[6]

I wanted the Lord to be the architect of my plans because He held the eternal perspective. Heavenly Father acts as our architect, and we get to fashion the future. I prayed to Heavenly Father about which goals to set for myself that would bring me happiness. The inspiration I received surprised me. I set goals inspired by the three-fold mission of the Church: proclaim the gospel, redeem the dead, and perfect the Saints. Pursuing these three goals over the period of a year brought me many unexpected blessings. The best blessing is that they brought me outside myself to concentrate and concern myself with my fellowmen.

Proclaiming the Gospel

I set a goal to become a more effective missionary. I began talking about the Church on airplanes, in grocery stores, and whenever I felt the Spirit prompt me. I began carrying the Book of Mormon and a stack of pass-along cards in my purse. Once at a cosmetics counter talking about perfume, I knew I was to testify to the lovely salesclerk. I felt her hunger for purpose in life. At Kinko's my heart was touched by the counter girl with green hair and multiple body piercings. I felt of her goodness and pulled out a pass-along card. With a friend's help, I even invited a group of fifty newly arrived Russian immigrants to a picnic to fellowship them. I loved proclaiming the gospel.

Redeeming the Dead

To redeem the dead, I made a pledge to do weekly temple work, which often meant a 5 A.M. session on Saturday. I wanted the power of the priesthood in my life, and I felt it by attending the temple. It became my favorite place. I shared with Elder Oaks how much I loved the temple. I believe that my love of that sacred place is one reason he married me.

During my times of personal sadness and need I came to learn of the healing and revelatory power of the temple. The temple literally can serve as a place of revelation and refuge for those in need. We can experience a variety of different blessings from our visits there. I would receive inspiration for work, resolve personal problems, be given added emotional and physical endurance, or feel a joy and contentment in the love that Heavenly Father has for all His children. No other place on earth can provide such comforting solace. It is a holy haven where the power of God is manifested to men and women on earth. Go there often to be close to your Heavenly Father.

The temple is a place of learning. In Doctrine and Covenants 110, Joseph Smith recorded that in the Kirtland Temple, "the veil was taken from our minds, and the eyes of our understanding were opened" (v. 1). My attendance in the temple gave me similar experiences. The Lord would always provide solutions and inspiration or, at the very least, clarity of mind and peace in my soul. Time spent in the temple is transforming. The serenity I felt enabled me to function so much more effectively. Even in the times when I was discouraged and tired, I left feeling clean and renewed, strong enough to cope with what lay ahead.

There is great equality in the temple. In our white clothing we are all equal before the Lord. There is great power in being prayed for in the temple. The dying, weak, afflicted, and heartbroken know this. In this world, prayer is sometimes the only remedy for pain that seems overwhelming and devastating. There are moments, minutes, and months when pain seems unbearable and beyond our capacity to endure. Often in those times that I went to the temple seeking help from Father in Heaven, I prayed for myself and others I knew to be in need. I always came away strengthened and uplifted and encouraged.

Perfecting the Saints

I decided to direct my energy to a weakness I wanted very much to change—forgiveness. I had walked around reliving and preserving past injuries. My goal was to devote my year to developing forgiveness. I knew that I had to repent and ask Heavenly Father to forgive me of my sins and shortcomings to accomplish this. The Savior taught His people in the Americas: "Your Father knoweth what things ye have need of before ye ask him. After this manner therefore pray ye: Our Father who art in heaven, hallowed be thy name. Thy will be done on earth as it is in heaven. And forgive us our debts, as we forgive our debtors" (3 Nephi 13:8–11).

Heavenly Father knew what I needed before I recognized it myself. My experience of repenting daily brought me closer to my Father in Heaven. No effort is perfect, but I kept trying. I also firmly believe the more we repent of our own weaknesses, the more capable we become of accepting and forgiving others of theirs. Having my debts forgiven meant changing and trying to be a better person.

One young sister, a convert to the Church and the only member in her family, taught me the great value of forgiveness. She had moved from the East Coast to attend Brigham Young University, fell in love with a worthy young man, and was married in the temple. Shortly after her marriage, she was diagnosed with leukemia. The treatments and the effects of the disease were overwhelming to her new husband. Bed pans, bloating, and blood exchanges were not what he had bargained for. He asked for a divorce, telling her that he had never loved her. I watched her friends, as they attempted to console her, criticize her husband. All she would ever say was, "He is young and didn't know how to handle the situation. Because of him I am where I am spiritually."

The real depth of her faith and soul shone through a few months later when her nonmember mother read at her funeral from her journal: "I would not change a thing about my life. Because of the trials and adversity I have experienced, I know I can stand before Jesus Christ and Joseph Smith and look at them eye to eye and say I tried my best." Her forgiveness of her husband and her loving nature became a sermon to everyone who knew her.

She was a great teacher to me. I also prayed to forgive anyone I held negative feelings for. I can remember partaking of the sacrament and letting go of past wounds and concentrating on my blessings. During that sacred ordinance it was almost as if I could physically sense shackles of concern and hurt falling from me and simultaneously feel a more powerful ability to focus on the present and its beautiful possibilities.

So many acts of obedience are indelibly tied together. As I read the scriptures I realized my efforts at missionary work increased my ability to be near to my Heavenly Father and to be forgiven by Him. The Lord says, "For I will forgive you of your sins with this commandment—that you remain steadfast in your minds in solemnity and the spirit of prayer, in bearing testimony to all the world of those things which are communicated to you" (D&C 84:61). The more frequently I bore my testimony to others, the more I qualified for the forgiveness I so desired. All that we do really does work for our own good.

An Eternal Perspective

When we have an eternal perspective our use of time changes dramatically. We are constantly choosing between the temporal and the eternal. Our choices are of consequence. Should we spend an afternoon shopping or doing service, watching television or attending the temple, surfing the Internet or reading the scriptures? These daily choices seem insignificant, but cumulatively they define the depth and breadth of our spiritual fiber and commitment. Be careful with your time. Do you have a video group, a ski group, a book club, a dinner club, a racquet club, or do you retreat, as I did sometimes, to my own television and large combination pizza? Don't isolate yourself or fritter your time away on frivolous pursuits.

Your use of time as a single woman is of great consequence to the wife and mother you wish to become. My friend Sandra shared with me how her use of time helped her develop into a capable woman of covenant. She dated her husband prior to his mission. He was and is dynamic, charismatic, and handsome. Everywhere they went and everything they did was with his friends and according to his interests. People gathered near him, laughing and listening and totally enthralled. She adored being with him but at the same time felt almost like an appendage, someone beside him but not really contributing. When he went on his mission, she felt miserable and lost and realized her almost complete dependence upon him.

While he was serving the Lord, she reached out to others, made friends of her own, dated, served, and was called to be the Relief Society president in her student ward. That calling blessed her life. She felt herself blossom into someone who made decisions, someone who could lead and teach others, and someone who could be charismatic in her own right.

When her future husband returned from his mission, he found her a more confident and self-assured woman to marry. They had both grown spiritually and emotionally during their separation, and the bond of love between them was greatly increased. They were now equally yoked. Sandra recounted, "Those additional single years not only helped me to become a better person to marry but also a more secure mother of five children during the many times my husband left to perform his duties as bishop and then as stake president. I am so thankful for that time alone."

Another example of someone whose eternal perspective and choices have refined her into a woman of covenant is my friend Emma. She is a woman in her early thirties who has faced major loss and personal tragedy and become stronger and more determined for it. In her short life, she has witnessed the death of her mother in an auto accident; married her Ivy League sweetheart, only to find him addicted to pornography; and later, as a divorcée, experienced rejection by a man whose family would not accept her.

Emma has known trial after trial. She has had heart-wrenching moments and has had to stop and seek to confirm the Lord's love for her. She has spent many hours on her knees and in the scriptures. Yet none of her adversities has weakened her commitment to Heavenly Father and her firm faith that He is watching over her. She spoke to me of her love of her family, of how she is a mother to younger sisters, and of her temple attendance. She has become a master gardener and an incredible cook and is pursuing further educational opportunities. She's even planning a summer in Europe to learn about architectural garden design. She loves to learn and make her life vital.

I asked her how she does it, and she simply said, "I take it one day at a time. I worry sometimes about what the women in my ward think. I don't want them to feel sorry for me or wonder why I'm single. I just keep trying and keep believing that Heavenly Father is leading me to something better."

She keeps going forward. I love Emma because when we are together my love for my Heavenly Father is increased. She attends church and finds strength in her ward family and in her covenants with the Lord. She is exceptional because every situation, from loss of a loved one to divorce to disappointment, has drawn her closer to members of her ward.

Emma perseveres because she maintains an eternal perspective, which enables her to keep her trials and feelings in perspective. She also loves others. She knows she is a work in progress. In a letter to close friends, she wrote: "I just want to take a moment and thank all of you for allowing me to learn and make mistakes, be forgiven, listen, wonder, and be captivated at certain moments for who you are and what you bring to my life. I am grateful that this life is a learning process and that every day we have opportunities to change. I am continually reminded of my imperfections and the amazing people that reach out to help me by their living examples of faith, humor, empathy, and loving kindness."

We are all climbing the learning curve. Mortality is designed to present challenges for us. Facing and dealing with problems alone, without the advice and support of a companion, can at times be almost incapacitating. I remember another dear friend who compared her ordeal with sewage backing up in her basement at irregular intervals to a ride on an "emotional rollercoaster." She was constantly worried about the next turn of events and had only herself and her income to depend on. She coped by studying general conference talks and frequently attending the temple. She found that she could take a step at a time with the Lord beside her.

We need to make time to spend with other people. Too much time alone allows us to dwell on our problems and weaknesses and to magnify them. We can lose perspective and begin to wallow in our personal problems. Many singles find themselves alone and lonely. Viewing our highly sophisticated society with its often-fleeting relationships and our lack of concern for one another, Mother Teresa said, "The biggest disease today is not leprosy or cancer or tuberculosis, but rather the feeling of being unwanted, uncared for, deserted by everybody."7 Any one of us can be crippled by loneliness. It is not good to be alone.

When we are isolated we can indulge in false assumptions about ourselves—believing that everyone else has friends, feeling socially inadequate or socially unskilled, being convinced that something must be wrong with us, feeling that no one understands our situation, or feeling reluctant to attempt to change or to try new things. Worse, we may stop feeling anything at all.

Being with others provides protection. Friends can help us avoid little embarrassments—telling us we have lipstick on our teeth or our slip is showing. They can serve as personal confidants with whom we can share heartfelt thoughts. They can prod us to good works and lovingly kick us when we need a good kick. In our down times the optimism and positive comments of others can make us laugh and regroup. And, as my single neighbor Linda says, "Having people around can keep us from going crazy. They keep me from being too eccentric or self-absorbed. I like feedback from people. I need their wisdom and their impression of me to stay sane."

In various ways all of us unknowingly assist others without our realizing it simply by our example of activity in the Church. During our mission in the Philippines, I sat with a group of single sisters in their early thirties as we waited for a program to begin. We began to chat. These women had become very dear to me during our service there. The conversation turned to my marriage. At first it was a bit disheartening to learn that the personal quality that most endeared me to them was the late age of my marriage. One sister said, "Sister Oaks, you have saved us. Now that people know that you married late, they don't tease us and ask us questions about being single as they did before you came. You made getting married later something people accept better now in the Philippines." The other sisters nodded their heads and said, "Much less teasing. Thank you, Sister Oaks." These words and their smiling faces made me thankful for the time Heavenly Father had allowed me to be without a husband.

When we combine our experience, we can help others. As I sat with these young Filipina sisters, they continued to ask about my marriage to Elder Oaks. I shared from my personal experience, telling them that a good man doesn't have to be perfect. He may still be a work in progress. Look for the basic important qualities of character. I told them the story of a young friend who had prayed to meet the man of her dreams, someone devoted and loyal, who loved the Lord and who would love her. She had known a boy from high school who had assisted his mother in caring for his disabled father, had helped to support the family financially and emotionally, and had been diligent in his Church attendance. I remember when she pointed him out to me at a dance. To many in the room he would have been seen as a tall, gawky, newly returned missionary wearing white socks and trousers that were too short. In her eyes, however, he was an Adonis in training and the answer to all her prayers. Her intuition was correct. Now he is an extremely successful corporate lawyer, a loving companion, and the devoted father to their four children.

I told the sisters to depend on Heavenly Father to be their adviser and to listen to the whisperings of the Holy Ghost. I also advised them, "Don't settle for someone with values different from yours, someone that you don't respect and love with all your heart. Eternity is a long time to live with someone who does not share your most basic values and who is not seeking to improve. Anyone who does settle for less in this essential area will only live to regret it. Never proceed in a matter this important without the confirmation of the Spirit."

I know from experience that it is worth it to wait for a man you love and respect but that the wait can be intensely painful and lonely. I also know from friends who have confided in me that their marriage to someone who chooses not to honor his covenants or who is abusive can be much more painful.

In this life we will all wait for someone—children involved in addictions, loved ones making destructive choices, or family members struggling to succeed. Only a few close friends knew how difficult my wait for marriage was for me. I know that friends who offered a listening ear and an understanding heart provided perspective and made even monumental concerns seem less significant.

We should take care not to isolate ourselves; extreme loneliness can increase stress, illness, and negative self-talk. We can retard our own abilities to cope by telling ourselves that we can't, that this is too hard, or that we shouldn't even try. Somehow the perspective and fellowship of others helps to alleviate and lift our burdens.

For me loneliness was an enormous challenge, though this may not be true for others. I kept busy, occupied, and anxiously engaged, but there were moments and hours that I found to be extremely painful. I wanted to be with a husband and family. It was often in these moments that I reached out to Heavenly Father and prayed to Him for comfort. It was also in these hours that I found the most solace and depended on my faith that the Lord was there for me. I may have been weak, but I knew my Heavenly Father was all-powerful and I could trust Him.

Elder Dennis E. Simmons spoke of this: "Shadrach, Meshach, and Abed-nego . . . knew that they could trust God—even if things didn't turn out the way they hoped. They knew that faith is more than mental assent, more than an acknowledgment that God lives. Faith is total trust in Him.

"Faith is believing that although we do not understand all things, He does. Faith is knowing that although our power is limited, His is not. Faith in Jesus Christ consists of complete reliance on Him."[8] My faith in the Lord helped relieve my pain.

Women especially need close friends. It is our nature to nurture one another. It is much easier to be objective about someone else's predicaments and problems than our own. We can provide wise advice and comfort to each other. Friends help illuminate situations so we can see them more clearly and make tribulations seem less insurmountable. Also, a good friend can bring variety and spice to our lives.

Linda told me of a dear friend with a charismatic personality who would help her can fruit, do quilting projects, go to political rallies, and share ideas with her. This friend made her feel of worth. Being valued by someone you respect and think is a valuable person buoys you up and increases your sense of joy.

Heavenly Father will direct us to people who will help us. A dear friend, a popular and vivacious ward Relief Society president, came down with a virulent flu and was home sick in bed for over a month. She found herself becoming lonely and extremely depressed. Nothing she did, from reading the scriptures to praying, seemed to help. Finally in prayer she asked Heavenly Father what to do. She felt impressed to make phone calls to friends she loved and tell them how much she appreciated them. These calls brought her joy as the friends shared how much they missed her and loved her. She just had to be the first one to reach out. She learned that we are never alone and that the Lord is mindful of each of us.

We are never too old to make new friends. One wise older widow, who had left behind all her friends and associates and moved into a new ward, stood up in fast meeting to share her testimony. She told me later, "I knew if I bore my testimony people would know me and know my heart. I left that meeting having connected with the members of my new ward, and I was not alone."

We can fend off loneliness by being accessible to those around us who are different from us. President Gordon B. Hinckley exemplified this. The more different a person was from him, the more he was interested in the person. He befriended others of varying ages, interests, and backgrounds. He found different people fascinating. His example is a good one for all of us and provides a recipe for creating a life that is rich and varied. Too often we try to befriend only those who reassure us of the status quo, who are exactly like us, and who may not contribute as significantly to our growth and balance. This is a wide wonderful world. Be open to all the friends and associates it has to offer.

Our prophet, Thomas S. Monson, has long been well aware of this great battle against loneliness and reminds us that we are constantly watched over. In 1997 he counseled the single women of the Church: "Death, divorce, and indeed lack of opportunity to marry have in many instances made it necessary for a woman to stand alone. In reality, she need not stand alone, for a loving Heavenly Father will be by her side to give direction to her life and provide peace and assurance in those quiet moments where loneliness is found and where compassion is needed."[9]

Time is a precious commodity. Make your moments count, first, by making an effort to stay close to the Spirit so you can function at your best; second, by planning and setting goals for a more balanced life; third, by cultivating an eternal perspective; and fourth, by spending time with other people.

When the winds are whistling around us and we feel assailed by life, may we remember the Savior. I love the song "Master, the Tempest Is Raging."[10] There exists in all of us the ability to persist with patience one day at a time. When the clock is ticking and the tempest is raging, consider it an opportunity to rise up with all the beauty and strength and wisdom within you to become the woman the Lord wants you to become.

CHAPTER 8

NEVER A SINGLE
DULL MOMENT

We all have the capacity to make our lives wonderful.

A single friend requested that I not forget to write about the giggles and joys and happy times that are part of *singlehood*. She said, "Kristen, when we are single the Lord is providing us additional time to enjoy and prepare for life in the eternities. Never let anyone think that being single is only about being sad and feeling depressed and deprived."

She went on to share her philosophy: "Being single is like being given a box of Legos. You can complain that you wanted the super deluxe medieval castle set or decide to be happy that you received a different box—and make a fantastic clipper ship. You can build something wonderful. You can share it with others. You can develop all sorts of imagination and skill. You can have a wonderful adventure—maybe just not the building you'd anticipated. You'll have a different adventure building a clipper ship rather than a castle."[1]

The giggles and the joys and the happy times will come to us but not as we seek to simply amuse ourselves in trivial pursuits. Singles are sometimes accused of partying and declining to take responsibility. We may travel the world in search of fun, endlessly trying to entertain ourselves or seeking exotic diversions. But no cruise, amusement, or other pastime can strengthen character and help with self-knowledge. The deep-seated joy we seek comes as we get to know who we are—our unique creativity and divine capabilities—and then use these gifts to enrich our lives and those around us. When we *become* the women and men the Lord wishes us to be, the journey is joyous.

Our lives become about as sweet and fulfilling as we allow them to be. The better prepared we are and the more we respect and know ourselves, the more we can develop our individual talents and also serve and bond with others. The visions we hold for our futures can become reality as we build our lives. Heavenly Father is the source of divine inspiration. He is the source of all knowledge. Our major purpose on this earth is to prepare to meet God.

The choice to do that is made on an individual basis, between each of us and Him. One by one we go to Him.

Most Experiences Are Individual

No matter what our relationships with others may be, many of life's greatest experiences take place individually. Joseph Smith walked into the grove alone, Moses ascended Mount Sinai alone, and Nephi sought spiritual enlightenment alone. In like manner, Sarah, Rebekah, Mary, and Elizabeth were informed of miraculous births by heavenly messages. Other holy assignments were issued individually. Esther was told to save her people, Emma Smith was directed to compile a hymnbook, and Eliza R. Snow was inspired to write such songs as "O My Father."[2] Our deepest spiritual communion with Heavenly Father and His Son occurs on an individual basis.

A valued single friend has written: "When we come into this world, we are alone. When we enter the waters of baptism, we do this as individuals. We are confirmed one at a time. One by one we bear our testimonies. Each of us is endowed in the temple as an individual. Our Church callings usually come to the one. And when we die, it will likely be a lone experience. I think we expect that so much of life is about being a couple or with others that we ignore all the times that Heavenly Father expects us to stand alone, to be counted as an individual, and to personally bear witness. We shouldn't be surprised that so many of our key experiences come to us alone. Likewise, salvation comes to one soul at a time."

Because salvation comes individually to us, we had better like ourselves and feel comfortable with who we are. It is vital that our relationships with ourselves be whole and healthy ones. Our integrity, our stability, our ability to love rests on our respect for and knowledge of who we really are. Shakespeare wrote of this truth:

> *This above all: to thine own self be true,*
> *And it must follow, as the night the day,*
> *Thou canst not then be false to any man.*[3]

Only if our relationship with ourselves is intact and sure can we be caring and trusted friends to others. If we honor that which is good and pure within us, we will find and honor that in others. It follows too that if we don't love ourselves, we cannot love anyone else.

Trust in Your True Identity

The gospel of Jesus Christ teaches us that we are daughters and sons of a Heavenly Father who loves us. When we really understand that relationship, it changes all that we do, all that we say, how we react to others, and how we use time. Our relationships with others become more celestial. We won't be going through the motions of doing right; we will be right. Our inner substance and nature will become right. That is more important than looking right to others.

"Are you just active in the Church or are you active in the gospel?" Elder Oaks asked during his address in a stake conference broadcast for northern Utah. "In contrast to just attending meetings, people who are active in the gospel are making and keeping covenants and going toward eternal life."[4] He referred to President Boyd K. Packer, who said, quoting a stake president, "Church meetings and programs are becoming a substitute for a testimony."[5] Merely showing up at church is a hollow action, while seeking to know the Lord is a hallowed, intensely meaningful and personally sanctifying process.

We all have to consider why we are doing what we are doing. Our testimonies are fragile. Consider the husband of an acquaintance who has betrayed both himself and her by denying his former beliefs. Instead of leaving her marriage and feeling inadequate and devastated, she has responded by being more loving toward her husband, by trying to understand him more, and by strengthening her own relationship with Heavenly Father and Jesus Christ. She told me recently, "If I sat around and worried what others thought about me and my marriage, I would fall apart. It would be like being on a roller coaster at the mercy of someone else, constantly going up and down. With the Lord I am steady."

Some Young Women leaders from a neighboring stake told me that a few of the girls in their program announced that as soon as they had completed the program they were going to stop attending church. The leaders realized that somehow these girls had fulfilled the requirements of the program but found no personal fulfillment in themselves. The Young Women values of integrity and faith had somehow not transferred from the activities done in the Personal Progress pages to the hearts and minds of the girls. They did not really believe that they were daughters of a Heavenly Father who loved them.

Anyone who does all the right things to look right to others in order to receive a reward will feel similarly. Our trust in the Lord should not be superficial. If our display of obedience is for others and not for God, we will develop a hollow faith that will not sustain us. If we proceed through life living in this semirighteous state, the trials of life will overcome us because, seemingly, not only do we not expect to be denied blessings, feel rejection, be betrayed in marriages, have rebellious children, suffer debilitating diseases, or have our dreams crushed but we also lack the spiritual strength to endure such experiences.

Part of the plan is that we will be tested, and the only means to pass the test is through genuine devotion and dependence on our Heavenly Father. When difficulties arise, the first reaction of many of us might be, "Why has God allowed this to happen?" We should not forget that other people have their agency or that afflictions may be opportunities for growth and development.

Heavenly Father became my best friend. As a single woman I saw that when I depended on Him, I increased my capacity to handle disappointment, conflict, and rejection. More important, I learned how I would not do certain things again or do them in another way, and I learned how to respond in a more mature manner. That is called growing up. As I turned to Heavenly Father, I came to see my trials and inconveniences as growing experiences. As I witnessed my ability to cope, to change, and to improve, I longed to share the lessons I learned with those I loved.

When my nieces and nephews encountered a challenge—from learning how to tie their shoes to making cakes to rollerblading to doing homework to getting along with peers—I used the challenge as a teaching moment. I often said to them, "Just say, Ho-ho-ho, I have a problem." I wanted them to embrace their difficulties, attack them head on, and not sit and cry and mope. I knew that if they began as small children to believe they were capable of solving problems by themselves, in the future they would learn to rely on their inner resources. Not one of them appreciated my help at the time, but in retrospect they do so as adults. My niece told me she still remembers those words, and they still help her.

Our Godly Identity

It has been said that "the unexamined life is not worth living." We have to constantly ask ourselves what a godly identity means. It is far more than completing Personal Progress, graduating from seminary, finishing a mission, or progressing from deacon to teacher to priest. It means deep inside we come to know who we are, what we stand for, and what we believe—and then being true to those beliefs in every situation. The truer we are to what we espouse, the more internal integrity we have and the greater our external ability to cope with difficulties and find happiness.

We need to understand God's plan for us. President Boyd K. Packer taught us so clearly about this plan: "The course of our mortal life, from birth to death, conforms to eternal law and follows a plan described in the revelations as The Great Plan of Happiness. The one idea, the one truth I would inject into your minds is this: *There are three parts to the plan. You are in the second or the middle part, the one in which you will be tested by temptation, by trials, perhaps by tragedy.* Understand that, and you will be better able to make sense of life and to resist the disease of doubt and despair and depression.

"The plan of redemption, with its three divisions, might be likened to a grand three-act play. Act I is entitled 'Premortal Life.' The scriptures describe it as our First Estate. (See Jude 1:6; Abr.

3:26–28). Act II, from birth to the time of resurrection, the 'Second Estate.' And Act III, 'Life after Death or Eternal Life.'

"In mortality, we are like one who enters a theater just as the curtain goes up on the second act. We have missed Act I. The production has many plots and sub-plots that interweave, making it difficult to figure out who relates to whom and what relates to what, who are the heroes and who are the villains. It is further complicated because you are not just a spectator; you are a member of the cast, on stage, in the middle of it all! . . .

"Until you have a broad perspective of the eternal nature of this great drama, you won't make much sense out of the inequities of life. Some are born with so little and others with so much, some in poverty, with handicaps, with pain, with suffering, premature death even of innocent children. There are the brutal, unforgiving forces of nature and the brutality of man to man. . . .

" . . . When you know the plan and purpose of it all, even these things will manifest a loving Father in Heaven."[6]

The more certain our knowledge of the eternal plan, the clearer our picture becomes of who we are, why we are here, and where we are going. The more we comprehend our divine selves, the stronger our focus and faith become. We can more fully comprehend our godlike identity.

When we understand that God has a plan for us, we can endure with dignity. My friend Sarah shared, "I think that being happy is a matter of how I define life's timeline. If my timeline begins and ends with this earth life, it is easy to complain and find fault. I catch myself succumbing to spiritual shortsightedness. 'Life isn't fair! Where are my blessings?' However, if I focus on a premortal existence and an eternal timeframe, everything comes into perspective. If I truly believe that this lifetime is a period of testing and probation, then it is my responsibility to recognize the challenges that will come to me. I can choose to be faithful or to 'dwindle in unbelief.' I can decide to be happy, productive, and bless others' lives, or I can choose from a large and diverse temporal menu. I just haven't found anything on that menu that rivals testimony and faith."

To maintain our testimonies and faith, President Packer also cautioned us to constantly "immunize our minds and our spirits with *ideas,* with *truth.*"[7] We immunize ourselves by knowing God's voice.

My friend Patrice often says, "Individually, as children of God, we need to learn how to recognize His voice. He speaks to us through His scriptures, His prophets, and our patriarchal blessings. The Lord teaches us, 'My word shall not pass away, but shall all be fulfilled, whether by mine own voice or by the voice of my servants, it is the same' (D&C 1:38)."

Patrice continued, "We need to learn to recognize and distinguish His voice from other voices around us. The two main other voices I think of are the voices of Satan and our own pessimistic inner voices that habitually speak negative thoughts to us. These are two sources that will not take us to a good place. I have noticed that women especially are so hard on themselves. Often if we are not focusing on the voice of the Lord, we let our minds spin at random, and we can get into some personally destructive and demeaning cycles. We might begin to think that we are incapable, ugly, fat, or even too tall. Our natures are sensitive and we focus on all the can't comparisons, the put-downs, and the negative thoughts that run through our minds.

"Negative thoughts are not born of God. God would never humiliate, debase, or say anything to destroy our faith and confuse us. He would lift and edify us and fill us with hope and faith and charity. We can't recognize His voice unless we are familiar with his scriptures, to see how He operates and talks to us. We can't differentiate the counterfeit voices if we aren't familiar with His voice. We have no other standard by which to judge. That does not mean the Lord won't say the hard things to us or that He won't be demanding of us, but He will do it by way of loving invitation, encouragement, and bringing to our remembrance who we are. When we hear and recognize His voice, we can accomplish whatever He asks of us as we enter into and keep covenants."[8]

President Spencer W. Kimball taught that each woman should seek her divine potential: "Drink in deeply the gospel truths about the eternal nature of your individual identity and the uniqueness of your personality. You need, more and more, to feel the perfect love which our Father in Heaven has for you and to sense the value he places upon you as an individual. . . .

"There is no greater and more glorious set of promises given to women than those which come through the gospel and the Church of Jesus Christ. Where else can you learn who you really are? Where else can you be given the necessary explanations and assurances about the nature of life? From what other source can you learn about your own uniqueness and identity? From whom else could you learn of our Father in Heaven's glorious plan of happiness?"[9]

Remain Optimistic

When we are optimistic and positive we function at our best. The Lord has instructed us to be so: "Let us cheerfully do all things that lie in our power; and then may we stand still, with the utmost assurance, to see the salvation of God, and for his arm to be revealed" (D&C 123:17). As we set out cheerfully and full of courage and try to do our best, the Lord promises tremendous blessings of fulfillment, peace, and confidence that all will be well.

"In September 1842, the Prophet Joseph Smith wrote the following in a letter to the Church, later recorded in the Doctrine and Covenants 128:19, 22: 'Now, what do we hear in the gospel which we have received? A voice of gladness! A voice of mercy from heaven;

and a voice of truth out of the earth; glad tidings for the dead; a voice of gladness for the living and the dead; glad tidings of great joy."[10]

Of all people on earth we have the greatest reason to rejoice and go forward. Time is an especially precious commodity because we know its great worth. The glad tidings are that we know who we are, and we know where we are going. Our moments are bright and hopeful because we have a purpose for life.

On a personal level, the more optimistic and positive we become, the more our burdens will be lessened, the greater our influence will be to uplift those around us, and the more capable we will become of making every moment count.

Learn to Be Comfortable with Yourself

Joseph Smith was an example to everyone in the Church. He was true to himself. Every account of him tells of his natural affable manner, his love of children, and his majestic leadership and prophetic power. He was comfortable with who he was. He was multidimensional and whole.

We can all become comfortable with who we are. By *comfortable*, I mean much more than just accepting ourselves—weaknesses, warts, and all. I mean digging deep inside ourselves, finding core beliefs, and relying on them. One friend I love to be near is magnetic and charismatic and warm because she knows herself. People gravitate to her because she has made peace between herself and the difficulties life has shown her. She has made Heavenly Father her best friend, and she is a friend to everyone else. She loves herself and cares for herself. She surrounds herself with very simple good things: lovely paintings, good music, fresh fruit, a cat who adores her, and time to ponder her spiritual self. She has mastered the art of living well, savoring every moment, and relishing good books, noble ideas, and meaningful conversations. She is totally comfortable in her own skin—even down to her toes in her comfy Birkenstocks. Her contentment is contagious.

Distinct and Different Women of the Church

I have many single friends and acquaintances who understood the plan and have depended on Heavenly Father to guide their lives. Despite crushing circumstances they have created lives of great worth and joy.

I have chosen to share only a few stories of Latter-day Saint women whose inspiring examples can bless us all. They desired not to have a single dull moment. Their choices and actions created happy, significant moments and had eternal consequences for those around them. They realized that their singular efforts could make a difference in God's kingdom here on earth.

Stella H. Oaks

My husband's mother, Stella H. Oaks, was a remarkable, whole, and secure person. A widow left to raise three young children, she was at first overwhelmed and even incapacitated by an emotional breakdown after her husband's death. Through faith and priesthood blessings she recovered her health and rose above her despair to earn a graduate degree from Columbia University, raise her children in joy, become a teacher and administrator, serve as a stake Relief Society president, and become a member of the Young Women General Board. She was twice elected city councilwoman in Provo and served for a time as acting mayor of Provo.

She made her life a delight. She was a working mother who

struggled to support and rear her family. Her three children recall going to the refrigerator every morning and finding three prepared meals so they could eat breakfast, lunch, and dinner in any order they chose and enjoy every bite. Meals were an adventure. One night Stella dropped a newly baked cherry pie in the middle of the kitchen floor. Instead of bursting into tears and indulging in self-pity, she remained true to her frugal nature and called her young children to grab forks and eat the pie off the floor. In every arena Stella was a positive and dynamic example to those around her.

Lucille Sargent

In the grand design of life our single status may provide us with opportunities to serve Heavenly Father in a unique way. Over the years Lucille Sargent came to the attention of Elder James E. Faust, who was then serving as president of the International Mission. Elder Faust said, "Each year as I reviewed the tithing, I noticed that as regularly as the months came and went, we received an envelope and tithing contribution from Lucille Sargent in Peking, China. Her faithfulness was exceptional because she was the only member of the Church in Peking."

Elder Faust mentioned her to then-Elder Gordon B. Hinckley, who informed Elder Faust that "Lucille Sargent has been in the Foreign Service of the United States for over twenty years, living in remote areas, behind the iron curtain, most of the time alone. She never married. She was placed in some areas at the very time that the Lord opened up those countries for the preaching of the gospel. She was most helpful in every instance."[11]

Her professional standing, mobility, and faith made her a great instrument in the hands of the Lord. Her life reminds all of us that if we are working to build the Church and help our fellowman, we should never underestimate the good we can do.

Allyn Rogers

My friend Allyn Rogers often comments on pursuing our divine destiny. Every six months, since she was eighteen years old, she has started a new hobby. Over the years these hobbies have added meaning and enriched her life experiences. She would "set a dream" for herself to accomplish—these dreams have included learning to sail, becoming an expert photographer, and learning to play the guitar. I especially enjoyed the year she learned to smoke a turkey; the results were delicious.

The dream I watched unfold from beginning to end was the building of her cabin. A single mother who supports herself and her children on a teacher's salary, she wanted a mountain retreat to escape from the world, be with friends and family, and enjoy nature. Allyn found a picture of a beautiful cabin. She taped that picture on her refrigerator, where she could constantly see it. She enlisted six close friends and inspired them with her dream. They set about to make their dream come true. She and her friends memorized that picture and visualized building it themselves. They drew up floor plans and went to a contractor for help. He saw their plans and quoted an exorbitant price, telling them it could not be done for less.

Undeterred, they went to Allyn's brother, who is a builder and who teaches the building trades. He said he could build it for half the price if the women did the work themselves. They determined to do just that. Allyn bought a leather tool belt and a metal hammer. She informed me, "You can't build a house with a wooden hammer." First, her brother insisted they make a miniature model of the cabin. This took the six women six months to build. Next, with their vision in mind and the model prepared, they commenced to build the real thing, which took only three months—from footings to insulation to sheetrock. They hauled rock, poured cement, and laid brick. They "set a dream" and made it a reality through their positive attitude and persistent effort. As friends they have enjoyed the sweet fruits of their labor.

Allyn says, "Making the most of our talents and gifts not only enriches our earthly existence but also prepares us for progression through the eternities."

Cécile Pelous

I first remember hearing of Cécile Pelous from Ed Borrell, the missionary who taught her the gospel in France. He told me that when he went to her door she already had a positive impression of the Church and she welcomed him in, a unique occurrence for a missionary serving in the Paris France Mission. In her teen years, ten years earlier, she had traveled throughout the United States. At the conclusion of her trip, when she gathered with her friends to discuss their favorite spot in America, Cécile remembered the warm enveloping feeling she had experienced on her visit to Temple Square. That feeling had remained with her and made her an eager investigator.

Cécile was a fashion designer, a *modéliste,* in Paris. She put her vision of beauty on paper, designing for the finest names in fashion—Ricci, Dior, Cardin. For Elder Borrell, finding, teaching, and baptizing Cécile, such an exceptional and talented investigator, was the highlight of his mission. After leaving his mission he kept in touch and watched the Church influence and bless her life.

With her Parisian passion for life, Cécile had a great desire to build God's kingdom. She longed for more than living in a charming apartment and designing lovely garments for wealthy patrons. In a short time she contacted Mother Teresa in India, explained her situation, and asked to volunteer for six weeks. To her surprise, Mother Teresa invited her to join with the Missionaries of Charity and the Little Sisters of the Poor in Calcutta "helping with sick children, the elderly, and the handicapped."[12] Cécile filled suitcases with medicine, bandages, and antibiotics, packed a few clothes, and set out to serve.

In India, Cécile saw human suffering on a scale she had never imagined. It was physically draining and emotionally overpowering. Immersed in the pain and suffering of those dying around her, Cécile became sensitive and weepy. After a short time, the sisters of Mother Teresa's order approached her, saying, "Stop crying. These people need your help, not your pity. You must get control of yourself, or you will have to go back home."

Cécile did gain control and increased focus. Her magnificent internal resources and vision helped her succeed with patients, especially the children. Mother Teresa, observing Cécile's innate gift with youth, sent her to assist a doctor in Pilkhana, a Calcutta slum, working among young orphan children too destitute to merit the attention of the Indian government. Cécile worked her magic with these children of India. They gravitated to her. She taught them games, sang, and played with them. She assumed she had finally discovered the place God wished her to serve.

But the Lord had a larger mission for Cécile. She set out on a second quest, this time to Banipur, where she "lived and worked in an *ashram* (a religious retreat) in . . . one of eight orphanages for children ages five to twelve."[13] Cécile found herself among those who really needed her. Working with these children she felt a personal satisfaction and a joy so pronounced she wanted to devote the rest of her life to helping and serving them. "The conditions there moved me so deeply," Cécile commented later, "that I knew I had to find a way to get back again to help."[14]

Cécile, who supported herself and was in need of funds, returned to Paris, but she was determined to help her beloved orphans. She prayed to somehow find enough financial backing to help those she had come to love so deeply. Providentially, a large commercial real estate developer began a project near Cécile's home on the outskirts of Paris. The location of her home near a Metro station caused it to escalate in value. Cécile declined to sell it, but the price doubled and then tripled and then skyrocketed. She prayed to Heavenly Father and heard, "Sell it!" She sold when the real estate prices in Paris were at their peak.

In 1988, on another break from work, "Cécile returned to Salkhia, near Calcutta, and taught orphan girls ages twelve to seventeen to print batik designs on material, which they could then sell to provide funds for the orphanage." In 1989, a Catholic priest who had observed her ability to soothe and entertain children suggested she go to Nepal.[15] Using the proceeds from selling her home, Cécile helped found "a day-care center in Belari for forty children, ages three through five, expanding her circle of love."[16]

Cécile has recently retired from working with the world's finest fashion houses and devotes herself to raising funds and directing the affairs of charities she has established. She has made her time on earth count, opening opportunities in the lives of children half a world away and providing an example to us all.

Dini Hansma

Dini Hansma was born in Hoogeveen, Netherlands. She was eight years old when World War II broke out. She remembers the green flood of Nazi soldiers entering her town, the falling bombs, the sirens blaring during air raids, and her friends being taken away in the night. The admonition of her parents was to talk to no one because no one was to be trusted. Her father was taken into forced labor in Germany, and she was left with a single mother.

In time, Dini became a certified teacher, and for a number of years was employed as headmistress of a kindergarten. In the early 1960s she took her savings and, seeking adventure, traveled on a visitor's visa to the United States. Staying with friends in Vernal, Utah, she attended church because, she said, "There was simply nothing else to do." Within the year she was baptized. She returned to Holland, saw her family, and in 1964 returned to the United States, this time as an immigrant. "The hardest thing," she recalls, "was to leave my mother and the rest of the family behind and realize that we might not meet again."

Dini believes that everything in life happens for a purpose, whether we know it or not. It was no small miracle that Brigham Young University accepted her Dutch teaching credits and certified her in just two semesters rather than four years. She found a teaching position in the Provo School District and went to live in the home of Stella H. Oaks. There she was a loyal friend and considered a member of the family.

Dini developed a passion for genealogy. She gathered about twenty thousand names in her own lines. Reaching an impasse when there seemed to be no more records for her family, she decided to look into the family lines of friends who were taken away by the Nazis during World War II.

She told me, "I was interested in the friends I had played with in my younger years. It really started with them. I decided I wanted to build a genealogical 'monument' to them. During the war I was too young to be in the Resistance, but it is never too late to do something. I started with Rika and Sara Phillipson. I gathered all the names in my town, went on to gather names from the whole province, and ended up gathering the names of families living in the four northern provinces. In all, I have gathered fifty-one thousand names on fourteen thousand family group sheets, and I am not finished yet."[17]

Dini adds, "For many years now I have volunteered my expertise in the Family History Library at BYU. Since 1972 I have been supervisor of three shifts." On June 7, 2007, Dini was awarded the Lifelong Presidential Service Award, presented by the White House for having served over twelve thousand volunteer hours.

Dini writes, "Being single in the Church has sometimes been a challenge. People have said some very funny things to me: 'How come you were skipped over?' 'Someone is waiting for you in heaven.' Or, more often, 'I want to know why you aren't married.' I have used various comebacks to end the conversation. The answer that usually stopped people in their tracks was: 'Funny thing that. I guess nobody wanted me.' I then get all kinds of compliments, and people have no more to say to me on the matter.

"My motto is: You will receive in life comparable to what you give. Single people especially need to reach out to others. Sitting back and waiting to see what others will do for you might mean you have to wait for a long time. Nobody is served by being depressed about it or having a depressed person on their hands. There is so very much to do. Help unconditionally, because if you expect rewards you will not get them and you will be disappointed. Count your blessings, and really name them one by one. Then thank the Lord for all you have and for all you can do. Ask Him what you can do for Him, instead of the other way around."[18]

Knowledge of Self Helps Us Bond with Others

The gift of knowing ourselves and developing our talents is that we attract others like ourselves, and we are led to those who need us. The more we honor the divine natures within us, the more our actions are in harmony with Heavenly Father, and the more compatible we become with others around us.

Our goal is to enter into successful eternal relationships. To do so requires more than just completing a wish list of what we desire in a mate. It requires that we become a person of virtue ourselves. The more thoroughly we have come to know ourselves—how we react in times of stress, what we do when we are tired and frustrated, how we react to boredom, what we do when we are down and depressed—the better able we are to cope with our lives and our relationships. We often do not see ourselves as others see us. The more opportunity we have to interact with others and get their assessment and feedback about us, the more successful we can become at evaluating ourselves, and if that evaluation is not as good as we would like, the more possibility we have to change and improve.

This internal evaluation process will be ongoing. We do not become stagnant on our wedding day. An eternal relationship entails much more of a couple than just making it through the front door of the temple. Veon G. Smith wrote of myths that plague marriage. Many people think, "'If I have my wedding in the temple, the marriage will take care of itself.' But it won't. Marriage is a dynamic interaction between two growing, changing people, and it requires constant focus on the quality of that interaction if the marriage is to be close and meaningful. A temple marriage does not automatically guarantee a celestial marriage—or even a pleasant one."[19]

Start now to prepare. The success of our present associations and of our eternal relationships hinges on our knowledge of how we present ourselves, how we react, and how we treat others around us. We need to observe ourselves and invite—and be open to—feedback.

Recently I observed two examples of how feedback can help us with future relationships. Others provide feedback, but we alone can act on it. The first was a young relative who has been interviewing for internships with large corporations. He has asked his possible future employers how he did, even during the interview. Many comments and suggestions made to him have helped him perfect his interview style so that he has now qualified for a prime internship. A second example was a volunteer worker who treated others with disrespect and harshness. When approached by his supervisor for being nasty and inconsiderate, he denied it. The supervisor then gave specific examples of his bad behavior. The volunteer buried his face in his hands and wept. He had not realized his own rudeness and harsh treatment toward people he genuinely hoped to assist. He asked to try again and asked for continual feedback.

We are surrounded by great teachers who, if we pay attention to them, will help us become magnets for the gospel, as President Spencer W. Kimball taught. One friend, Kris, has helped me so much to become a more diplomatic and tactful communicator. I often speak directly from my heart, and the words sometimes spill out without careful consideration for others. Kris, on the other hand, can address problems with great finesse and kindness. When there is a disagreement and Kris is around, others come away reconciled and understanding because of her wise words. I have learned much by watching her and listening to her.

As our capacity to know ourselves increases, so does our influence for good. I believe that single sisters, especially, because of their mobility and visibility throughout the world, will be an enormous influence for good. President Kimball said, "My dear sisters, may I suggest to you something that has not been said before or at least in quite this way. Much of the major growth that is coming to the Church in the last days will come because many of the good women of the world (in whom there is often such an inner sense of spirituality) will be drawn to the Church in large numbers. This will happen to the degree that the women of the Church reflect righteousness and articulateness in their lives and to the degree that the women of the Church are seen as distinct and different—in happy ways—from the women of the world. . . . Thus it will be that female exemplars of the Church will be a significant force in both the numerical and the spiritual growth of the Church in the last days."[20]

It should be no surprise to anyone that increased numbers of women will enter the Church because they are drawn by the good example of women within the Church. They will need to be tutored and loved and welcomed into The Church of Jesus Christ of

Latter-day Saints. The women of the Church have a great destiny and responsibility ahead.

In some way you have just such an influence on others. There are talents and contributions only you can make. Dig deep into yourself to discover what they are. Pray and fast to find out. The Lord may inspire you to write a book, a song, or a movie. You may be given an idea to begin a business or start a preschool. Each of us has a dream. Our patriarchal blessings and revelations from Heavenly Father can forever change the course of our lives. God is not limited by our education or lack of it. He's not limited by what we have or do not have. If we believe, God can assist us toward our righteous goals.

Sister Sheri Dew refers to righteous women as the "Lord's secret weapon" and says that as "covenant women during this culminating era, every one of us has a unique opportunity to change the world." She invites us to do just that: "If we would unleash the *full* influence of covenant-keeping women, the kingdom of God would change overnight. . . .

". . . Let us be the generation of women that finally walks away from the world. If we will Awake to who we are, Arise by making of our lives ministries, and Come unto Christ by steadily becoming more holy, we will have a degree of influence the world and the kingdom of God have never felt before—an influence that has no limit and no end."[21]

The more we rely on Heavenly Father to lead and direct us, the more we look into ourselves—at our strengths and talents—the more we can be used as a unique instrument in His hands as an agent for good. As we turn to Heavenly Father for direction and purpose in our lives, we can become an "instrument in the hands of God" and "show forth good examples" and bring "salvation [to] many souls" (Alma 17:9, 11). When we seek to do His will, He provides us with "a portion of that Spirit" (Alma 18:35). Heavenly Father can inspire us and help us to enrich our lives.

Life is meant to be a joyful experience. Use your individual talents, faith, and efforts to make it so. Adopt the mantra "Never a single dull moment," and use the Legos given you to build a happy and fulfilling life.

CHAPTER 9

THE SINGLE BEST THING YOU CAN DO

*The single best thing we can do is to
remember our divine identity.*

Sometimes we find loving ourselves is very difficult. In our adversity we can lose sight that we are the divine children of a Father in Heaven who loves us. We can become preoccupied with our personal weaknesses and allow them to hinder our eternal progress. We can allow our own self-doubts and personal misgivings to diminish us. A friend told me what young singles in her ward reported in sacrament meeting about their experience at a multistake conference for young single adults. One young single sister said, "I loved how Elder Holland says the Lord looks at us and sees the best, because I often look at myself and see the worst." This friend had not realized how critical young people are of themselves.

These young people did not know how precious they were to their Heavenly Father. The first great commandment is to love God with all our heart. Surely the great commandment is not for Him; He already loves us. This commandment is for us so we can understand the depth and immensity of His love for us. God is the source of love. It is not just a suggestion that we love Him; it is a commandment. When you begin to comprehend your eternal value, when you know you are validated by the Creator of the world, you don't let other people define you. Your security and your sense of who you are allow you to tap into Heavenly Father's love until it fills your heart deeply, not just in a partial or temporary manner.

So often we are seeking to feel the love Heavenly Father has for us, and there is a disparity between how we feel about our physical, outer selves and our divine, inner selves.[1]

One friend who is a psychologist shared with me that she speaks with many people of varying ages and backgrounds, and every one of them has the same basic worry: they all wonder if they are really okay. No matter how accomplished or wealthy or popular or talented they are, they all question their own worth in the eyes of others. They are still searching for a validation of personal worth. The psychologist continued, "That inner validation and sense of worth will never come from an outside source. It can never be dependent on the opinions others have of us."

Beauty Is More Than Skin Deep

An anonymous letter with only a post office box address was delivered to Elder Oaks. The letter expressed a concern so decisively that he felt to share both it and his reply with me. They state very well the struggle with self-worth so many of us feel in this life.

From the anonymous letter: "I am writing to you because I am unhappy and have been unhappy for years. I am at the point right now that I need someone to give me clarification and guidance so I can begin to exercise faith to change my life; otherwise, I feel I'll never change.

"I am in my upper twenties and am single. Being single is not the underlying problem. The problem is that I am not a [physically] attractive person. I don't have any abnormal growths or anything, but

I'm just not what girls would call good looking. Most girls think I have an awesome personality, super genuine and nice, and have everything going for me. The phrase I often hear is, 'He's perfect in every way, but I just don't have those feelings for him.' I can't work on my jaw line or the shape of my eyes or other features of my face. I just want to be attractive and have my wife think I'm attractive. What this means is that I have had very little opportunity over the years to date girls that I am interested in."

This young man writes not only about his unattractiveness and the toll it is taking on his dating life but also about his unhappiness. I would like to know something about the young women he wants to date. This raises a delicate question about whom any of us choose to date. We have to be realistic about whom we can attract and whom we find attractive. An analogy could be made about a five-foot-six-inch man with adequate basketball skills aspiring to be a member of the NBA Dream Team. It probably won't happen.

This topic is treated poignantly and humorously in Joseph Stein's *Fiddler on the Roof* when two sisters sing dreamily of the fine marriages to rich, intelligent, and handsome men the matchmaker might make for them. Their older sister, more aware of how matchmaking works, asks her younger sisters if they are great beauties from rich families. She provides a much clearer picture of what a young woman in their circumstances might expect of a matchmaker's efforts.

In a similar way, many young men seem to be looking for Barbie with a testimony, when they themselves do not look anything like Ken, Barbie's counterpart, and are perhaps only marginally active in the Church.

Looks are somewhat important, but once we get to know someone well, our ideas about their appearance may change. A person we thought beautiful may, because of an unpleasant disposition, become unattractive to us. Likewise, someone who has gone unnoticed may suddenly, because of some inner nobility or other asset of personality, become very attractive to us.

It is interesting that men will befriend men of different levels of attractiveness. Men choose male friends whose company they enjoy, who have the same interests, and whom they respect. Handsomeness is rarely the basis of male friendship.

In contrast, when choosing someone to date, a man pays quite a bit of attention to looks, sometimes choosing "arm candy"—someone to bolster his ego by looking good on his arm. His dating, then, is not about companionship and compatibility but about the swelling pride of the connection and the impression he will make on others by being seen with a beautiful woman. More often than not, the woman he is dating realizes this is the case. The consequences of dating only for physical attraction are twofold: either the woman loses regard for the man, or, if she is less scrupulous, she uses the man to benefit her by some means other than the development of genuine affection.

The young man continued his letter by complaining about the body Heavenly Father gave him:

"As a result of this, my faith and patience with the Lord have been tried. I keep telling myself He *could* have made me handsome, but He didn't. Why? Why am I ugly and a lot of my close friends are attractive (and married, too). At this point in my life I have very little hope of ever being happy. I feel like what's the point of being good? What's the point of keeping the commandments? To what end? To what end?"

I felt the discouragement and disorientation of this young man. His concern over his physical appearance has become all-encompassing. He does not make any connection between keeping the commandments and personal happiness. He is beginning to give up on himself.

Often when we give up on ourselves we make the assumption that God has given up on us when He is just beginning to work on us. Our Heavenly Father promises that if we endure our adversities well, He will strengthen us in them and that ultimately these struggles will become sanctifying experiences that will qualify us for exaltation (D&C 121:7–8).

In our discouragement we sometimes forget the words of the Lord when He counseled Samuel as he was trying to find a king for Israel: "Look not on his countenance, or on the height of his stature; because I have refused him: for the Lord seeth not as man seeth; for man looketh on the outward appearance, but the Lord looketh on the heart" (1 Samuel 16:7).

Sister Susan Tanner, as Young Women General President, said that in the early months of her marriage "my husband said quite often, 'I didn't marry you for your looks.' Finally I teased him a bit by saying, 'That really doesn't sound too flattering.' He explained what I already knew, that this was intended to be the highest compliment he could give me. He said, 'I love you for who you are intrinsically and eternally.'"[2] His appreciation of her went far beyond anything external and fleeting. He loved her for her character and goodness.

Take a moment to look around at those who influence you most and whom you love. It is not because of their exterior beauty. It is because of their unique and caring, even quirky, natures. External appearances have only limited impact. When I worked as a consultant, one manager would always tell me, "Dress your best and look your best, but know you have only seventy seconds for people to care what you look like before they notice who you are and what you are saying."

The young man writing the letter had not yet taken time to love himself "intrinsically and eternally" or to look for anything beyond exterior beauty. Ironically, by not recognizing his own inner beauty, he lost the ability to love anyone else for theirs, and in his depression he made bad decisions.

In his letter the young man admitted that he was struggling with the commandments. He was living a life he was not proud of, and he had approached his bishop to correct his mistakes.

"Every one [of my mistakes] stems from all this [my ugliness]. I get so depressed being turned down, again, by girls that my resolve to be obedient is gone. I find repentance pointless. The only reason I am still trying is because of the great peace it brings into my life. But while I may have peace, I am still unhappy. It reminds me of my mission. I was squeaky clean and had a measure of peace accompany my life, but I was never happy. I have never been happy."

In his discouragement this young man tried the ways of the world, seeking to ease his dissatisfaction but finding only more pain. He had felt the Spirit and had been blessed by the peace of it, yet he now has great self-loathing and feels unhappy. He is fixated on his own weaknesses and has forgotten his real eternal identity.

At times we are all unhappy with ourselves. Nothing is more demoralizing for young people than to feel that no one finds them attractive. Everyone has been discouraged with some aspect of themselves—from looks to brains to athletic ability to ability to relate with others. Each of us has felt moments of frustration, devastation, or limitation. That is part of our earth-life experience. How we react to those situations makes all the difference. Heavenly Father has blessed us with eternal perspective, and if we live worthy of it and trust in Him, that eternal perspective can ease the burdens of life.

In closing, the young man wrote: "P.S. Do you ever think about what you will look like in the next life? Are you 100 percent comfortable with how you look? I would ask this same question to everyone, not just you."

Elder Oaks wrote a wise reply to the P.O. box number given in this young man's letter. (No name was given—only a post office box):

"Dear Brother:

"Though we don't normally respond to anonymous letters, I am responding to your letter expressing your concerns and unhappiness with your physical appearance. You say you 'just want to be attractive.'

"I will not say that looks are not important, but I do think you have built a definition and pedestal for attractiveness that is far higher than it should be. We teach that true beauty is founded on righteousness, virtue, and gospel living.

"All one has to do is look around an old folks home to see how transparent skin-deep beauty is. Or compare the attractiveness of some people before twenty and after fifty. The long-term beautiful people of the world are people of generosity, thoughtfulness, and all the other basic Christian values. Further, when you look at the skin-deep beautiful people of movie stardom and see how often they move in and out of marriage, it is apparent that attractiveness is not synonymous with happiness.

"To highlight this truth consider this description of the Savior in the fifty-third chapter of Isaiah:

"'Who hath believed our report? and to whom is the arm of the Lord revealed? For he shall grow up before him as a tender plant . . . *he hath no form nor comeliness; and when we shall see him, there is no beauty that we should desire him.*'

"Even in the life of Christ himself, physical beauty was not important; and consequently, we should not let it become too important to us.

"You ask if I am concerned about what I will look like in the next life. I spend no time fussing about this relatively unimportant matter. I work on conducting my life in a way that reflects my testimony of Jesus Christ. I recommend you do the same."

Remember Your Divine Identity

We are children of a Heavenly Father who loves us, and to reap the blessings of that love takes consistent obedience and prayerfulness. If we make that effort, we will have a powerful weapon against discouragement. It is one of the devil's greatest tools. He knows that discouragement diminishes our capacity to act. It robs us of energy, motivation, and confidence. It confuses our thinking and causes us to make stupid decisions.

It is common for us to be critical of one another and ourselves. I felt so often that something must be wrong with me because I was not yet married. I had to be too fat, too involved in my work, or just not pretty enough to attract the man I wished to marry. I believe every person, single or not, at times succumbs to feelings of inadequacy.

When criticism about being single comes from sources outside ourselves, it can be very difficult not to be offended. Few people who married in their early twenties really understand the concerns of a never-married older single. They found it easy to marry, and they wonder what could possibly be holding up anyone else. Unless they are close to someone who has struggled for many years with being single, they may not be aware of or even sensitive to the struggles of single people. Whether explicitly spoken or not, many believe that the single person is somehow inadequate or just not trying hard enough to find an eternal companion, when quite the opposite may be true.

Not understanding the struggles of single members of the Church, a neighbor commented to me about her niece—intelligent, lovely, accomplished, and single in her mid-forties. "I wonder what is wrong with her?" she asked. I answered, "Nothing is wrong with her. She just hasn't yet found an eternal companion equal to her."

Many assume that those who are single are just not making themselves available enough. College girls have confided in me that their mothers told them to sit in front of the business building or to start studying in the law library to meet eligible men. They found these suggestions insulting.

We are children of a loving Heavenly Father, and we look to His timetable and direction. Only in that way can we be in the right situation to make the right things happen in our lives.

In different seasons of our lives we have different expectations of whom we should marry. I remember one elderly sister in a former ward who was marrying for a second time. In Relief Society she announced her joy in finding a new mate. She hoped to encourage us by saying, "He still has his hair and can drive at night." For many singles these are not the definitive qualifications we are looking for, but for this sister, marrying a devoted priesthood holder who had those additional qualities was just icing on the cake.

Others watching us wait to meet our companions give advice or make suggestions that are hurtful when they only mean to help. I received a letter from a young woman who felt herself becoming embittered by her single state and by her reaction to the advice given her. She said, in part:

"During the time of life when I was suffering because of lack of dates and direction in my life, my younger married sister offered some unwanted advice. At the time of 'the talk,' I was told of the many personal faults that prevented anyone from wanting to marry me. She said, 'The whole family thinks so.' It was devastating. During this talk all of my faults and shortcomings were discussed, and I was told that 'if I changed these horrible attributes, I stood a chance of marrying.'"

She goes on to say she was humiliated and more bitter because of the "biting words." Obviously, her younger sister had sought to motivate her through criticism, a motivation very few appreciate. I remember feeling sensitive about my situation, and at times mention of it did not roll off my back but penetrated my heart.

Yet it is sometimes wise to listen to our well-meaning critics. They may provide valuable feedback that we can receive in no other way. We should carefully evaluate the counsel given us because it might help us go forward.

Our leaders have great concern for the single members of the Church. President Spencer W. Kimball responded to this need with very wise advice:

"Make yourself attractive as a marriage partner. How nice and easy would it be if we had a magic wand! But we haven't. You might take a careful inventory of your habits, your speech, your appearance, your weight, if it is heavier than most people appreciate, and your eccentricities, if you have them. Take each item and analyze it. What do you like in others? What personality traits please you in others? Are your dresses too short, too long, too revealing, too old-fashioned? . . . Are you too selfish? . . . Are you too anxious or disinterested? . . . Are you dull or are you too exuberant? Are you flashy or are you dis-interesting? . . . Scrupulously clean both physically and morally? . . .

"What are your eccentricities, if any? I think nearly all people have some. If so, then go to work. Classify them, weigh them, cor-ral them, and eliminate one at a time until you are a very normal per-son."[3]

Respect yourself enough to be as attractive as you can be. Women feel paranoid enough about how they look that I hesitate to increase consciousness of appearance. Every magazine on the news-stand writes about losing weight (interestingly, often coupled with an article on cooking), and every form of entertainment seems to fea-ture the beautiful people. I do, however, want to remind us that when we look good, we feel good. Taking care of ourselves can increase our respect for ourselves. We wash our car, vacuum our home, and do our dishes—we shouldn't neglect to maintain ourselves.

This is a process, "line upon line, precept upon precept" (D&C 98:12; 128:21) in which we need to be patient with ourselves. Heav-enly Father would have us look at ourselves the way He views us. Each of us is beautiful and unique. Think about your best asset. Concentrate on your strengths, and work from there. We are handmaidens of a Heavenly Father who loves us. Always keep that focus in your mind.

Make every effort to be the best you can be. If you feel unattractive, make every effort to be attractive. Whatever makes you feel better about yourself, do it—from improving your hygiene to losing weight to exercising to finding clothes that make you look and feel good. If we are less than pleased with some aspect of our personality, we should go to work to change it. The important thing is to keep trying. It is all part of eternal progression. If we are unhappy with our situations, whatever they are, we have the capacity to change our lives for the better. That agency is central to the plan of salvation. As a child of God, you have this capacity—if not to change the physical you, then to ask Heavenly Father's help to change the internal you and any negative feelings you harbor.

To keep healthy, my friend Sally and I would walk every morning around Liberty Park. We became familiar with the others who walked there. One couple especially touched our hearts. They walked slowly, hand in hand, smiling. The husband walked especially slowly because he was afflicted with severe scoliosis.

We always smiled back as we passed them. Sally would whisper, "Trying, trying," and that became our mantra—"Trying, trying." We were doing our best every day, and so were the people around us. We became cheerleaders for one another.

Setting realistic goals and expectations for ourselves can help us overcome discouragement. "Ye shall know the truth, and the truth shall make you free" (John 8:22). Research from dating statistics indicates that "despite the wide spread myth that men prefer skinnier women, a survey by psychologist Paul Rozin proves differently. When men were asked to indicate the body type they are most attracted to, they typically picked the average female figure." Dating statistics "also show that looks are not that important. 67% of U.S. single men, and 86% of U.S. single women find that someone who smiles a lot" is much more attractive than "someone who is physically attractive, but has no personality. . . .

"Aside from physical beauty, singles are looking for intelligence, optimistic attitudes, self-confidence, and partners who enjoy the same hobbies or interests they do. Similar levels of intelligence are also important. Well-matched couples generally have similar levels of education. People tend to look for partners with whom they can converse at the same level."[4]

All this data indicates that it is what is inside that counts. We have control over that part of ourselves. In Primary we learn to sing "I Am a Child of God."[5] In Young Women we recite as part of our theme that "we are daughters of a Heavenly Father who loves us and we love Him." And in Relief Society we again affirm our identity as women of God. The important thing is that we retain the memory of who we really are.

Heavenly Father would have us look at ourselves in the way He views us. As His children, we all possess beautiful and unique qualities, but ultimately our potential to improve does not lie simply in our own hands. Contrary to what the world teaches us, we need not despair over our shortcomings. The Lord instructs us to recognize our weaknesses and to be humble and faithful:

"If men come unto me I will show them their weakness. I give unto men weakness that they may be humble; and my grace is sufficient for all men that humble themselves before me; for if they humble themselves before me, and have faith in me, then will I make weak things become strong unto them" (Ether 12:27).

The Lord is on our side. He is literally our Father in Heaven and He can guide us, direct us, and lift the burdens from our backs if only we listen for His voice and hearken to His command.

In the scriptures there is specific instruction on how to draw closer to our Father in Heaven and become more like Him. In Helaman 3, we read, "Nevertheless they did fast and pray oft, and did wax stronger and stronger in their humility, and firmer and firmer in the faith of Christ, unto the filling their souls with joy and consolation, yea, even to the purifying and the sanctification of their hearts, which sanctification cometh because of their yielding their hearts unto God" (v. 35).

Learn to recognize when the Lord responds to your pleas. During one fireside a bishop shared how he had counseled a struggling young couple who doubted themselves and were being destructive to one another. He offered simple advice to bring a greater measure of the Spirit into their home. He asked them to study the scriptures together, to pray together, and to use kind words when speaking about themselves and each other. The young couple returned in a month to visit with him. They had experienced greater personal peace and harmony and love for themselves and for each other.

One thing they shared surprised the bishop. The young wife said, "Bishop, I started to feel so good about myself. The sadness and dislike I had felt for myself and our home was lifted from me." She asked, "Is that what people are talking about at testimony meeting when they say the Spirit has healed and comforted them?" This positive feeling had been her first recognizable experience with the Spirit. Her bishop, overcome with emotion, nodded yes. The bishop said it was one of the few times he knew his counsel and direction had changed a life.

I also have a testimony that many times as I reached out to my Father in Heaven, He carried me and comforted me. Belief in Him is what gives us self-worth. The single best thing we can do is to remember our divine identity and in faith yield our hearts to Him.

PART FOUR

Religious Life and Church Experience

CHAPTER 10

SINGLE AT CHURCH

To remain active, a single member has to develop
a deep and abiding testimony of gospel truths rather than
depending solely on Church programs for happiness.
—Anonymous Church member in Los Angeles

*W*hen we are single our Church associations become especially meaningful to us. We look to our wards to provide not only a place to worship but also a place to socialize and be part of a ward family. Single members have high expectations that their wards will be places of refuge, of personal growth, and of spiritual renewal. The expectations for fellowship are high because we live in a world where social isolation is increasing. Reports from the U.S. Census Bureau show that one-fourth of American households now consist of one person living alone. As Robert B. Putnam, a Harvard political scientist sees it, America is fraying as people spend more time alone, commuting to work, watching TV, and spending less time with friends and neighbors. We are becoming a nation of loners.[1]

Our wards are unique because they are living examples of the kind of social group Putnam sees disappearing. They provide the kind of social experience many Americans aren't getting any more. They bring together people of different ages and backgrounds, build on shared beliefs rather than on narrow self-interests, rely on voluntary participation in meaningful callings, and provide a place where people can support one another. They provide a sense of religious and personal connectedness.

Our wards, however, are not immune from the social forces reshaping America. Americans are spending increasing amounts of time alone during commutes, at work, with computers, and in front of videos and television. We are becoming more insular and having less outreach in our lives. The result is that members—single members in particular—may receive less fellowship than they anticipate or desire. In the Church the consequence of feeling isolated and alone is often inactivity. Members who feel no bonds of fellowship, who are not integrated into a ward, do not stay active for long.

President Gordon B. Hinckley said, "We speak of the fellowship of the Saints. This is and must be a very real thing." He added, "We must never permit this spirit of brotherhood and sisterhood to weaken. We must constantly cultivate it. It is an important aspect of the gospel."[2]

In the fraying society that surrounds us, a single member of the Church, to remain active and involved, has to develop a deep and abiding testimony of the truths of the gospel and not depend solely on the programs of the Church for happiness. Our outreach to others becomes extremely important. Our singleness should not deter us from that. One single sister in our stake confided to me, "During my youth I always planned on getting married and never focused on becoming a disciple of Christ."

Our purpose must be very clear. At baptism we covenanted "to be called his people, and [to be] willing to bear one another's burdens, that they may be light" (Mosiah 18:8). We need to base our commitments on the Savior and on our relationships with our brothers and sisters in the gospel, not on our marital status.

The Singles Ward

There is no separate Church for singles. There may be wards, branches, or classes for singles, but they are all part of the same Church. There can be much joy in attending a singles ward— opportunities for leadership, callings to teach, service projects, social activities, firesides, and spiritual guidance. There are opportunities to bond with others of similar interests and age and to meet new friends. It feels comfortable to be in an environment and to associate with others having common concerns and needs, where being single is the norm. It is easy to feel accepted when our lives are so much like those around us.

Yet there are unique challenges in a singles ward as well. In this environment of possible future mates and with only a short window of time, some focus almost all their energy on searching for a husband or wife. Instead of enjoying this unique time to meet with others in a similar single situation, some become preoccupied by a nagging fear that marriage is escaping them. They become more frustrated and concerned with their single condition.

A bishop came to repair our furnace, and we talked as he worked. He told of the sadness, isolation, and despair some single people spoke of as they counseled with him. They saw no hope for marriage, and they felt abandoned and unwanted. They felt they did not fit in anywhere. They were too old to spend most of their time with their parents, and they often had no group of true peers that felt comfortable and supportive. Sadly, a few often spoke of how they wished that this life were over and that they could return to their Heavenly Father and be free of their pain and loneliness. "I would have been less empathetic and even critical if I had not experienced some of the intense discouragement they spoke of myself," he explained.

He then told me how Heavenly Father had prepared him to be

their bishop. A few years before, he had grown depressed as he suffered from a stomach condition that robbed him of sleep. The less he slept, the more depressed he became. His world grew darker and darker. Sometimes he felt assaulted by self-destructive thoughts. But he loved the scriptures, and he knew the power of prayer. His knowledge of true doctrine literally provided him with the will to live. The next months were difficult for him, but his condition was finally diagnosed and treated medically. He regained regular sleep patterns and began to enjoy life again as a wiser and empathetic man. Of this period of his life he said:

"I did not enjoy my suffering, but through it I learned that Heavenly Father always cares for me and that He is on my side when all else is against me. I can tell the members of my ward with a deep certainty that their Heavenly Father is aware of them and that He will not forsake them, even if He does require them to continue in the struggles they would prefer to escape. Heavenly Father blessed me with those experiences so that when I counseled young men and women, I could understand how they felt in a situation that was difficult and from which they saw no escape. I knew how they felt.

"Also I try to teach them long-term perspective. We are all in the same boat; there is no boat marked 'single and not married.' There will always be what I call 'divine discontent' because life is not perfect. We are not here just to accumulate toys and treats; our time here is a test. All of us may long throughout our lives for blessings we do not have: one may lament a parent lost in childhood, one may want a child, one may lose a child, one may have limited opportunities, one may not have an eternal companion or have lost an eternal companion to death. All of us, single or married, long for eternal blessings and to be part of a celestial whole.

"Young single men and women are often very fragile because they are just emerging as adults. It is a tender time, a time when they need to be treated with love. A snide remark, a rejection, or a harsh word can be devastating. I worry that too often the members of my ward have not learned the great power of being kind to one another. It makes such a difference. I try to make my ward a place where we feel fellowship and love, where we come together as true followers of Christ."

A Need for Greater Kindness

The bishop's words echoed the admonitions of President Howard W. Hunter: "We need to be kinder with one another, more gentle and forgiving. We need to be slower to anger and more prompt to help. We need to extend the hand of friendship and resist the hand of retribution. In short, we need to love one another with the pure love of Christ, with genuine charity and compassion and, if necessary, shared suffering, for that is the way God loves us."[3]

Unfortunately, many of us live in a harsh world and try to fit in by being cool. We sometimes bring the ways of the world to Church with us. Cool does not suggest human warmth and is often characterized by arrogance and emotional indifference. Cool may mean using sarcasm, cynicism, or ridicule. The common response in this human ice age is to create distance, to become defensive, and to protect ourselves. This defensiveness often makes unattainable the warmth and joy that we desire. Simple kindness and genuine caring can rekindle that warmth. To learn principles of kindness we need only look to the gospel and the teachings of our Savior Jesus Christ, which are clear on how to treat one another.

One winter when my husband and I spoke at a University of Utah Institute fireside, I felt impressed to slip in a story about kind words and the ability they have to shape lives. I told of Bryce, who complimented his wife on all she did and how his loving remarks brought confidence and dignity to a woman who had previously thought herself of little value. It was only a very short reference in my talk, but the young man who gave the closing prayer repeatedly referred to speaking kind words. He prayed that we would all be kinder in our speech and more considerate with our words. After his prayer he had tears in his eyes as he shook hands with Elder Oaks and me. I did not know if he felt he was the victim of harsh language or if he desired to stop using it himself. I did feel the depth of his feeling.

A Call to Worship

It is important to attend church to worship Christ. Without this we may miss a multiplicity of blessings and lose our sensitivity to the power and direction of the Holy Ghost in our lives. Unfortunately, we can take the ways of the world to church with us. One single sister confided in me that to her, singles wards seemed more like social units than places of worship. She felt that many times members were more worldly than Christlike and more concerned about sociality than they were about the Savior.

A friend told me about a conversation she struck up with a young woman seated next to her on an airplane going to New York. When my friend spoke of the Church, the young woman replied, "Oh, I learned about your Church from the missionaries in New York, and I even joined it, but when I went to church and saw people concentrating on dating and jockeying for social position, I stopped going. I didn't fit in. I went to worship and learn more about all the marvelous things that the missionaries had taught me."

She had been looking to find spiritual refuge with other believers and instead felt like part of a meat market, where men were looking to date the most attractive women. Because this sister did not experience the fellowship she needed and expected, she took offense and stopped going to church.

One bishop of a singles ward expressed other concerns to his congregation. "Many of the members of my ward are so valiant and do such a tremendous job in their callings, but when it comes to many of the activities, these same young people come only if they have nothing else better to do. They are surrounded by a culture that concentrates on personal needs and not the needs of the community. I want them to realize that church is much more than a social organization and should not be confused with a shopping spree, where we come to pick and choose what fits our needs. We are here to learn the gospel of Jesus Christ."

Wards reflect the level of spirituality of the ward members. Members may be vulnerable to insensitive remarks or careless actions. Anyone with hurt feelings can become discouraged and critical. We need to remember that each of us will experience good days and bad days. The only true constant in any of our lives is our Savior. We go to our places of worship to feel His Spirit and to renew our covenants.

Unspotted from the World

In his November 2007 Church Educational System fireside to young adults, Elder Oaks spoke about keeping the Sabbath day holy. The more I reflect on his talk, the more benefit I see in it for all of us. When we keep the Sabbath day holy, we are promised blessings that can prove transforming to our lives. "And that thou mayest more fully keep thyself unspotted from the world, thou shalt go to the house of prayer and offer up thy sacraments upon my holy day" (D&C 59:9).

We can be cleansed and protected and made unspotted from the evil influences of the world. We can also be more blessed with a disposition to care for and love one another as brothers and sisters.

The very core of our church experience is meant to center on the Atonement of our Savior and on our partaking of the sacrament. This is a sacred life-changing privilege because we covenant to always remember the Savior, to take His name upon us, and to keep His commandments so that His Spirit will always be with us. The routine of partaking of the sacrament should never indicate to us that it is a commonplace or mundane act. We covenant with Heavenly Father weekly because our covenants serve as our defense and protection against the world. Our fragile human natures require such routine.

Thomas B. Griffith, president of a Brigham Young University stake, recognized the need of his flock to have a greater understanding of the Atonement of Jesus Christ. He explained: "Like all stake presidents, I worried about the members of the stake. I worried about the things one might expect a priesthood leader of single adults to worry about, but I also worried about whether the members of the stake had a 'testimony of the Atonement of Christ and of His role as Savior and Redeemer.' I had the sense that most of them loved Christ—no small thing—but I worried that not enough of them knew Him as their Savior (one who had saved them) or their Redeemer (one who had bought them)."[4]

President Griffith asked that every lesson, activity, talk, enrichment night, and family home evening make reference to the Atonement and connect with it. "We made it clear that we expected the teachers to teach the approved curriculum. . . . We had two suggestions.

"First, we urged teachers to find examples of principles being taught from the life of Christ. . . .

"Second, we encouraged teachers to see how the principle taught was either part of Heavenly Father's effort to draw us to Him through Christ . . . or a principle that could draw us closer to our fellow humans through Christ."[5]

An amazing thing happened. The Atonement was on the mind of each member of his stake. They reflected on it, thought about it, and appreciated it, and they came to revere it. The level of spirituality in their stake rose dramatically. Concentrating on this one principle fortified every member. They began to be "of one heart and one mind" (Moses 7:18).

President Griffith described the effect a similar emphasis had on a Book of Mormon people who really came to know their Savior: "They were now prepared to be organized anew into a church community, to hear and put into practice the teachings of the Sermon on the Mount, to learn how to serve those who were powerless: the sick, the disabled, the children. This group transformed their society from one that had been divided by race and class and opportunity into a society in which 'they had all things common among them; . . . there were not rich and poor, bond and free, but they were all made free, and partakers of the heavenly gift . . . because of the love of God which did dwell in the hearts of the people' (4 Nephi 1:3, 15)."[6]

Singles wards were created for young people, often in their years of schooling, to come together to learn of their Savior. They come also to make friends and find companions. These wards can be places of great fellowship and learning. The Church is also organized to help single members at age thirty-one to transition back into family communities and to associate with myriad age groups and backgrounds. This transition can prove traumatic for some.

Transition from a Singles Ward

As members in a singles ward, we may have gone for months or even years without interacting with children or youth or the aged.

Our comfort zones and perspectives can become narrow and limited to the world of adults. Our Heavenly Father wants more for us. After we reach a particular age, we have been counseled to return to home wards with families, children of varying ages, and members with a variety of needs.

This transition is not always easy. Singles often become more comfortable in the company of other singles. They know that certain questions and conversations are off limits. Their fellow ward members are facing many of the same challenges. These ward members also have time to spend developing friendships and talents. For some, a move to a family ward can seem like separation from a surrogate family and close friends.

One single young man, faced with his return to a family ward, confided to his family, "I am now thirty-one, and I am going to ward hop. I cannot bear going back to our home ward and have everyone question me about the fact that I am not married." The danger of continual ward hopping to avoid pressure from ward members is that with no records in a ward, this young man cannot be called to a position of service. By avoiding discomfort and occasional awkward questions, he denies himself the opportunity and blessings to serve and connect with the members of his home ward.

A person who chooses to ward hop becomes very vulnerable. Consistently attending wards without a membership record is a dangerous practice. We place ourselves in a position where we have no bishop to watch over us, no line of authority to report to, and no one with a constant knowledge of our spiritual and temporal dealings. Worst of all—we distance ourselves from the Spirit.

One bishop lamented that those who ward hop often attend only sacrament meeting, skipping Sunday School and Relief Society or priesthood meeting. They miss the opportunities for camaraderie, friendship, and bonding opportunities found in these meetings. They make no meaningful connections. He said, "They come to take a quick survey, look for the chicks or eligible men, and then disappear. I worry that their testimonies will weaken and that they are headed for inactivity."

This what's-in-it-for-me approach to church attendance is the antithesis of true worship and devotion to the Savior. Instead of blessing others and building the kingdom, those who ward hop emphasize narrow self-interests. Instead of serving and loving, they focus on themselves. We cannot reach out to others if we are concerned only about meeting our own immediate needs.

A friend who has great empathy for those who ward hop explained, "Many people ward hop to increase their chances of meeting a mate." She confided, "My life has become a balancing act. I feel if I'm not out looking around, I'm not doing everything I should be, and then when I am so overly preoccupied with looking around, I am not living my life with any real purpose. I have to constantly check and regroup my priorities, and it is exhausting." Sadly, during this transition, many just disappear off the radar screen.

One sister told me, "I'm taking a break from church." Knowing her family and being a friend of her mother, I asked, "What does your mother say about that?"

The young sister told me, "My mother said if I stop going to church, it will break her heart."

I continued, "Why do you think she said that?"

The young sister replied, "Because she knows the Church is true."

Because she knows the Church is true—that said it all.

We need to concentrate on the truthfulness of the doctrine. Church attendance will seem exhausting and meaningless for anyone whose social concerns triumph over love of the sacrament. Focus on the things of God, trust in Him, and renew your sacred covenants weekly.

As we serve in the Church we come to know it is true. The

mission of The Church of Jesus Christ of Latter-day Saints is better fulfilled when all of its members are working to build the kingdom of God. Single people need the Church and the Church needs the testimonies and talents of its single members.

"It is not enough to know that God lives, that Jesus Christ is our Savior, and that the gospel is true. We must take the high road by acting upon that knowledge. It is not enough to know that [the president of the Church] is God's prophet. We must put his teachings to work in our lives. It is not enough to have a calling. We must fulfill our responsibilities." The truths of which we testify "are to motivate and guide our actions."[7]

The Home Ward

Single members faced with the decision to return to their home wards should trust in the wisdom of their leaders and depend on the guidance of the Spirit to help with their transition. As with any change or new environment, there may be a period of adjustment. It takes time and effort to develop new relationships and discover ways to make meaningful contributions. The transition will likely not be painless. Yet, if we are obedient our lives will ultimately be blessed.

Recently my husband and I spoke with a group of young singles who transitioned into their home wards with a large group of other young singles. They found adequate fellowship with others of their own age; more important, they felt the bishop's love. They felt watched over, and they connected with their wards. They received callings, made new friends with members of varying ages and interests, and strengthened their testimonies. They felt needed and validated. One said, "When I decided to move forward and embrace the options ahead of me, I felt such a sweet peace and happiness. It was only when I clung to the past and stood still that I felt anxious and out of step."

I know what a tremendous difference it made to me as a single member of the Church to have a calling, to feel needed, and to contribute to the welfare of those around me. I also remember how removed I felt when I did not have a calling. Callings place us in a position to meet others and to help others. Accepting and fulfilling Church commitments and serving each other bind us together and make us stronger. It is so much easier to move forward in the Lord's plan for us when we are connected with others who have the same desires and when we feel that we are a vital part of the Lord's kingdom. President Hinckley said every new member should have "a friend, a responsibility, and nurturing with 'the good word of God' (Moro. 6:4)."[8] His words are true.

In counseling Church leaders, President James E. Faust told them that the best of all possible experiences for single members as they enter a home ward is to be given a calling. He urged them to "ponder the needs of single members regularly in leadership meetings and include them in meaningful callings, assignments, and activities."[9] In many wards and stakes, single sisters and brothers are given significant responsibilities because their testimonies and talents are widely visible to priesthood leaders.

As a single sister, I was called as a Primary president. Others of my single friends served as Young Women and Relief Society presidents and counselors. Still others were called as teachers in Gospel Doctrine and Gospel Essentials classes, early-morning seminary, and institute. Each of these individuals became an integral member of the ward and found Sunday a day of great strengthening, service, and sociability.

As one close friend commented: "Nursery children do not look to see if you have a ring on your finger as you wipe away their tears. It doesn't take a wedding license to feed hungry Scouts or missionaries or shut-ins. Nowhere on the tithing slip do you indicate marital status as you contribute to the Church's humanitarian service or the Perpetual Education Fund. And they don't have two doors at the temple—one for couples and one for singles. We are a Church that needs faithful workers. I've been blessed because I have had priesthood leaders who knew this."

I have learned from happy and sad experience that if we wish for our ward experience to be a happy and fulfilling one, we have to help make it so. In most cases, we must volunteer and extend ourselves to be welcomed into a ward. That means signing up for service projects, babysitting, and providing dinners. It means making a deliberate and consistent effort to be part of the ward community. I have one friend who says the best way to make friends is to work in the kitchen. She signs up for every table-setting, cleanup, and serving assignment she can find. The payoff for such effort is magnificent. Many of the best Church leaders and teachers I have known were examples of this kind of involvement.

A Covenant People

We learn to become a covenant people through our attitudes. Andrea, a young single woman, shared her account of an interview with her bishop in her singles ward. He asked how she was doing, and he was surprised when she answered, "Bishop, I just love this ward. It is so much fun. I love coming to the activities, I love the Relief Society lessons, and I love the women I visit teach." The bishop replied, "Andrea, you love this ward because you participate and contribute so much to it." He then went on to relate a story he shares with many of the single members during his interviews.

A family was moving to a new town. They came to a crossroads with a sign that directed them to the town. At the crossroads sat an old man. They asked him about the town. The old man replied, "Did you like the town you came from?" They answered, "We loved it, we enjoyed our neighbors, and we had many friends. It was so difficult to leave and come here." The old man then declared, "Take this road. You will find this town as wonderful and welcoming as the one you just left. The people are friendly and helpful. You will like it here."

Later that day another family moving to the same town came to the same crossroads and asked the same old man which road to take. He asked the same question: "Did you like the town you came from?" The family answered, "No. We had few friends, and the people were cold and distant and uncaring. It was miserable." The old man then gave the same reply: "Take this road. You will find this town as unfriendly and miserable as the town you left."

As single members of the Church and especially as older singles, we must remember that our attitudes are all-important. We, in large measure, determine how happy and fulfilled we will be. The Church is family-centered. We know where we are going eternally and what our ultimate purpose will be. What if marriage and having children are not in our realm of experience right now? Do we give up, complain, and become bitter and discouraged? Do we avoid church, become critical of our leaders, or shy away from group activities? Or do we reach out to the Savior?

We are a covenant people. The highest and holiest covenant is marriage. As an unmarried single who had not made this covenant, I sometimes felt less mature or adult. I also had divorced friends who were anxious because of broken covenants, often through no fault of their own, and who sometimes became self-critical and cynical. Consistent temple attendance became very healing to me. The temple became a haven for me, and its promises and teachings provided great security when I felt alone. My frequent temple visits also provided me with the strength and guidance to serve in my callings to the best of my abilities. I felt I was a contributor in my ward and not just someone waiting for my life to begin.

Many families have members who became inactive as they grew older and felt that the Church had no place for them. During our mission in the Philippines, a senior sister missionary wept as she spoke of her unmarried nieces in their mid-forties who had stopped going to church because they felt they no longer fit in with their ward members. She asked for advice about what to say to them. Faced with an unexpected challenge—death or divorce or sickness—and confronted with the "mists of darkness" described in 1 Nephi, any of us may question where we fit in the plan that Heavenly Father has laid out for us. We fit in because we love our Savior Jesus Christ. He desires to bless us, and our partaking of the sacrament helps ensure that He can.

Everyone has challenges. I shared with the sister missionary how difficult it had been for me as a single to sit alone in church every Sunday. (Even now that I am married, I still sit alone every Sunday!) I knew how her nieces felt. Every Sunday I would peer into the chapel and decide whom to sit by or to sit alone. I remember slipping late into meetings and sitting alone in the back because I didn't want to draw attention to myself.

Sister Gerratt, the wife of one of my husband's counselors in the Philippines, heard me share such an experience. The weeping sister missionary kept asking us how she could help these women in her family come back to church. The simple solution for these women did not escape Sister Gerratt, an Idaho farm girl who has great faith and lots of good common sense. She said, "When the time comes to go to church—you just go." She then shared something about her own life. Despite her shyness as a young woman, she continued to attend church. Too insecure to raise her hand to contribute to a lesson in Relief Society, she just persisted, and through the years she gained confidence and strength. She said, "To this very day it is still hard for me to enter a congregation and sit alone while my husband is on the stand. No one knows me. I just go in and do it and begin to feel the Spirit of the Lord." That day Sister Gerratt became one of my heroes.

We need to depend on our Heavenly Father to help us maintain our perspective and preserve our faith. We need to realize that our attendance at church and our devotion to our calling is a matter of eternal consequence. Elder Jeffrey R. Holland spoke to mission presidents about the price we must pay to return to Heavenly Father. His advice applies to anyone struggling to know and serve God. He said:

"Presidents, you will have occasion to ask, and your missionaries will have many occasions to ask, why is this so hard? Why doesn't it go better? Why can't our success be more rapid? Why aren't there more people joining the Church? It is the truth. We believe in angels. We trust in miracles. Why don't people just flock to the font? . . . Why isn't it easier, President?"

Elder Holland continued: "I have thought about this a great deal. I offer this as my personal feeling. It's not Church doctrine. . . . I am convinced that missionary work is not easy because *salvation is not a cheap experience.* Salvation was *never* easy. We are the Church of Jesus Christ, this is the truth, and He is our Great Eternal Head. Why would we believe . . . that it would be easy for us when it was never, ever easy for Him? In turn, how could we possibly bear any moving, lasting testimony of the Atonement if we have never known or felt anything of such an experience? As missionaries we are proud to say we are disciples of Christ—and we are. But mark my word. That means you must be prepared to walk something of the path He walked, to feel something of the pain He felt, to at least occasionally sometime during your mission shed one of the tears of sorrow that He shed."[10]

"Salvation is not a cheap experience." We should remember that. Never let any trial stand between you and your allegiance to your Heavenly Father. Never let any unintended slight or insult separate you from partaking of the sacrament and lead you to spiritual weakness and possibly toward spiritual death. Hold fast and remember what you know to be true. A friend said it better: "If I don't endure now, I'll have an eternity to think about why I didn't."

During challenging times we need to call on our Heavenly Father for help. We need to remember our many blessings and to realize that others seldom mean to offend us when they question us about our single condition. There is a reason many valiant and lovely women are single. It often escapes even the brightest married people that there is a shortage of good single men. Every faithful and wise woman wants a husband she can respect and trust, a man who desires to serve the Lord and keep his covenants, who honors his priesthood, and who is able to support a wife and family. Because such men are in short supply, no wonder there are large numbers of worthy single women. Conversely, many young men complain too that the women they wish to date and marry are preoccupied with education, career, and personal development and are not interested in relationships.

One key benefit of this gospel for all members of The Church of Jesus Christ of Latter-day Saints is the enormous blessing of the Spirit and the direction and peace it supplies in our lives. The more we cling to the gospel, obey the commandments, and attend church, the more the Lord can bless us. In 1998, before I was married, I wrote in my journal: "Today was not an easy day for me. I felt so worn and dejected. Yet in sacrament meeting I felt the comfort of the Spirit. I know that I won't be facing the problems at work all by myself. I am not alone, and Heavenly Father is aware of me."

There Will Be Challenges and Blessings

We need to constantly monitor the state of our hearts. We carve out a comfort zone for ourselves, develop habits, and continue in those habits. For me, Sunday was often the most difficult day of the week because I thought about being alone when I saw families at church. I say this also because so often I found myself or others I love going home to a lonely house and often being too shy to accept invitations when they were offered. One friend told me, "Sunday is the loneliest day of the week for single members of the Church because they leave a loving environment and return home to a lonely house and a meal for one."

Contrast that reaction with a comment from another friend: "I can't think of an Easter, Thanksgiving, or other holiday when I didn't receive invitations to dinners from members of my ward and stake. Every Monday night I have dinner and family home evening at the home of long-time ward members. Because I work, I always get the 'salad assignment.' These wonderful friends include me and other singles in summer barbecues, holiday dinners, and museum outings. We have served together in ward and stake auxiliary presidencies. Serving together in the Church has led to strong friendships."

Look for someone who might need you and whom you can serve. Organize activities that pull people together. One dear friend invites her married siblings over for a special dinner she prepares every week. Her purposes are multiple—to keep her family close, to allow her to serve and be with others, and to hone the domestic cooking skills she loves. She is making her single house a home. Happiness is not determined by circumstance; it is determined by attitude.

Rather than being inspired by talks and lessons at Church, some singles find themselves more discouraged and desolate. How could this happen? Recently in my home ward a young couple was given the speaking topic "Being instruments in the hands of the Lord." The young mother related how overwhelmed and consumed she was with raising and caring for her three young children. She had come to the realization that teaching them about their Father in Heaven was her service to Him. I watched the single, never-married, professionally successful sister sitting next to me wilt as she listened because she felt she would never have the opportunity of motherhood. She longed for those blessings. If the story were to end here, it would, indeed, be a sad one.

Three weeks later I watched the same single sister settle into the seat next to mine as sacrament meeting started. She looked happy and radiant with a big smile on her face. Her glow was so apparent that I asked where she had been. She answered, "Oh, I've been called to work with the seven-year-olds. I love it; they are an experience and a half. It has been a delight. I love teaching them." When we seek to serve, we truly become part of a ward family. This single sister learned that sacrifice precedes the law of love, and she too had been given the opportunity of teaching children about their Heavenly Father.

We will all be challenged, and during those challenges we need to turn to Christ and remain active and involved in our wards. We need to make the decision to stay happy and positive. One young sister with several small children concluded that divorce was the only solution open to her when her husband could not give up his addiction to pornography. She told me, "I knew that I would be divorced in a church that values family, eternal marriage, and marital harmony. I knew that I believed in those things and that I would still believe in them after I became divorced. I determined, for my children and myself, that I would not become bitter or discouraged or angry because those blessings were not currently a part of my life. I treasure those values, I honor them, and someday I want every blessing for my children and myself. I determined to just keep going to church, to listen to every lesson, and not to become bitter and disenfranchised. I have been divorced for three years. At last the Lord has lifted the pain of my divorce from me. Through all this time I have never resented any talk or activity I have attended because I know that this is the true church of Jesus Christ on the earth, and I have been and will continue to be blessed if I remain faithful."

We have to always consider the blessings we have and the unique contributions we make. Singles should never forget what a powerful force for good they can be. Church attendance can come to seem hollow if we fail to maintain the big picture that we are all on the way to returning to our Father in Heaven. The Church is the best vehicle to get us there.

Being part of a ward family, especially with members of varying interests and ages, can be fulfilling. Our congregations provide us the opportunity to interact with others of different economic backgrounds, ages, needs, and interests and to become brothers and sisters in the gospel. Our *lifescapes* become enlarged.

Emily, a dear single friend, loves the diversity of her family ward and the chance to connect with the youth and children. Her singleness is a wonderful vehicle because she has the time and energy and desire to help and nourish others.

Kathryn could be recognized as Sunbeam teacher of the year. She went from stake Young Women president to teaching the three-year-old Sunbeams. She did not consider this a less important calling. She told me, "In this church we don't go up and down; we just move around to where we are needed." Instead of looking upon her calling as an assignment that she could prepare while going out the door on Sunday morning, she regards her calling as holy and important. I know because when I visit her we spend time preparing for her class. To Kathryn, no one is as important as those three-year-olds and their families. She takes time in class each week to listen to each child answer the question: "What made you happy this week?" She makes photo albums of her class for all the parents. She loves her class because she serves them.

Another dear single friend, Allyn, prayed about the members of her ward. She was single, and yet she was the one helping married couples—cleaning up basements after floods, delivering dinners, and visiting the sick. She looked at the basic needs of friends around her and listened to the Spirit as her guide. She blessed the lives of everyone around her.

Suzan, a single sister in my home ward, ministers emotionally to everyone around her. People gather near her just to hear her laugh and feel her appreciation of them. She is a healer of the brokenhearted and the lonely. Nothing limits her. Married and single sisters gravitate to her side for help and counsel.

The inspired programs of the Church were created to include and benefit everyone. Many of the programs are intended for families, and these families include single parents. Single parents can receive great support from those who serve and teach their children. These same programs also benefit the single members who serve as the Primary teachers, the Young Women advisers and teachers, scoutmasters, and early-morning seminary teachers. The more all of us involve ourselves in the organizations of the Church, the more we gain a testimony of their truthfulness and, more important, the more cohesive bond we build with the members of our ward.

Single members often have a richness of life and work experience that makes them invaluable to a ward. Often they have the flexibility and time to serve. I will never forget a Primary program where the assigned pianist decided the morning of the program to stay home with a sick child. A talented and confident single sister, Louise, stepped in to save the day. She saved the program and endeared herself to all of us for years to come because the program still went on.

Singles can become Saviors on Mount Zion when they overcome their trials and bless the lives of others. One of the most powerful testimonies of the Atonement I have witnessed was given by a young divorced mother with two children as she taught her Laurel class. She testified to the young women how the Lord had lifted her burdens and taken her pain following her divorce. She told them that the Lord loves His people and how He is always ready to help us. She was living evidence of her lesson. I studied the faces of the young women in her class and saw how her wisdom penetrated their hearts and how her happy countenance evidenced the truth she was teaching them. I thought how fortunate they were to have such a valiant example of a noble sister who increased in faith during her suffering and was teaching her Laurels that they could do the same.

Our service and care for others live beyond us. Thirty-year-old men in our ward still speak of "June Bug"—my husband's first wife, who was their Primary teacher—because she taught them, loved them, had parties for them, and watched over them. We all have the capability to magnify our callings, and the major result is that our own hearts expand in the process and our testimonies become strengthened. We learn we are not alone.

Of all the programs that blessed my life as a single sister, home teaching and visiting teaching head the list. Having someone care and knowing that I mattered to even one person made life brighter. One-on-one attention provides us with a connection to our ward family. Organizations may benefit us, but individual people love us. In every way, my home teachers and visiting teachers have blessed my life: emotionally, as friends; spiritually, by giving me priesthood blessings when I faced stressful situations or illness; and physically, by moving me out of an apartment and then by driving my furniture across the country to a new home. There are no other programs in the Church so effective for reaching the one. Loving and committed home and visiting teachers have the capacity to make an enormous impact for good in the lives of others.

President Gordon B. Hinckley called us a happy people. "Why are we such a happy people? It is because of our faith, the quiet assurance that abides in our hearts that our Father in Heaven, overseeing all, will look after His sons and daughters who walk before Him with love and appreciation and obedience. We will ever be a happy people if we will so conduct our lives."[11]

Church Leaders Make a
Great Difference

A Church leader can make a tremendous difference by caring, being attentive, and making a special effort to stay close to single people. My favorite wards have been the inclusive ones, where bishops encouraged activities that would include the entire ward. My home ward of twenty years had consistent, regular get-togethers that I could depend on attending. Our bishopric also was deliberate in their fellowship of all members. They made sure every widow and other single sister had a ride to every activity. It meant so much to me to be constantly remembered.

Singles, because they have no spouse, often depend on their ecclesiastical leaders for direction and advice. Many times I was helped by caring bishops who offered wonderful and wise counsel. But I am also aware that singles need to be careful not to overtax and burden bishops with their needs and concerns by demanding too much of their time.

I love the following account because it reveals the great devotion of a bishop for his flock. Because he was spiritually in tune, he could see the strength, radiance, and potential in an inactive single woman who wanted nothing to do with the Church.

"When I first visited with Sister White [not her actual name] I found her to be a woman with a radiant spirit and a bright and engaging intellect, but she had become quite discouraged in the course of her Church involvement and had largely withdrawn. A long-time member, she served a valiant mission in the Philippines and was quite active for a time thereafter. Although she had been given many priesthood blessings in which she was promised she would enjoy a happy marriage, these blessings were not realized, and she became discouraged and progressively more isolated. She told me it was no use trying to activate her. She knew the gospel was true, but she felt she didn't fit into the Church, and she didn't think that was going to change. She basically asked me to leave her alone.

"Her spirit was so strong and her goodness so radiant that I felt emboldened to proceed. I felt inspired on the spot to call her as the Laurel class adviser. I told her we needed her very much and said that I had come to give her a calling. Surprised, she abruptly refused. She was sure the young women would not take to her and felt that she would probably not like them. She said this was the last calling she could imagine accepting. I told her the call had come from the Lord, that He loved her and wanted her service, and that whether she chose to accept or not was a matter between her and Him. I asked her to ponder and pray about it.

"Her nobility of soul won out, and before long she accepted the calling. She was a singular blessing to our young women and to the ward as a whole. Yet I believe the person most blessed by Sister White's newfound activity was me. As I came to know her, I marveled at her profound and mature soul. We became friends, and she grew comfortable speaking to me in direct and open ways.

"Once, while discussing another matter with me, she stopped and said, 'Bishop, I want to teach you something. I know you give a lot of counsel to people about marriage. I told you that I had been repeatedly promised a happy marriage. That has not happened, but I have had opportunities to marry that I have turned down. At first that caused me a good deal of self-doubt and even fear that I might have forfeited my promised blessings by refusing these marriage proposals. But they were not really fitting proposals, and they would not have led to good marriages. From these experiences and from my exposure to others' marriages, I have learned an important truth. Since you are a bishop and you are in a position to have influence and to give counsel in these matters, I want you to understand this: It is better to be single than to be badly married!'"

The bishop said, "I pondered Sister White's counsel at the time, and I have had many occasions since to ponder it and to share it. She was absolutely right. No woman should feel any obligation to marry a man who does not offer her the prospect and probability of a loving, eternally happy home. I thank Sister White for her goodness, her wisdom, and her willingness to teach her bishop."[12]

Continued Effort, Commitment, and Blessings

Our goal is to help one another, build one another, and assist one another. Now is the time, more than ever before, for us to reach out and try to understand one another. And yet we must also accept an occasional bump or bruise. Life is going to give us a few slings and arrows. Some of these will be minor—a bad haircut, lost luggage at the airport, a flat tire—and others more significant—loss of a job, illness, or low self-esteem. Some of these bumps and bruises may involve ward members. A thoughtless comment, a thorny question, or an awkward situation could occur at a grocery store, family reunion, or work convention. Yet when they occur at church, they may be particularly difficult. We often expect our wards to be safe harbors from life's storms, but we need to be prepared for unintentional slights or oversights. One friend calls it "putting on my rhino skin."

Yet, in attempts at understanding one another, we must also remain true to our core doctrines. When a divorced and frustrated sister tearfully left a lesson on achieving a celestial marriage and ran to the bishop for advice and comfort, he counseled her, "Our Savior, Jesus Christ, taught us how to achieve the highest state of happiness. We can't teach something less. It is doctrine. It is true. Our challenge is to keep aiming for that highest state regardless of where we are." That is the challenge for all of us. It is the only road to happiness.

Another single friend has made the decision not to walk out or become tearful over lessons that are uncomfortable. She says, "I don't want the abridged gospel or 'singles edition' that edits out potentially offensive material. I signed up for the full program." She gave an example. "In this Church we celebrate Mother's Day. It is a day that can pose a challenge to singles, and it is a day of decision. (See chapter 4, "Every Single Holiday.") As a single person you basically have two choices: stay home and mope, or show up with a smile and be grateful for the wonderful mothers that have influenced you. You can recognize that it is also a day to celebrate Eve, Rebekah, Rachel, Sarah, and Mary. You can choose to think of your own mother and grandmothers. You can view it as a day to be happy for those women in your ward who have been blessed with children.

"I have friends who simply get depressed and don't leave their homes. And I have other friends who focus on the contributions of all mothers. All of us have the same doctrines. We can decide that specific lessons or topics are offensive or difficult, but that doesn't make the subject less truthful. You're going to be missing a lot of sacrament meeting talks and conference addresses if you decide you don't want to hear about eternal marriage and children. If this is painful, you have sizable wounds to lick. I think it's a matter of deciding to be happy and not miserable."

We belong to the Church of Jesus Christ. Our goal is to become Christlike, and that requires years of continued effort and commitment. I admire every single member who, even when feeling out of the mainstream, stays active in this Church, where the family is revered and marriage is acknowledged as an ultimate celestial blessing. I believe this doctrine need not offend single members of our Church. To the contrary, they can embrace it and desire it with all their hearts. It is difficult to be different, to long for the blessings of eternal happiness, and to perceive that you have been denied them, if only for the time being, while so many around you seem to be enjoying them. The great blessing is that in our wards we are surrounded by others who are striving to draw closer to our Heavenly Father.

CHAPTER 11

SINGLE CONNECTIONS

Because Christ is prepared to stand by each of us always,
we can be sure that He expects each of us to stand by one another.

In our church the terms *sister* and *brother* are meant to truly sig-
nify that we are one church family. All of us—different in background, culture, marital status, and age—are meant to come together
as one body in Christ. We are all children of a loving Heavenly
Father, yet at various times in our lives we may struggle to fit in and
feel we truly belong. That may happen following a move and having
to make new friends. It may happen when we transition from one
program to another—for example, from Young Women to Relief
Society or from a singles ward to a family ward. It may happen when
we have a difficulty with someone in a calling or a misunderstand-
ing with those we are called to work with. It may happen when we
find ourselves single in a ward full of married couples with families.
There may be times when you are the one asking or being asked, "Is
there room in this Church for me?"

We are meant to cherish and love one another. The powerful
faith of two pioneer sisters, Emily and Julia Hill, connected their
spiritual knowledge to their earthly relationships. The experience of
Emily and Julia, whose loyalty and devotion carried them through

trials that left them more sanctified, connected, and united has had a profound effect on me. A descendant of Julia, Sister Debbie J. Christensen, shared more of their story with me.

In 1856, Emily and Julia Hill had finally earned enough money to pay for their passage to America. They were early converts to the Church and longed to come to Zion, having been disowned by their parents. Upon their arrival in America, they were assigned to the Willie handcart company, and during their journey to Zion they suffered torturous weather and near starvation.[1]

Debbie related a dream she had of their experience. "I saw these women lying in the snow at Rocky Ridge. I somehow felt what they were feeling. Emily—weak, freezing cold and starving—lay on the snow and knew that if she did not get up she would die. More important, the Spirit whispered to Emily that her sister, Julia, would also die. For Emily, life without Julia would be only half a life. She felt responsible in a very eternal way for the welfare of her sister. I could feel Emily lift herself and then Julia from the snow with an almost Herculean effort. I could hear Julia making desperate little sounds; she was so weak that she could not speak or cry out. I knew that Emily would die to preserve the life of her sister; it was all or nothing."

Debbie spoke of the spiritual might and healing potency of the Atonement: "Because of their sincere belief in Jesus Christ, they could act with strength and love. Even those in the direst circumstances, those in the Willie handcart company, were given strength to minister to one another. Think how different their experience was from those in the Donner Party, who faced very similar trials and began to degenerate emotionally."[2]

The Spirit in the Willie camp taught them there was a better way to care for one another. We can become sanctified in our trials rather than bitter, judgmental, and uncaring. Even in the hardest of circumstances we can reach out in a tender way to those who are suffering around us. We can all heal through the Savior's Atonement.

Needed: Small and Consistent Acts of Love

We have an obligation to lift and love one another. Small and consistent acts of love can make a very great difference in the lives of others. My husband and I travel often, which causes us to attend church away from home frequently. One person whose outreach has transformed my life and ensured my connection to our ward is my eighty-year-old visiting teacher and her companion, who phone early in the month and give me multiple options for a visit. The older sister is precise about her appointments because of the effort she has to exert to reach me. When the snow is piled high against the porch and the cold winds are raging, I often see these two sisters struggle to make it to my porch. When they enter my home I feel the genuine love they extend to me, and they always present the monthly message in a most personal way. These sisters' loving care is my link to my ward. They are my connection to the fellowship and activities I often miss. I love them for it.

We attend church in part because we are seeking love, acceptance, and spiritual support. Too many cease to come because they have yet to feel this love. Our purpose as sisters is abundantly clear: as followers of Jesus Christ we have the capacity and the obligation to reach out in loving ways to one another. On a much more sacred level we are to be of one heart and one mind.

Our capacity to minister to and cherish one another is often diminished by the harsh world we live in. Our society is one of changing values and worldly distractions. Members who adhere to Church standards and principles may find themselves under scrutiny or as targets of discrimination. Single members, especially, with their opportunity to interact among diverse groups of people, may find their ethics and values questioned. It is an ideal time to be a missionary and also an ideal time to be perceived by others outside our faith as a peculiar people.

Interestingly, in a world of shifting values or skewed standards, it may appear much easier to navigate as a single Latter-day Saint. In many communities there is little pressure to marry because many are not marrying. Marriage is viewed by some as unnecessary, and children out of wedlock are common. For many in our world, marriage and children are viewed as a hindrance to personal freedom. Divorce is common. The single life may be viewed as unencumbered and free of responsibility.

Married persons with this point of view may, in fact, envy those who are unmarried. Single members of the Church may find themselves living in the gap between the world's view of single life and the Church's emphasis on marriage and families. They may find greater acceptance among friends and colleagues outside the Church. While searching for the love and support of ward members, they may not feel entirely a part of the gospel community.

Disconnections

Ironically, some singles may find difficulty forging relationships within the Church because such high and ideal expectations of marriage and family are stressed. These are God-given ideals, and we aspire to them. But if we have not achieved the ideal marriage and family, we can become very critical of ourselves and misunderstood by others. Some say because of their singleness they have been classified as a breed apart.

In England a recently widowed sister with three children was approached by a counselor in the bishopric. He said to her, "You won't be attending any of the married activities anymore; you will be involved with the older singles. Here is the phone number of the person you should call." She was devastated. She still considered herself married. She felt most comfortable with the other married couples in her ward, but after his comment, she felt she no longer belonged. Feelings change, and a person once accepted as part of a couple is sometimes less welcome as a single person.

There is a happy ending to this English widow's story. She was obedient and followed the advice given to her by her priesthood leader, attended her singles' group, and, after some years, met and married a wonderful man. Together they have gone on multiple missions and now serve as mission leaders in Asia. She told me, "Only by being in that singles group did I meet my husband."

There are other surprises for the newly widowed. A young sister reported that while her husband was homebound in the final stages of cancer, her married neighbors, both male and female, came to deliver food or to check on her family. After her husband died, the wives continued coming but almost never did their husbands come with them. This new single sister found herself in a unique niche and felt coolness and distance from her married friends.

Many of my single friends—charming, beautiful, intelligent, accomplished, and fun—have a deep need to feel part of a whole; yet they frequently say they do not quite fit in. A friend of mine who converted from Judaism compared herself to a spoon in her parents' kosher household. She said, "In our house we had multiple drawers in the kitchen. One drawer was for kosher and another for everyday. If a spoon had dropped on the floor or had been used for meat instead of milk, we considered it contaminated. It could not be used any longer, so it was stuffed in the middle drawer and was never seen again." Being single, my friend felt like one of those spoons—she had been placed in the middle drawer.

I know some divorcées who have also known the middle-drawer experience. Discouraged and overly self-critical, they say their divorced status made them undesirable. One friend, a perceptive and adept psychologist, taught Gospel Doctrine in her ward during her divorce. She felt this calling helped her maintain her sanity during that awful time in her life because it required that she study and try with all her might to stay close to the Spirit. She was sometimes aware of resentment from class members who had once been good friends. It took great personal strength to stand before them and teach each week.

One man in particular seemed cold and was critical of her when she taught her weekly lesson. While she still held that calling, this man was called to be the president of her stake. Because of the way he had treated her and because she was concerned about his opinion, she made an appointment to talk with him. What he said when they met surprised her. He had felt very uncomfortable with a divorcing sister in such a visible position teaching the entire ward. He was concerned enough that when he was called as stake president he had gone to the Lord about the matter. The Lord told him she was to remain in her calling.

This evidences several things to me. First, the Lord knows us—our hearts, actions, and worthiness and our needs, concerns, and strengths—no matter what our circumstances may suggest to others. Second, the Church is run by revelation. When our priesthood leaders ask to know the Lord's will for His people, He will tell them. Third, I think this suggests that the Lord would like us to love more, condemn less, and rely more upon His wisdom. We cannot know people's hearts as the Lord does, and to truly do His will in regard to them, we need to seek the gift of discernment and His guidance.

This same sister found that after she was divorced, a large number of the ward members she had been close to, even some she had worked with and known before she had married her husband, broke off contact with her but maintained ties with her husband. She mourned not only the failure of her marriage but also the loss of her friends. In her wisdom—in part the result of her professional training and experience—she understood it was not personal. She also understood that all of us are works in progress. Her friends needed to follow the teachings and example of Christ. The Savior provides a loving and active example of someone who ministered to, included, and valued others in their greatest times of need.

The great wonder of the gospel is that it can empower us with an inner resilience and determination to reach for higher ground. So many who have served most valiantly, reached out to others, and consecrated all they had are sisters who had encountered distress in their own lives. Transitions in our lives can be tedious, but they can also allow us to blossom into people of great strength. When I spoke to one young sister, whose smile and happy manner magnetized all around her, she said, "Sister Oaks, I am divorced and still looking." I asked her how her life was going. She replied, "The gospel just makes me happy. The more I dedicate myself to it and the more I interact with those around me and serve them, the more the Lord blesses my life."

The more we extend ourselves in the service of the Lord, the nearer we draw unto Him. We have a sure promise from the Lord that He will stand by us if we stand by Him. I had no husband to lean on, so I came to depend on the Lord as my best friend, and I know now that is what the Lord wanted for me—to love Him first before all else. He desires the same for each of us. I have also come to believe that since Christ is prepared to stand by each of us always, we can be sure that He expects each of us to stand by one another.

Developing a Community of Saints

We strive to be a community of Saints—working to "bear one another's burdens" (Mosiah 18:8). This requires that we extend to all the hand of fellowship and love. We teach that there should be no *isms* among us, no artificial barriers based on age, nationality, background, interests, and marital status. It has been my experience that spending time working, serving, and growing together results in misconceptions melting away. Stereotyping and misunderstandings are replaced with friendship, insight, and genuine love.

I asked older married women friends about their friendships with single women in their ward. Many of them said, "A lot of the single people in my ward seem so independent, so self-sufficient. They seem less personal with me. I look at them and see their manicured hands and no runs in their hose, and I feel a little dowdy. They seem so put together and so able. I'm at home in my sweats, chasing after teenagers and surrounded by mounds of dirty clothes and piles of grimy dishes. They could never identify with my life."

Another sister commented, "I'm not talking about everyone, but some of the more professional women seem so reserved and quiet, almost untouchable."

When I asked if they were close to any of the single sisters in their ward, most said they had close friends who are single. One added, "We've had wonderful times together, and some have become almost a part of our family." I questioned, "How did these friendships grow?" Without exception, all said the friendships grew not from attending Relief Society meetings on Sunday but from serving in a small group or auxiliary committee or from visiting teaching.

I can understand why some ward members perceive single sisters as somewhat distant and unapproachable. As a single woman, I had no control over whether I was married, so I put extra effort into controlling myself. I focused on how I looked and how I projected myself. With no children or husband demanding my time, I spent my energies on my occupational and academic achievements. I was not exactly a domestic diva, and I was a bit out of my element at some enrichment activities. My skills were creating PowerPoint presentations, and I emphasized that I had difficulty even boiling spaghetti. My point is not about technology versus pasta—it is about familiarity and the attributes in which we grow to feel competent.

We gravitate to and accentuate those things. We feel at home in our personal comfort zones.

As members of the Church we have to be careful not to judge one another and to suspend any previously held assumptions that might cripple our ability to accept one another on any level. Carlfred Broderick, who was a professor of sociology at the University of Southern California and a stake president, wrote of his inaccurate assessment of a sister in his ward whom he had known for years. In his judgment, she had made a series of very poor life choices. She had married a handsome and charming man who later converted to the Church and took her to the temple but never went back. He gambled and drank and chose other activities that were unhappy and unwholesome. Worse, her children, seeing his example, began to follow him. They adopted his attitude, values, and lifestyle.

When this sister asked for a blessing to sustain her in this awful situation, Carlfred Broderick's thoughts were on this order: "'Didn't you ask for this? You married a guy who really didn't have any depth to him and raised your kids too permissively. . . . ' I had all those judgments in my head. I laid my hands on her head, and the Lord told her of his love and his tender concern for her. He acknowledged he had given her (and that she had volunteered for) a far, far harder task than he would like. . . . She . . . had signed up for hard children, for children who had rebellious spirits but who were valuable; for a hard husband who had a rebellious spirit but who was valuable. The Lord alluded to events in her life that I hadn't known about, but which she confirmed afterwards: twice Heavenly Father had given her the choice between life and death. . . . Twice on death's bed she had sent the messenger away and gone back to her hard task. She stayed with it."[3]

President Broderick wrote: "I repented. I realized I was in the presence of one of the Lord's great noble spirits, who had chosen not a safe place behind the lines . . . , but somebody who chose to live out in the trenches where the Lord's work was being done, where there was risk, where you could be hurt, where you could lose, where you could be destroyed by your love."[4]

"The Errand of Angels Is Given to Women"

We are surrounded by many forces that divide us: inaccurate perceptions of each other, overscheduled busy lives, and a lack of meaningful opportunities to communicate. Without a spiritual connection to bind us, we may drift from Church activity and risk the loss of our salvation. As sisters in the gospel we are meant to minister to one another and watch over each other—and not just in a cursory or obligatory manner.

How important is it that we extend the hand of love and understanding to everyone around us? The principle of loving and accepting those around us has profound ramifications. Brigham Young taught, "It is folly in the extreme for persons to say that they love God, when they do not love their brethren; and it is of no use for them to say that they have confidence in God, when they have none in righteous men."[5]

President Gordon B. Hinckley told us: "Be loyal to one another, your friends and associates. Look for the good in those about you, and emphasize that good. Never go around gossiping about your associates or speaking unkind words concerning them."[6] It is even worse to ignore their presence.

President Hinckley continued: "What I am suggesting is that each of us turn from the negativism that so permeates our society and look for the remarkable good among those with whom we associate, that we speak of one another's virtues more than we speak of one another's faults, that optimism replace pessimism, that our faith exceed our fears."[7]

Just as Debbie J. Christensen dreamed that Emily Hill innately knew that she had no real life unless her sister, Julia, survived, our happiness and emotional well-being hinge upon the unity and loyalty we have for each other. We are not saved in isolation. In this dark world we need to minister to one another, pray for one another, and, like Emily, reach out for one another.

We all have the capacity to bring great joy and relief to the lives of those around us by doing small acts of service. One friend takes an elderly sister shopping. Another friend makes dinners and delivers them just as exhausted neighbors come home from work. Still another carries her computer with her when she visits friends so she can help them make calendars, family books, and DVDs. She is preserving memories for others and validating and connecting them to their loved ones. Great happiness comes when we lift others from the doldrums of life, and best of all, we become more happy and satisfied ourselves.

Years after her handcart experience, Emily captured in her hymn "As Sisters in Zion" the essence of sisters committed to and caring for one another:

> As sisters in Zion, we'll all work together;
> The blessings of God on our labors we'll seek.
> We'll build up his kingdom with earnest endeavor;
> We'll comfort the weary and strengthen the weak.
>
> The errand of angels is given to women;
> And this is a gift that, as sisters, we claim:
> To do whatsoever is gentle and human,
> To cheer and to bless in humanity's name.
>
> How vast is our purpose, how broad is our mission,
> If we but fulfill it in spirit and deed.
> Oh, naught but the Spirit's divinest tuition
> Can give us the wisdom to truly succeed.[8]

The visiting teaching program is unique in the entire world because it sends women to the homes of their sisters to carry the message of Jesus Christ. Our purpose really is vast and our mission is broad. With the Spirit, we can magnify our ability to discern and understand the needs of those we are sent to teach. We can discuss fashion or politics or weather with other friends, but as visiting teachers our visit is no ordinary one. We come to share testimony and truth and to strengthen each other.

In many countries outside the United States visiting teaching can appear to be a foreign experience. For many it is no easy thing to travel across the city to make a Church contact. In India, when I was trying to teach a group of sisters the concept of *watchcare* and what we do for our sisters in the gospel, I relied on an idea given me by my good friend Kris. I simply asked the sisters to get up, turn to the sister next to her, and give her a hug. They hugged and smiled and laughed; the love in the room was palpable. In this Church we love each other and care about each other. That day everyone felt the spirit of visiting teaching and understood what it meant to be a visiting teacher.

I wish I could claim I was always a noble and effective visiting teacher, but on occasion I have been, and I treasure the friendships and blessings that resulted. I know if we have one friend who genuinely cares and reaches out to help us, that friend can alter the course of our lives. One afternoon when I felt distraught with worry over a situation, my visiting teachers arrived at my door. I had even forgotten they were coming. I remember so distinctly the sweet reassuring spirit they brought into my home and how their message seemed to offer a solution to my anxious heart. As children of God we are interconnected and responsible for each other.

Being of One Heart and Mind

The desire to be connected is key to our happiness and sense of purpose in life. I asked my friend Carol what was most important to her. She replied, "Just to know that I matter, that my life matters, that I am not alone, and that someone cares." Maybe we all have a chance to become more gentle and human by letting our sisters know that they matter.

We practice the skills of caring in all facets of our lives. We have been taught that we don't have to look across the world to serve others; we have only to go across the street. There seems something more noble and exotic about serving when it entails a travel opportunity, and we may fail to notice the neighbor across the street who feels marginalized and suffering. There are also multiple opportunities to nurture and minister to others both inside and outside our faith. Perhaps the greatest care I ever gave to others was to those I met when I was teaching school.

After my mission, I went with two friends to teach high school in Wyoming. We were very energetic and excited to serve. It was a new school, and we selected the furniture for our rooms as well as the student materials. Teaching was a joy. Planning excursions and activities and helping with the school play were my dream come true. The students became very dear to us. We cared about their grades, their lives, and their friends. We also worked with Vietnamese refugees and taught English as a second language. We were invited to their homes and invited to dine with their families. I remember eating my first set of pig's ears and loving every bite. To this day I receive letters and calls from our students. They knew we loved them, and we felt their love for us. They made our stay in that tiny Wyoming town a rewarding and rich one. We can all create such opportunities to care for those around us.

Like Emily Hill, we can reach out to others around us and lift them. Our ultimate goal is a united sisterhood. Small considerate and caring acts can have enormous significance. Each sister needs to know that her life matters and that she is of worth. One newly widowed sister in our stake began taking dinners to others whom she saw suffering. She was a talented cook and wanted to escape her grief by giving to others. She delivered a dinner to a sister whose husband had recently left her and her five children. On a cold, snowy evening the distressed and abandoned sister opened the door to see the widow and burst into tears. She said, "You are delivering this to me when you have a broken heart. I can't believe it. Thank you, thank you. It means so much more to me because I know this is not an easy time for you, either." These two became fast friends. Each rose above her sadness by serving and caring for the other.

Is There Room in This Church for Me?

Everyone wants to feel at home when attending a branch or ward. We want to be part of a caring community that nurtures and nourishes. Sometimes it takes a large dose of faith to reach out and help build that community. But we must do it because it is part of the Lord's plan to build His kingdom. That doesn't mean we are immune to a careless comment or prickly question. Yet it is through this kingdom-building process that we become more perfected and better able to face these situations. We are strengthened, others are blessed, and we show Heavenly Father that we understand what it means to serve Him.

We are in reality children of Heavenly Father, and we are inseparably connected to one another. It takes great faith and great courage to love and reach out and continue reaching out to others different from us. But when we do, our connections of caring are deeply intensified, and we become joined at the heart.

President Marion G. Romney taught: "It is the mission of the Church of this last dispensation to develop another people who shall live the gospel in its fulness. This people are to become 'pure in heart.' . . . They shall be the Lord's people. They shall walk with God because they shall be of one heart and one mind, and they shall dwell in righteousness, and there shall be no poor among them."[9] We will accomplish this one single connection at a time.

The Lord would have us united as one body, serving and loving one another. President Hinckley reminded us, "As we are one, we are his.

" . . . We pray for one another that we may go on in unity and strength. If we do so, no power beneath the heavens can stop the onward progress of this great kingdom."[10]

You may be asking, "Is there room in this Church for me?" The answer is a resounding *yes!* There is room for every one of Heavenly Father's children. But we need to recognize that truly understanding this comes at a price—for every member, not just singles. The price is paid as we build caring relationships, serve and sacrifice, strive to live gospel principles, and develop Christ-centered love. And it certainly helps if we develop increased patience and forgiveness. It is through this process—and paying this price—that we find our place in the Church.

CHAPTER 12

A SINGLE STANDARD

*Most of us know well the sustaining doctrines of the great plan
of happiness, and yet we may fail to make connections between sacred
truths and practical applications we should employ in our lives.*
—*Elder Cecil O. Samuelson*

*N*o women try harder to be the best they can be than do Latter-day Saint women. Eternal progression seems programmed into our DNA. But each day we are in the presence of the "great and spacious building" (1 Nephi 8:31) described in Father Lehi's dream, and often it is very alluring. Sister Susan W. Tanner spoke of a society that mocks modesty and violates virtue, making followers of Christ a prime target.[1]

For women of covenant there is a single standard—the standard established by Heavenly Father. We are each unique and individual, and as we apply the doctrinal guidelines to our lives, we can prevent the subtle persuasion of worldly influences from diminishing our unique goodness.

We are desperately needed as examples of goodness in a very dark and confused world. We are "to trust in the living God, who is the Saviour of all men. . . . [and] be . . . an example of the believers, in word, in conversation, in charity, in spirit, in faith, in purity" (1 Timothy 4:10–12).

We all have had times when the way we presented ourselves was not in harmony with the beliefs of our hearts. It may have been an unkind comment, a poor choice in reading, or harsh language. We live at a time that requires us to establish and live standards, to determine guidelines that set the bar by which to measure our conduct. We want to be the very best women we can be. The question becomes how we can ensure that all we do reflects our testimony of the gospel so we are not, as Elder Quentin L. Cook said, "in camouflage to [our] neighbors and co-workers."[2]

Good and noble women and men are being pulled and bombarded by the world in unexpected moments and ways. The time has arrived for us to boldly share our convictions. That is not always easy. In my late thirties, following a merger in my company that I successfully navigated, I was sent with a group of other consultants to a Caribbean island as a reward for a prosperous sales year. I knew few people, and I was the only Latter-day Saint in the group. During the first day I attended professional seminars conducted by my new colleagues and associates. They were adept and bright and capable. I wanted to be just like them.

After work in the early evening I gathered with a group around the pool to socialize. To my surprise, these people whose friendship and professional acceptance I so desired began to talk of provocative and explicit experiences. There was laughter and drinking and a real sense of camaraderie among the group. I knew I didn't belong and rose to excuse myself; however, my escape route was directly in front of everyone seated at the pool. I remember standing and walking away, hoping to go unnoticed. That was not to be. One man called to me, asking, "Does our talk offend you?" It was so unexpected that I had no prepared answer. I had no immediate words to share the truths and doctrine I believed. I simply turned to the group and said, "I am tired. Please excuse me. I'm going back to my room."

They knew and I knew why I was leaving. That moment to testify, in a way that would not offend but share truths that might have blessed lives, will always be lost to me. I think I remember it so clearly because I believe someone in that group needed to hear another voice proclaiming a better way, and I missed my opportunity. I also believe that if I had depended on the Spirit to give me words, I would not have offended them but would have cemented stronger and surer relationships. Yet I was silent.

I told this story to a dear friend who is a bold missionary and extremely valiant. She shared some words from her patriarchal blessing that relate to each of us: "Many will want to know what makes you so different, and you will have a chance to teach the gospel and bring them into the Church and help build the kingdom of God upon the earth." In these times, when your voice is needed, do not miss your chance to speak.

Living Up to a Heavenly Standard

We can prepare ourselves to be better examples by measuring our personal actions by the gospel standards our Church teaches in the scriptures, in publications such as *For the Strength of Youth,* and in the teachings of our leaders. These standards are not for Sundays only. They guide our day-to-day choices and activities on subjects as diverse as physical health, personal honesty, modesty in dress, and appropriateness of entertainment, viewing, and reading. When we measure our behavior and thoughts against these standards, we can know whether we are preparing to return to our Heavenly Father's presence. A thorough examination allows us to make corrections and align ourselves better with the Lord's desires for us.

Brigham Young University president Cecil O. Samuelson noted the gap between knowledge and behavior in his message "Outward Expressions of the Inner Self": "Most [of us] know well the sustaining doctrines of the great plan of happiness, and yet we may fail to make connections between sacred truths and practical applications we should employ in our lives."[3]

Instead of experiencing an identity crisis, singles can experience an identity check, bringing their lives into harmony and balance with all the truths they know. A widowed sister, feeling disoriented and not knowing quite what to do, told me that she had decided to "live the gospel as she had never lived it before." She desired to feel a deeper connection and more protection from her Heavenly Father. For her that meant increased scripture reading, service, and temple attendance. She prayed more ardently, concentrated on her blessings, and sought to care for all those around her. She not only desired very much to fit into her ward but also to marry again. She told me, "The Spirit directed me to act and think and dress in ways I had not before."

Applying a heavenly standard to our lives is no easy thing, but it sends a message that we are indeed women of God. The more we seek to perfect our relationships with others and to conduct ourselves as women of God, the more we will find balance and success in life. One man remarked, "What makes a woman beautiful to me is not that she is just pretty; in fact, she may not be what many consider pretty. Rather, it is the dignity with which she conducts herself and the goodness reflected in her countenance that make her attractive."

Making Wise Choices

Speaking to BYU students, President Samuelson said, "I have assumed, and still do, in large part, that you understand the doctrines underlying modesty, personal appearance, and agency and that you will make correct decisions and judgments when you take time to think about the issues before you. My purpose today is to help all of us seriously and personally consider the specific matters of modesty and deportment in dress and appearance as well as the broader issues related to what we represent externally to others as a reflection of our inner selves."[4]

President Samuelson reminded his audience that our acts and speech and dress have the potential to greatly influence our places of employment, our places of worship, and our homes. External appearances indicate so much about us, whether our dress is that of the military, an athletic team, a gang member, or a missionary. Others know what we represent simply by looking at us. "Although the specific messages, both good and bad, are usually intended by clothes worn, makeup applied, hairstyles, jewelry, and the like, it is also true that we may inadvertently send signals by our appearance that we don't intend to send to others."[5]

Of course we wish to be attractive and appealing. But the world invites us to be alluring and sometimes beckons us to be inappropriate. Societal standards of personal conduct and dress consistently morph, often to a lower and more seductive norm. Society entices us to become and act like less than we are. Church members know the doctrines of the Church, including the plan of salvation and eternal marriage, and yet we somehow experience a spiritual disconnect between "sacred truths" and what President Samuelson calls "the practical applications we should employ in our lives." We may appear and act in ways that do not represent what we sincerely believe.

As consumers we are often manipulated by the evil in the world, which has us think that because something is fashionable it is desirable. The media has collected the sensational and seductive and presents them as a lifestyle to be emulated.

Some may have a tendency to spend more time counting calories and working on their external appearance than counting their blessings and cleansing "the inward vessel" (Alma 60:23). But if we seek more after external beauty and fashion than faith, how will those in our community know what else is important to us? Ask yourself two questions: "Am I dressing for others (to conform to worldly trends or to attract a potential mate)?" or "Am I dressing for myself in clothing I find modest and consistent with my standards?"

"Today more than ever before, [we] need clear guidance in dressing modestly. In many modern societies, standards of modesty and even decency in dress have all but vanished. Styles that once might have been seen only in a cocktail lounge or an inappropriate magazine are now being marketed" to us on every level.[6]

The more we deviate from gospel standards, the more we lessen our ability to feel and be influenced by the Spirit. The more we become like the world, the less sensitive we become to goodness and promptings of the Comforter.

Inappropriate speech and behavior will elicit an inappropriate response. Take care not to become someone who reveals more flesh than faith. If a dress is too tight or a neckline is too low or a gesture is too familiar, the Spirit cannot be present. One young friend worried because her Laurel teacher was teaching about modesty while wearing revealing clothing. Her attire contradicted her message.

A mission president's wife shared with me a letter from one of her returned missionaries, thanking her for her and her daughters' examples of modest dress. He wrote that modest dress "is something crucial that I look for as I am dating. I have a story to share with you. I met a young woman a couple of weeks ago, and as I went to pick her up (we had met once before), she was very immodestly dressed in a low-cut shirt. We went to meet up with my two roommates and their dates. The whole time I was uncomfortable because of this girl's choice of clothing. Not only was I uncomfortable, but also the whole group noticed and was uncomfortable.

"After the date, I apologized to one of the girls in our group for the way my date was dressed. My friend's girlfriend did not know me that well. She said something that really struck me. As I walked in with my date, she thought to herself, *So that is the type of guy John is.* I learned immodesty affects not only the one wearing the clothes but also the one who is with her. Taking out a girl who shows up immodestly dressed shows others that I support that mode of dress. I was embarrassed because I am not like that. I felt so bad the whole evening because the Spirit wasn't as strong as it could have been. Not only does it affect a young woman but also all around her. I am so thankful for the standards that you and your family live, especially your daughters. . . . The way a woman dresses attracts a certain type of guy. And the guy attracted to immodesty is not one that is magnifying his priesthood."

This young man wants a righteous and modest companion. The Lord's way is the antithesis of the world's way. The Lord wants the very best for us. He wants us to magnify our calling as women. We acknowledge this by the way we dress. In selecting films, searching the Internet, and making other choices, we should remember the following:

- I am a dearly loved child of God. He has given me the sacred gifts of a sound mind and a healthy body for a specific purpose—to do His work.
- God wants me to uphold His high standards. My behavior, language, appearance, and thoughts should reflect my divine origin and purpose.
- Living gospel standards helps me be an instrument in building the kingdom of God on earth, and it allows others to treat me with respect as a daughter of Heavenly Father.

Personal dignity is a fragile thing. Our speech, dress, language, and other choices affect how others perceive us and act toward us. Wise women realize this and practice restraint. My husband often quotes President Boyd K. Packer's statement that "the devil does not practice restraint."[7] I remember that principle when I try to evaluate my own behavior and thoughts.

As an example of practices aligning with standards, how we dress

lasting relationships because it admonishes us to reach out to others and away from ourselves. The gospel teaches us to "bear one another's burdens" (Mosiah 18:8) and to engage in acts of service one to another. There is no better formula for developing solid personal relationships and individual happiness.

Conduct

Margaret D. Nadauld, as Young Women General President, reminded us that "women of God can never be like women of the world. The world has enough women who are tough; we need women who are tender. There are enough women who are coarse; we need women who are kind. There are enough women who are rude; we need women who are refined. We have enough women of fame and fortune; we need more women of faith. We have enough greed; we need more goodness. We have enough vanity; we need more virtue. We have enough popularity; we need more purity."[9]

The way we conduct ourselves tells much about us. Rules of conduct vary with culture, occasion, and situation. For example, an affectionate, effusive person might need to pull back in some situations instead of touching or saying terms of endearment that come naturally to her.

Generally, we learn the rules by watching the interactions of others. You may know someone who is quite adept at social situations and who serves as an outstanding role model. There are numerous books (in fact, bookstores are full of them) about how to behave in various social situations, including those of newfound singleness. However, our best teacher is the Holy Ghost, whose subtle promptings can bless our lives and actions in all that we do.

Sometimes the temptations of the world cause us to look to the world instead of to Heavenly Father and the promptings of the Holy

Ghost. Loneliness and our hearts' longings may create great problems for us. When there is no one suitable to marry inside the Church, some may begin to look outside the Church. You may come to care for a man—Church member or not—who would like you to dress more suggestively and revealingly to please him. I have had experiences with a few such men. My heart would hurt because I hated being alone, but I loved my temple covenants and my testimony more than I wanted to be attractive to those men. If anyone asks you to demean yourself or to be less than you are, run away from that person as quickly as possible, just as Joseph ran from Potiphar's wife. This action and its consequences were extremely painful in the short term, but he gained far more blessings in the long term as he proved himself loyal to God.

Some think of marriage as a powerful, passionate, romantic connection. Some imagine that life is designed to be "happily ever after" as opposed to "endure to the end." While the Disney screenplay may conclude with the former, the gospel teaches the latter. Hollywood fiction does not present suitable images of real relationships, real problems, and real solutions. We cannot hold onto fantasies that we think will make us happier when in truth fantasies blur discernment and intensify loneliness.

One single sister rejected a worthy young man because, in her words, "He didn't give me goose bumps when he walked into the room or make my eyes sparkle at just the sight of his smile." She had convinced herself that love would come at "first sight," and her heart would "skip a beat." When asked how she had adopted these ideas, she responded, "I've seen this in movies and on television. I know all the signs of 'Mr. Right.'" Sadly, her views of attraction, love, and marriage had been misshapen by the media.

One young single sister shared with a close friend that she was tired of waiting to be married. She was tired of being alone, tired of supporting herself, tired of making all the decisions by herself, tired of waiting for her dreams. The wait was getting her nowhere. She wanted all the right things. She wanted to be a wife, to be a mother, to have a family, but in her desperation she went about it in all the wrong ways. She was looking for someone who had that special spark, not realizing that such a relationship would go up in flames. She decided to pursue a relationship with a man outside the Church and had a physical involvement. She discovered too late that he did not share any of her values. She shared the story and wept as she told of how she had decided to change her standards to meet those of the world. Her compromise had brought her only profound sorrow, remorse, and despair. She learned—through mistakes and bad choices—the cost of peace and happiness.

Like this sister, we can make incremental decisions that weaken us bit by bit. She did not decide overnight to make destructive decisions. Instead of turning to the Lord, she allowed herself to dwell on the deficits in her life. She diminished her ability to do what was right because she was so consumed with her lack of blessings. She sabotaged her own ability to carry her load.

God has designed all of us in His image. "Through the foreknowledge of God we have been designed to be successful in carrying our loads of trial and tribulation if we stay within God's design limits. . . . We have been designed to succeed. However, when we compromise our spiritual strength through sin or when we deny or ignore our personal talents and gifts that God has given us . . . we risk spiritual buckling and catastrophic failure" in our own lives.[10]

Maintain your spiritual integrity. You do not have to lower your standards to find the company you seek, although the blessings you desire may come after your commitment is tried. You may have to forego the company of those who would drag you down before you meet those who will lift you up, but that is consistent with the Lord's law of sacrifice. Many converts to the Church have commented to me about their transition from their past life to their new Church life. They had to leave old friends and habits behind and search out new ones. They experienced real sorrow and loneliness as they separated themselves from these former friends and established themselves on more holy ground. Every person I know who has made this journey also told me that in the end the struggles brought an inner peace and joy never experienced before. The sacrifice was well worth it.

If we do our best to keep our thoughts and behavior within the standards the Lord has set, we will surely receive blessings. My husband told me that during our courtship, as he left the home of a married daughter, she playfully called out, "Now, Dad, remember who you are and what you represent." He and I have laughed about this daughter's loving admonition as she mimicked the exact things her father had said to her when she was dating. We also knew that her words were true and that Heavenly Father would bless our courtship as we conducted ourselves in a manner consistent with His commandments. He will do the same for you if you keep your courtships and dating experiences wholesome and within the parameters outlined by our gospel standards.

When I met my husband I met my best friend. There was romance, but more important, I found someone I felt comfortable with—someone with whom I could pull weeds in the garden, wash dishes, pray, and confer over problems. I enjoyed his company more than anyone else's and came to depend on his honest feedback and wise advice. I could confide in him, and I had complete confidence in him. He would also laugh at my jokes.

Trust is the basis of every loving relationship. All we say and do contributes to the trust we develop with our family and loved ones. Others will come to rely on us in direct proportion to our reliance on the Lord and our obedience to His commandments.

Single women would agree that there is a shortage of good single men. Our faith and dress and actions may attract a good man who is less active or of a different religious background. Stay close to the Spirit and open to inspiration and missionary possibilities—the Lord may be leading your husband to you. The same applies to good men within our religion—if you are not initially smitten, give them a chance. You may come to discover the love of your life.

A Holy Solution

When we live the gospel it is much easier to achieve trust and love in our relationships. We can maintain that trust when our actions are connected to gospel truths. Always remember your identity as a child of God. Always remember that someday you will be someone's wife and mother and that your actions will have a profound effect on all those who come after you. Both Heavenly Father and Satan know that our actions have eternal consequences. Heavenly Father wants us to keep trying our best. He may allow us to be stretched, requiring us to hold on a while longer, but unlike Satan, who will not deliver on his promises, our Father does not abandon His children.

Be worthy of and hold a current temple recommend. That recommend is an indication of how you live your life. Others around you will know you pay a full tithe, you live the law of chastity, you obey the Word of Wisdom, you are obedient to the laws and ordinances of the Church, and that you follow the prophet. Nothing else lets others know so quickly and comprehensively that you have connected your beliefs to the practical applications of your life.

The purpose of our sojourn on earth is to learn to apply the Lord's laws. Elder Neal A. Maxwell made an insightful observation about the blessings of fully living all gospel laws: "Obedience actually brings both blessings and additional knowledge . . . ; obeying correct principles accelerates knowing."[11]

Living to the best of our ability can accelerate our knowing the things of God. The more we connect sacred doctrines with practical application in our lives, the more abundantly we will be blessed by our Heavenly Father. When we align our beliefs with our actions, we are true to a single standard—the Lord's standard.

CHAPTER 13

EVERY SINGLE BLESSING FULFILLED

*Patriarchal blessings contain individual and unique promises
for this life and into eternity. Those promises are sure.*

As Latter-day Saints we cherish our patriarchal blessings.
Because of the precious and sacred nature of these blessings, many
members of the Church turn to them for words of help in times of
sorrow, indecision, and soul-searching.

President Harold B. Lee reminded us that our blessings are
"'paragraphs from the book of [our] possibilities.'"[1] Sister Julie B.
Beck applied this teaching when she said: "Because a patriarchal
blessing is not meant to be a prediction of all that will occur in the
life of the recipient, we should seek and follow the guidance of the
Holy Ghost to receive greater understanding for our course in life.
The teachings of the gospel are always a guide to a full understanding
of our destiny and privileges."[2] Patriarchal blessings are of an eternal
nature for this life and all eternity. Some promised blessings might
come to fruition after this mortal life is finished. The promises of the
Lord are sure. Our Heavenly Father loves and cherishes us, and He is
true to His word.

What, then, does a single sister do when the longed-for promises in her patriarchal blessing of marriage and family do not manifest

themselves in the time she expects? The years slip by, frustration mounts, and tears flow as she waits upon the Lord. We may be waiting for marriage or children or the promised peace and happiness that elude us.

One sister expressed her thoughts on the subject: "Life goes on and on, and I have yet to find my eternal companion. My patriarchal blessing says in a few years I would make that choice. A few years have turned into twenty-four years. I guess that is a few years to the Lord, but it is a long time in mortality. My patriarchal blessing also says I will make the choice in my mortal life."

She continued, "When I was young, President Spencer W. Kimball always said that we should marry in the temple and wait until we were married for intimacy. These days I'm finding myself wondering if that still applies at forty-five years old. I find myself wondering if I will still be desirable to a man, especially when I may not have my honeymoon in the next thirty years. It's so hard not to feel rejected because I have heard so many stories of men who say that they saw their companions and knew they were the one. Why hasn't anyone looked at me that way? It's hard not to feel like a left-over."

Her feelings of rejection and frustration rang true to me. The wait she describes can test us to our core. I remember thinking, *What is the "due time of the Lord"?* as I passed my twenty-fifth birthday and then my thirtieth, fortieth, and fiftieth birthdays. How could I have received such a beautiful patriarchal blessing assuring me of marriage and family and have none of these blessings be realized? What was I doing wrong?

I wasn't doing anything wrong. I had simply forgotten to maintain an eternal perspective. It is often said that we are not physical beings on this earth having a spiritual experience; we are spiritual beings having a physical experience. Heavenly Father's timing is not the same as ours, and we have to trust Him.

Many of my friends have also felt on occasion that the Lord had forgotten them. They carried their blessings with them to bishops and stake presidents in tears, asking, "Why has the Lord forsaken me? Why is my blessing unfulfilled?" They wanted relief from the sadness and frustration they were feeling. A young bishop in a singles ward in the East told me many lovely and talented young sisters visited him distraught because they were not married and had no prospects to be. He sensed their pain and knew how true and good these women were, and he knew that the pain caused by these righteous desires might continue throughout the lives of some of them. He advised them to pray and read the scriptures and continue to have faith in the promises of Heavenly Father—very simple advice that would lead them to unlock the sustaining power of the Atonement in their lives.

I believe his advice was excellent. Married or single, when we find ourselves asking questions about marriage or about children not yet born or blessings not yet realized, we need to remember that our patriarchal blessings are between us and the Lord. His promises are sure. These moments are opportunities to draw close to the Spirit, not to give up in despair.

President Wilford Woodruff taught: "The inhabitants of the earth do not realize the effect and benefit of prayer. The Lord hears and answers the prayers of men, women and children. Prayer has more power, a great deal, to bring down the blessings of God, than almost any other thing."[3] These words are true, and as we try them out, we will realize their truth.

How do we pray for the answers we seek? We need to pray with all the intensity of our hearts. There is no set formula. For some, that might be five minutes on their knees, and for others it might mean walking continually with a prayer in their hearts. Answers and relief and assurance and peace come in moments we least expect. These are blessed moments when we can connect with that which is holy. That can happen at age twenty or sixty—single, divorced, or widowed.

A friend, Emily, shared with me, "I was just repeating the same prayer over and over again about finding my husband. It seemed fruitless, and I wondered if my prayer was getting through. It was then that I decided to pray a different type of prayer. I wanted to understand what was happening to me. I told the Lord that I had covenanted with Him, and however He wanted to use me to build the kingdom, I would accept. I feel now that I have a purpose and a reason for my circumstances. This perspective has made me stronger and more patient, and I feel Heavenly Father's direction much more in my life. Of course, I still want to marry, but I want to do it on the Lord's timetable."

The same is true of our scripture study. The words of the Lord open our minds and hearts to understanding. If we read scripture and "study it out in [our] mind" (D&C 9:8), the Lord can more personally speak to us. Faith is a real and vital force, and we can magnify it through our actions. In fact, Elder Bruce R. McConkie taught: "Faith is a gift of God bestowed as a reward for personal righteousness. It is always given when righteousness is present, and the greater the measure of obedience to God's laws the greater will be the endowment of faith."[4]

Blessings Are Eternal

What about those who feel they have not been obedient to the counsel given them or who feel betrayed by others they chose to love? One divorced friend who had not followed the advice in her patriarchal blessing felt her life was doomed because she had not been obedient. She felt her disobedience had diminished or forfeited her eternal blessings. Misfortune seemed to plague her life: she discovered that while she was working to support her children, a neighbor had molested her boys. Everything else around her seemed dark.

In an effort to change her life, she turned to Heavenly Father and repented "with full purpose of heart" (2 Nephi 31:13). She became valiant and consistent in her church attendance. There were still struggles in her life. She told me she was still young and immature in gospel understanding when she approached her stake president for advice on her patriarchal blessing. She expected him "to fix everything because it's not going the way I want." She recalled, "I wasn't waiting on the Lord. I wanted a fortune-teller to let me know my future."

She asked her stake president for another patriarchal blessing because she felt her disobedience made receiving her blessings impossible. She shared with me the wise advice he gave her: "Anne, the Lord can instruct us and bless us in so many ways if we are obedient. If you want to know what your Heavenly Father has for you, place yourself in a position to hear it. Blessings and inspiration will come to you in many ways while you listen to spiritual music and read the scriptures, Church magazines, and conference reports. Go home and fast. If you still wish a blessing, return in two days."

Anne went home despondent about financial worries and concerns for her future and her children's; however, she did what the stake president had suggested. She fasted, prayed, and turned to her scriptures.

The Lord spoke to her in a specific way as she read in Matthew 6:31–32: "Therefore take no thought, saying, What shall we eat? or, What shall we drink? or, Wherewithal shall we be clothed? (For after all these things do the Gentiles seek:) for your heavenly Father knoweth that ye have need of all these things." She felt that the Lord was giving her fatherly advice, that He was aware of her specific needs and situation, and all would be well. She felt to let go of her stress and trust completely in her Heavenly Father. She returned to her stake president, smiling, and told him that she did not need another patriarchal blessing. She said to him, "You knew, didn't you, that if I was obedient my questions would be answered?" He replied, "No, but I hoped so."

Another dear friend, Marie, the mother of three children and now married to a man who is serving as a bishop, told me how much she cherished her patriarchal blessing. She said, "My first marriage was falling apart; my husband walked out on me. I remember leaving our small apartment carrying only my two small babies and my scriptures in my arms. I turned back because I could not leave without my patriarchal blessing—it was my beacon and compass. I was at such loose ends, my blessing seemed all I had to direct me. I remember putting the children down and searching through drawers until I found that blessing. I knew God had a plan for me, and if I was obedient He would bless me. Even today that blessing is upstairs right beside my bed. I keep it next to me and depend on it."

She trusted in her Savior and knew He meant it when He told us through his prophets that His purpose in coming to earth was to relieve the sufferings we would experience in this second estate. We are specifically told, "He shall go forth, suffering pains and afflictions and temptations of every kind; and this that the word might be fulfilled which saith he will take upon him the pains and the sicknesses of his people" (Alma 7:11).

Often as I waited on the Lord for the husband and children promised in my patriarchal blessing, I experienced heartache and longing. Only faith in the promises my Savior had given me relieved the pain I sometimes felt. The Lord is patient, and He wants us to be patient, too, and trust His timing.

We cannot demand blessings and expect them to be delivered on the schedule we specify. A friend of mine in California often says, "The Lord is not a short order cook on call to give us what we want.

Obtaining blessings is not like ordering a pizza." When we ask, "Why is this not happening?" and look enviously at others around us who have the blessings we desire, we are following a formula for unhappiness. Coveting always makes us dissatisfied. Perhaps we could instead consider that the Lord has placed us on this earth with a plan specific to us and that our current affliction may be part of that plan. Ultimately, we wouldn't want the Lord's work on us to go undone, even if it stretches us in ways that hurt. Even through the trials, we can be grateful that in His wise fatherly care He is preparing us for life with Him. As we think on ways the Lord is blessing us and will bless us, our gratefulness will increase and so will our happiness.

As we wait upon the Lord, our desires become all-important. There will always be things we long for and pray for that don't come to fruition. That doesn't mean we are not loved of the Lord. I recently received an e-mail from a dear friend in her forties. She had been so excited to become pregnant late in life. (I have never had the privilege of giving birth, but I know it is no small thing to take on the responsibility of a tiny infant later in life when you have reduced energy.) The anticipated birth of a daughter was especially joyous for this friend because she was married to a man who was not the father of her two boys, and she felt the little girl would secure and bless their marriage. In the e-mail she shared, "My physician tells me that the baby has not grown for several weeks, has no heartbeat, and is actually getting less distinct anatomically. It appears that I have miscarried but the miscarriage is incomplete, and I will need medical help to complete it."

A later e-mail arrived, saying: "Because I wrote you about my dilemma, I need to tell you that things seem to have resolved, or at least seem to be in the process of resolving. I had determined that my state of mind was being affected by the way the hormones alter during an incomplete miscarriage, and I decided to go ahead and take the medication to bring labor on right away, to go through what appeared to be required to get it over. . . . I delivered our tiny, tiny baby this evening. . . . We just don't know what Heavenly Father has in mind with who He takes and when. It is very frustrating, but I feel inclined to trust Him in this. I have a feeling this is part of His plan, although I don't know any more than that, and I feel a certain tenderness and generosity, even appreciation, for what I have experienced from Him. I have had a hard time emotionally, alternating between sudden illogical anger and tears, and I felt better right away once she was delivered. I think the confused and changing hormones were provoking a more chaotic state of mind. Now I feel peace, for which I am so grateful. It is amazing we can go through so much and never leave the house."

Her e-mail touched me deeply. Our dreams, whether we're single or married, can be crushed and our hearts broken, and we never have to leave the house. We all have so much private grief that the world is not aware of. President Ezra Taft Benson said, "Some of the greatest battles we will face will be fought within the silent chambers of our own souls."[5]

In all her heartache and desolation, this friend chose to lean on the Lord and trust Him rather than her own understanding. Her battle was real, and in her moments of greatest anguish she stayed true. She chose not to be angry with God but "inclined to trust Him in this."

After I received this e-mail, I called her to let her know of our sorrow and concern and that she would be in our prayers. When I passed the phone to my husband, he said to her, "It will be all right." He shared words he felt were given Him by Heavenly Father. "Your desire was to be a mother and to have this beautiful child. The Lord knows of your desire, and that is all-important." He referred to Doctrine and Covenants 137: "For I, the Lord, will judge all men according to their works, according to the desire of their hearts. And I also beheld that all children who die before they arrive at the years of accountability are saved in the celestial kingdom of heaven" (vv. 9–10).

The Lord judges us by the desires of our hearts. If we live good and devoted lives and desire to marry and have children but never achieve those goals, it does not mean our desires were for naught. It means that desires—the real intents and silent motives of our hearts—are what are precious to our Father in Heaven. We know that in the eternities all things will be set in order, but right now as we live and breathe in mortality we are laying a foundation for our eternal life. Every effort, every bit of faith, and every life—no matter how short—is extremely significant, and we should always stay focused on that. No desire for a marriage or a child or an opportunity to nurture and raise a family is futile. Our sincere desires are known to Him, and they have eternal significance.

While visiting a ward, my husband heard a sister in her mid-fifties comment on trusting in the Lord. She stood and told her Relief Society sisters:

"My patriarchal blessing says that my greatest accomplishment in life will be as a mother. I have never married and have no children, and so I have to trust in the Lord for that blessing to be fulfilled in His own time." What so impressed my husband was the strong spirit and happy countenance of the woman. Her faith and trust in future blessings provided strength to everyone in the room.

We are deeply loved by our Heavenly Father. A stake patriarch addressed the youth and told them how his calling had made him realize the individual love the Lord has for each of us. He said as he began each blessing, it was as if the Lord gave him insight to the pure goodness, potential, and motivation of the person he was blessing. He felt that each person was precious and unique. As more members came to be blessed by him, he also realized how it was possible for the Lord to love each one of us on a personal, individual level. He became much less judgmental of those who came to him. Their external appearance and manner often belied the beauty and goodness within. He simply learned to feel a more Christlike love, similar to the love missionaries have for their investigators and parents for their children.

This same patriarch said that middle-aged sisters often returned to question him about promises of marriage that were made in their blessings and had not yet been fulfilled. Sometimes these sisters would continually focus on a single promise and wait for that promise to be fulfilled. One single sister was very different from most. She too had wondered why marriage eluded her, even though it was promised, but it was not until she was in her mid-forties and was diagnosed with a very fast-moving cancer that she clung to the words in her patriarchal blessing. She had been promised specifically that "if she honored her parents, her days would be long upon the earth." She did not want to die. She concentrated on that phrase in her patriarchal blessing, and years later she is doing fine. She learned that promises are sure and that the immediacy of one promise precedes another.

We should concentrate on all the beautiful promises in our patriarchal blessing and do everything in our power to learn what the Lord has in store for us. There are many promises for each of us. If we read and reread our blessings we can unlock our book of possibilities to help us make decisions and maximum use of the talents the Lord has given us. The Lord placed us here to be productive and grow and be happy. He provides divine direction to us, married or single.

One young sister reported to me that her patriarchal blessing specifically blessed her to pursue an advanced education stating that she had much potential and would have many service opportunities. She is beautiful and bright. Many of the young men courting her have asked, "Why are you studying medicine when you should be pursuing a family? Don't you have any desire to marry?" She should not have to reference her patriarchal blessing to defend herself. In contrast, the young man she is now dating (finishing his MBA) has said, "I think it is wonderful that you are following your dream. Medical training involves so much time and energy, but as a couple, we can work this out because we love each other." She is realizing the significance of her blessing, and the Lord is providing her with abundant opportunities, personal and professional.

Gratitude is also a big component of happiness. We tend to expect our blessings immediately. I wonder if our gratitude is obscured by our high-tech civilization. Everything around us operates at breakneck speed, from our cell phones to the Internet to the television to the microwave. It says a great deal about us that we are a society in which our desires are fulfilled so expeditiously. The speed with which everything around us operates seems to magnify the wait and intensify the frustration and impatience we experience in matters that are beyond our control.

Our fast-paced environment compounds the difficulty of living as God's daughters on a timetable and with a perspective that are not part of this world. When we want things to hurry up, we should consider that the great gifts given to us by our loving Heavenly Father— the gifts of prayer, scriptures, the Holy Ghost, and the temple—are eternal.

Think of the time it took to write and accumulate the scriptures we now have. We have the condensed wisdom of ages. It is impossible to consume it all in a moment and be finished, and the prophets could not write it in a moment either. Paul promises, "The holy scriptures . . . are able to make thee wise unto salvation through faith which is in Christ Jesus" (2 Timothy 3:15). Acquiring wisdom takes time. That wisdom is accumulated by reading the scriptures one verse at a time, one page at a time, and one day at a time. We have to be patient.

As we wait upon the Lord for the desired blessings of love and family, we have a choice to make. Do we turn to Him, keep His commandments, pray to Him to direct our actions and ease our burdens, or do we give up? How do we handle ourselves when our desires and expectations do not come to fruition in the way and at the time we desire?

While Elder Oaks and I were visiting a mission, the mission president and his wife spoke to me about their daughter, a beautiful woman with a lifetime of exceptional educational and social experiences. Still single in her early thirties, she was emerging from deep depression after a failed romance. This precious woman aspired to marriage and motherhood and all the worthy promises in her patriarchal blessing, and she was suffering for having been disappointed thus far in realizing them. Her mother asked me for advice.

I shared with her the experience of a friend I will call Karen, a highly skilled athlete who had torn a tendon in her leg that required surgery to repair. She was sent to a counselor in the hospital before she went home. He said, "I have watched your determined and positive attitude. You persist and try to do your best in every circumstance, but in this circumstance, your physical abilities are different from what they were before. You have to accept that and go on." Karen asked him how to go on. He told her she would have to grieve her loss and then go forward. "How do I grieve?" she asked. He replied, "Feel sorrow, be sad, accept this, and then go on and use all the wonderful abilities you have left. You will not qualify for the Olympics, but your life can be very beautiful."

Like Karen, as I grew older alone my life was not what I had expected, worked for, or anticipated. It was a process for me to learn to depend on Heavenly Father and trust in His timetable for me. I allowed myself to let go of what was not and concentrate on the beauty of what could be in my life at that time, and that has made all the difference. I did not give up hope of marriage, and I did not doubt the promises of my patriarchal blessing. I would not want any single sister, no matter what her age, to give up or doubt. Rather, I encourage single people to embrace the beauty of the life Heavenly Father has given us.

Rather than measuring our experiences against our ideal and coming up short, we should enjoy the great blessings of the moment. When I let go of what I thought was supposed to be and began to accept what the Lord had planned for me, I let go of any disappointment and bitterness I felt.

We are all on a different page as our book of possibilities unfolds, and the best is yet to come. If blessings have not manifested themselves in your life as promised, they will. Our Heavenly Father has counseled us to "dispute not because ye see not, for ye receive no witness until after the trial of your faith" (Ether 12:6). Those trials may include experiences and opportunities to grow that we do not anticipate.

Sister Elaine Jack shared an essay by Emily Perl Kingsley, a mother who compared having a handicapped child to boarding a plane for a vacation in Italy but landing instead in Holland.

"'Holland?!?' you say. 'What do you mean, Holland? I signed up for Italy! I'm supposed to be in Italy. All my life I've dreamed of going to Italy.'

"But there's been a change in the flight plan. You've landed in Holland and there you must stay. . . .

"But everyone you know is busy coming and going from Italy, and they're all bragging about what a wonderful time they had there. And for the rest of your life, you will say, 'Yes, that's where I was supposed to go. That's what I had planned.'

"But if you spend your life mourning the fact that you didn't get to Italy, you may never be free to enjoy the very special, the very lovely things about Holland."[6]

Did you catch that last line? Emily Kingsley found that accepting reality freed her to enjoy her life and her handicapped child.

Accepting the unexpected reality that happens also frees us from the burden of despair and allows us to make our lives happy and meaningful.

There is sanctification in the wait if we turn to our Heavenly Father and through prayer find the peace we need. In fact we are commanded to pray in faith for what we lack. Our Savior asks us to "pray always, that ye may not faint, until I come" (D&C 88:126; see also Luke 18:1). Allow yourself to rejoice in the life you have.

Finally, we should read our patriarchal blessings, our book of possibilities. If we study the counsel given us and follow the counsel, we can rely on the promises the Lord has made. If we don't now have all the blessings we desire and have been promised, know they are yet to come. His promises are sure. If we are obedient, the Lord is bound to keep His commitments to us, and we will not be denied any blessing.

"Seek ye first the kingdom of God, and his righteousness; and all these things shall be added unto you" (Mathew 6:33).

CHAPTER 14

WITH AN EYE SINGLE TO THE GLORY OF GOD

When we focus "an eye single to [God's] glory," we become steadfast in faith and qualify for blessings.

I once attended a Sunday School class in which the teacher wrote on the board, "Right man, right place, right time." A single sister in her mid-twenties entered the room and declared, "Oh, another lesson on marriage!" The teacher said, "No, a lesson on Joseph Smith."

Sometimes we can become so fixated on our present desires that we lose our eternal perspective. As members of the Church, we believe the fullness of happiness comes with eternal marriage. Since my marriage, one question I have been repeatedly asked is, "Did you ever come to terms with being a single member of The Church of Jesus Christ of Latter-day Saints?" Yes, absolutely.

My husband felt I should write about my single experiences to share with other singles, especially sisters. The miracle of my life is not that I finally got married. My miracle was that I came to know that God loved me, and that great gift did and does bless my life every day. Heavenly Father provides us so many opportunities in this challenging world—some magnificent, some difficult, some painful. Each presents opportunities to reason, to choose, to experience, and to learn. His plan also provides us with the knowledge that

261

happiness and fulfillment are ongoing and that beyond this reality of mortality there exists the more important reality of eternal life. That is the message I have tried to share.

For me, contentment came gradually as I became more and more grateful for the opportunities and blessings Heavenly Father had already showered upon me. My single life was happy, and I felt loved by my Heavenly Father. If I were still single today, my life would still be happy and full—to the extent that I would continue to draw closer to my Father in Heaven.

When did this realization come to me? It happened as I turned my will over to the Lord, Jesus Christ. For single persons making their way in a wicked world, this is doubly important. We must never forget that joy is a gift. It is a "fruit of the Spirit," along with "love, . . . peace, longsuffering, gentleness, goodness, faith, meekness, [and] temperance" (Galatians 5:22–23).

President James E. Faust taught us, "The joy we seek is not a temporary emotional high, but a habitual inner joy learned from long experience and trust in God."[1]

Our happiness has the capacity to increase as we become more serene and reflective. One of my favorite scriptures is "Be still, and know that I am God" (Psalm 46:10; see also D&C 101:16). There came a time in my life when it just felt good to be still, rejoice in the Spirit, and enjoy my journey. I didn't need to travel extensively— although that is still great fun. I didn't need to frantically plan out every free minute. I didn't need to always be with others. I didn't need to fill up any empty spots I felt inside because Heavenly Father had already filled them. I did not feel alone and neglected. I felt complete as a daughter of God because I knew who I was. I was not looking for my other half or missing a link to someone else. I knew I was a whole, complete daughter of Heavenly Father. I knew the Lord loved me and watched over me.

In retrospect, my single years were such a blessing because they provided me the opportunity to seek out the Lord. What I initially perceived as an ongoing struggle to survive alone proved to be needed momentum to develop humility and trust in my Heavenly Father. Others, married or single, would testify of this principle as their unexpected challenges and disappointments were compensated by an increased faith. Challenging times can be profoundly character building when they increase our understanding of the power of the Atonement and our conviction that the Savior has taken our burdens and sorrows upon Him. As my trust and belief in Him grew, so did my personal happiness and satisfaction with life.

Everything of worth in my life I can attribute to my membership in The Church of Jesus Christ of Latter-day Saints. The Lord also provided me with meaningful work, good and loyal friends, and Church callings. Many other single persons will testify of similar blessings. I have so many single heroes who are devoted teachers who go the extra mile, accomplished artists who donate their time to the community, and fellow Church workers who sacrifice their time and talents to build others.

A Journey of Faith

I must not minimize the difficulty of the journey. Many of us, married or single, young or old, will face extreme tests of our faith. These tests may be so monumental and life-changing that we will have to call upon all of our inner spiritual resources to cope, to endure, and to overcome. I have come to believe that such testing is all part of the plan because the more we rely on faith and on our dependence on the Lord, the deeper and stronger our personal convictions become. We are here to endure—in afflictions (D&C 24:8), in faith (D&C 63:20), and valiantly (D&C 121:29)—and we are to be lifted up (1 Nephi 13:37), to be not cast out (Mormon 9:29), to endure to the end (D&C 10:69), and finally to be saved and exalted (D&C 18:22; 121:29).

When we focus "an eye single to [God's] glory," we become steadfast in faith and qualify for blessings. We are more peaceful and content. In the scriptures the blessings mentioned are the "remission of your sins," "a crown in the mansions of my Father," and a promise that "your whole bodies shall be filled with light, and there shall be no darkness in you; and that body which is filled with light comprehendeth all things" (D&C 55:1; 59:2; 88:67). We come to know that our Savior, Jesus Christ, is profoundly and eternally invested in us. He knows intimately our sorrows and sadness, and He ministers individually to each of us.

Know too that understanding and acting upon our relationship with the Savior is a lifelong process. This was reinforced for me by our grandson Hyrum. Following his mission, Hyrum, who had served as an assistant to the president, described a spiritual inadequacy he felt in himself in the first few months in the mission field. "I tried everything I could to be a good missionary," he said. "I followed all the rules. I tracted hours and more hours. I prayed and read the Book of Mormon. But it wasn't until I turned myself over to the Lord and His will and what He wanted for me that I really became a missionary."

I have reflected on his words often. They brought to mind the words of another person, who said, "You can do all the things a missionary would do without ever becoming a missionary." Hyrum became a missionary when he realized it wasn't just the things he was doing but the state of his heart that really made him a missionary. He had to realize that he was in the hands of a Heavenly Father who loved Him, and in faith Hyrum turned the work and himself over to Him.

We can do all the right things and still not feel like we are children of a Heavenly Father who loves us. The peace we seek comes as we consecrate ourselves with full purpose of heart—holding back nothing. When I think of learning sacred things, I compare that process to how Pavarotti, the great Italian tenor, explained how he learned opera. It was more than learning the music—the music had to become part of his soul. Our love of the gospel should be like that—it should become a part of us, engraved into our souls.

He Is Always There for Us

I know we have a Heavenly Father who loves us. My most powerful proof of that came two years ago upon the death of my dear daddy. He was my cheerleader and friend for over half a century during my single years. His example was the one I looked to when visualizing a husband. He was a physician, and even after he retired and suffered severe health challenges, he dressed daily in his dapper clothes and bow tie.

He was my confidant and friend. I would often go to him, even after he became blind and ill, and sit across from him at the kitchen table and pour out my joys and concerns to him. He would laugh with me and cry for me. He suffered from multiple strokes and heart attacks and became disabled, and yet I never heard him complain even once. For more than twenty years I feared losing him, and the very thought of it brought tears to my eyes. As many single people can attest, our ties to our parents become extremely strong because we have no mate with whom to confer. Before and after my marriage, my father was extremely dear to me.

On Friday, February 24, 2006, Daddy and I went out for our usual lunch date to his favorite fast-food restaurant, where he ordered the same sandwich, same condiments, and same drink. It was a set routine. The next day when I returned from a Relief Society meeting, my husband was at home waiting for me on the porch. He led me into the living room and asked me to sit on the couch. He then said, "Kristen, your daddy passed away suddenly this morning. I went up to help your mother, and his body is now at the mortuary."

My reaction to his words was so unexpected. I had always envisioned myself becoming totally inconsolable at this moment, breaking down into a torrent of tears. Instead, an intense warm assurance of peace and confidence filled my soul. I have never experienced such calm and love. I had a sure knowledge of many things—of my father being fine, of my Savior, of the truthfulness of the gospel, and of the plan of salvation. All was well with me. I was also given a testimony that all would be well no matter what I had to endure. A thought raced through my head that surprised me. I was convinced that no matter what disaster I faced or calamity ensued, all would be well— so deep was the peace I felt. I knew that our Savior, Jesus Christ, lives and loves us and knows us. I felt divinely watched over, and I knew that my daddy still lived and that I would be with him again.

Know That the Atonement is for You

I know that the Lord is especially mindful of those who are single in this life because they carry their loads alone. I struggled to write this book that it might be meaningful to those who have this extra burden. I prayed that I would have a listening ear and be directed to places and people who could help me write those things that would be helpful to His children. It was after just such a prayer that I felt impressed to go to an evening adult religion class that I sometimes attend when we are not traveling. I went late, hurriedly leaving a pile of dirty dishes on the table.

When I reached the class and found a seat in the very back of the hall, the teacher, Robert J. Norman, deviated from his assigned lesson and began with a new one. He said:

"In the temple we are allowed to see from the beginning to the end as if there were no veils. That should encourage us to understand that with the Lord there are no barriers to our progression if we put our trust in Him. Veils are doorways, not barriers. In the temple we see how to progress all the way back to the presence of God. The Savior has thought our salvation through completely and thoroughly from the beginning to the end and has made ample provision for each person who is faithful. . . .

"Sometimes we forget how powerful God is and how inclusive His plan of redemption is. The Millennium is a thousand years. There is adequate time to make things right. We know that all will be well for those who put their trust in the Savior. . . .

"No one in the Celestial kingdom will wonder why he or she is there or will say that it was easy getting there. They all stayed the course, fought the fight, and when they felt all alone, they turned to the Lord for help to accomplish what they had agreed to do from before the foundation of the world (Alma 13:3–5). I ask you to turn to the Lord to help you. He will answer your prayers for help."[2]

These wise words brought comfort, and I knew they needed to be shared.

Get on with the Business of Life

The important thing is that we keep pressing forward. Opposition in our lives may reduce this momentum, but we cannot afford to let personal setbacks, deprivation, or sorrow slow our spiritual momentum for too long. We maintain momentum by doing the things we know we should do: reading the scriptures, praying, attending church, keeping our covenants, going to the temple, serving one another, and fulfilling our Church callings.

"If we stop, it will take far more spiritual force to get us moving again than if we keep moving no matter how slow or minute that movement is."[3]

No one is immune from influences that could arrest spiritual momentum. "Henry Clegg, Jr., an early Mormon pioneer, discovered a similar spiritual principle (see Gayle M. Clegg, 'The Finished Story,' *Ensign,* May 2004, 14). While crossing the plains, he and his family contracted cholera. His wife died and was laid to rest in an unmarked grave. Henry carried his young son sick with cholera in his arms the rest of that day, only to have him die. Henry retraced his steps to his wife's grave and [buried] his son in her arms and then rejoined the wagon train, now five miles away. He stopped writing in his journal for a period of time. When he wrote again it was simply two words: 'Still moving.'"[4]

My husband faced a similar major loss. He was devastated after the death of his wife, June. They had had an extremely happy marriage and were best friends. It was painful for him to come home to an empty house without the sounds of her sweet conversation and the smells of her good cooking wafting from the kitchen. Some of those who knew him during this period have told me that instead of his usual brisk walk, he plodded, his feet barely leaving the ground. Every night he returned home to his vacant dark house, retired to his den, and worked on her history. He told me he would reflect on her great qualities and their happy times together and weep and write.

He finished writing June's biography a year after her death. That same month, during a visit to the temple, he felt a voice say to him, "Now it is time to get on with your life, Dallin." He knew that his time to mourn was over. He would always miss and love June, but he had to go forward to meet what remained for him to do.

When we encounter stressful situations and call upon our

Heavenly Father in faith, He strengthens us. He increases our natural ability to survive, and He helps us persist even in devastating circumstances.

Life is easier if we take it just one step at a time. My husband once said to me, "I read the Book of Mormon this morning, and I know that tomorrow morning I will get up and read it again." He was describing his lifelong pattern to maintain and increase his faith. We all need such patterns.

Focused on the Things of God

We live in a perilous time, but we have been raised up to live in it. It is no small task to remain focused on the things of God in an often godless world, but we came from heaven with all the qualities required to accomplish this. Stay on the path of goodness, and there will be no opportunities lost and no blessings postponed. Do what is right, let the consequence follow, and all will be well.

The qualities given us include our talents, testimony, and faith. We also have prayer and scriptures and priesthood power. We have patriarchal blessings that give us something to aspire to, leaders who love us, and, most important, the whisperings of the Spirit, the Holy Ghost, to tell us the truth of all things. We can know that we are always precious to Heavenly Father.

We also have the promise that in these perilous times the Church will go forward. It will continue to be a safe haven. It will come forth "out of obscurity" (D&C 1:30) and "shine forth fair as the moon, clear as the sun, and terrible as an army with banners" (D&C 109:73). Its strength will increase and spread. President Henry B. Eyring told Church members during a 2007 multistake conference of the northern Utah stakes that we should proceed with a "wise optimism." So much that is good and wonderful is ahead for all who put their trust in Heavenly Father. It is not a time to become bitter or discouraged when our personal lives are not quite what we wish them to be. If we join our life with the Lord's, only hope and joy await us.

We are unique in all the world because we know our origin and our destiny; we are part of an eternal family. Our relationship to God is defined in terms of an eternal family. We know where we came from. We know the nature of God; He is our father. We also have a Heavenly Mother. We know from the Proclamation on the Family that "each has a divine nature and destiny."[5] We know that our destiny is to return to God to have our own eternal family.

Glorify Heavenly Father

Glorifying our Heavenly Father and our Savior should come before all else in our lives. When Elder Jeffrey R. Holland interviewed Sister Ruth Faust after the death of her beloved James, he asked about meeting the many demands of her husband's calling and still being a wife, mother, grandmother, neighbor, friend, and member of the Church in her own right. Sister Faust replied, "As in all things the key is your relationship with your Father in Heaven and the Savior. We make a mistake if we think the answer is just in time-management or getting a better set of luggage. The answer for us and everyone else in the Church is 'Come unto me, all ye that labour and are heavy laden, and I will give you rest. Take my yoke upon you, and learn of me; for I am meek and lowly in heart: and ye shall find rest unto your souls.' When we do that then we really do experience the miracle that '[his] yoke is easy, and [his] burden is light.'"[6]

Sister Faust's words as a widow are of particular significance to me because my husband is some years older than I am. I was single for many years before we married and, because he is older, there is a statistical possibility that I will be single again. Whether life is long or short, married or single, I know the Lord has always been there for me, that He is watching over me now, and that He will be there for me in the future.

As followers of the Savior we can make a very great contribution in a very dark world. President Ezra Taft Benson testified: "Christ changes men [and women], and changed men [and women] can change the world.

"Men [and women] changed for Christ will be captained by Christ. . . .

"Finally, men [and women] captained by Christ will be consumed in Christ. . . .

"Their will is swallowed up in His will. (See John 5:30.)

"They do always those things that please the Lord. (See John 8:29.)

"Not only would they die for the Lord, but more important they want to live for Him."[7]

My prayer for all of us is that as we seek to serve the Lord, we become the "right women, in the right place, at the right time" and experience the peace and direction Heavenly Father so desires to extend to us. As we keep an eye single to His glory, I testify that He will bless us, even in the most unexpected circumstances, with the capacity to live glorious and fulfilled lives.

NOTES

INTRODUCTION

1. *Preach My Gospel*, 3.
2. Oaks, *With Full Purpose of Heart*, 206–15.

CHAPTER 1: MY SINGLE YEARS

1. Holland, "This, the Greatest of All Dispensations," 53–54.
2. Faust, "Welcoming Every Single One," 8.
3. Perry, *Face of a Stranger*, 147–48.
4. Lee, "A Sure Trumpet Sound," 78.
5. Ballard, "Great Shall Be the Peace of Thy Children," 59–61.
6. Perry, "Called to Serve," 39.

CHAPTER 2: THE WORTH OF A SINGLE SOUL

1. Holland and Holland, *On Earth As It Is in Heaven*, 85.
2. McConkie, "Agency or Inspiration?" 38.
3. U.S. Census Bureau, "Unmarried and Single Americans Week," *Facts for Features*, July 19, 2004.
4. Scott Marsh, KBYU radio interview, "Thinking Aloud: Children and Finance," September 5, 2007.
5. Wendy Ulrich, personal correspondence.
6. Ibid.

7. Beck, training meeting for wives of General Authorities, Salt Lake City, October 2007.

Chapter 3: Single Switch Points

1. Hinckley, "Watch the Switches in Your Life," 91.

2. Scott, "Learning to Recognize Answers to Prayer," 32.

3. Oaks, "Student Body and the President," 13–14.

4. Faust, "Power of the Priesthood," 42.

5. Eyring, "Education for Real Life," 18–19.

6. Samuelson, "Family, Education, and Careers."

7. Wendy Ulrich, personal correspondence.

8. Samuelson, "Family, Education, and Careers."

9. Monson, "Three Goals to Guide You," 120.

10. Holland, "This, the Greatest of All Dispensations," 54.

11. Newell, "A Lifetime of Learning," *Music and the Spoken Word,* April 13, 2008.

12. Hinckley, "Perpetual Education Fund," 53.

13. Donna Lee Bowen, personal correspondence.

14. Samuelson, "Family, Education, and Careers."

15. Oaks, "Student Body and the President," 13.

16. Sheryl Garrett, in Chu, "'Til Debt Do Us Part."

17. Wendy Ulrich, personal correspondence.

18. Taylor, *John Taylor,* 197.

19. *Worldwide Leadership Training Meeting,* 23–24, 30.

20. Hinckley, "Converts and Young Men," 47.

21. Hinckley, "Forget Yourself," 4.

22. Marian Baker, March 30, 1999.

23. Hinckley, "Dawning of a Brighter Day," 84.

24. Monson, "Whom Shall I Marry?" 4.

Chapter 4: Every Single Holiday

1. Quoted in Scott, "Glad Season of Hope and Caring," 3.

2. Beck, "A 'Mother Heart,'" 76.

3. Ibid.

4. "Dating Statistics."

5. Staheli, "Obedience—Life's Great Challenge," 81.

6. Quoted in ibid., 82.

NOTES

CHAPTER 5: A SINGLE DATE

1. Grossman, "Grow Up? Not So Fast," 44, 42.
2. Oaks, "Dating versus Hanging Out," 14.
3. Andersen, "Hold Fast to the Words of the Prophets," 6.
4. Peterson, "College Women Find the Non-Dating Game Confusing," 29, 5.
5. Oaks, "Dating versus Hanging Out," 13.
6. Bednar, "Quick to Observe," 33.
7. Cox, "Spiritual Gems of Life," 4.
8. Penn and Zalesne, *Microtrends*, 21.
9. Clyde Robinson, personal correspondence.
10. Oaks, "Divorce," 73.

CHAPTER 6: A SINGLE-MINDED WOMAN

1. Benson, "What I Hope You Will Teach Your Children about the Temple," 8.
2. Kimball, *Spencer W. Kimball,* 222.
3. Thayne, *As for Me and My House,* 27.
4. Mindy Davis, personal correspondence, May 22, 2007.
5. Romney, "Principles of Temporal Salvation," 3–4.
6. Kimball, *Spencer W. Kimball,* 217.
7. Beck, "A 'Mother Heart,'" 76.
8. Kimball, *Spencer W. Kimball,* 215.
9. Nibley, in Hafen, *Broken Heart,* 93.
10. Packer, "The Choice," 20–21.
11. Hafen, *Broken Heart,* 103.
12. Schlessinger, *The Proper Care and Feeding of Husbands,* 56–57.

CHAPTER 7: A SINGLE DAY AT A TIME

1. Frank, in Telushkin, *Jewish Literacy,* 367.
2. "Karl G. Maeser Honored as BYU Founder 2007."
3. *Preach My Gospel,* 146.
4. Quoted in ibid., 146.
5. Kimball, *Faith Precedes the Miracle,* 99.
6. Zwick, "Ponder, Pray, Perform, Persevere," 42.
7. Mother Teresa, *My Life for the Poor,* 52.
8. Simmons, "But If Not . . . ," 73.

9. Monson, "Mighty Strength of the Relief Society," 96.

10. *Hymns,* no. 105.

CHAPTER 8: NEVER A SINGLE DULL MOMENT

1. Mary K. Stout, personal correspondence.

2. *Hymns,* no. 292.

3. Shakespeare, *Hamlet,* 1.3.78–80.

4. Oaks, stake conference broadcast for northern Utah stakes, October 28, 2007.

5. Used by permission.

6. Packer, "The Play and the Plan," 3–5; emphasis in original.

7. Ibid., 3; emphasis in original.

8. Patrice Tew, phone conversation.

9. Kimball, *Spencer W. Kimball,* 222.

10. Smith, *Joseph Smith,* 352.

11. Faust, "Married or Single: Look beyond Yourself," 35.

12. "Portraits," 66–67.

13. Ibid.

14. Crucy, "Cécile Pelous," 8.

15. Jenkins, "Cécile Pelous," 26.

16. "Portraits," 66–67.

17. Dini Hansma, personal correspondence.

18. Ibid.

19. Smith, "Warning Signs of Infidelity," 58.

20. Kimball, *Spencer W. Kimball,* 222–23.

21. Dew, "Awake, Arise, and Come unto Christ."

CHAPTER 9: THE SINGLE BEST THING YOU CAN DO

1. Lockhart, "One Being Is As Precious," BYU broadcast.

2. Tanner, "Daughters of Heavenly Father," 108.

3. Kimball, *Teachings of Spencer W. Kimball,* 295–96.

4. "Dating Statistics."

5. *Hymns,* no. 301.

CHAPTER 10: SINGLE AT CHURCH

1. See Putnam, *Bowling Alone,* 212, 235.

2. Hinckley, " 'Fear Not to Do Good,' " 2.

3. Hunter, "More Excellent Way," 61.

4. Griffith, "The Very Root of Christian Doctrine," 3.

5. Ibid., 2–3.

6. Ibid., 5.

7. Oaks, "Be Not Deceived," 46.

8. Hinckley, "Converts and Young Men," 47.

9. Faust, "Welcoming Every Single One," 8.

10. Holland, "The Atonement," 8; emphasis added.

11. Hinckley, "What Are People Asking about Us?" 72.

12. Devn J. Cornish, personal correspondence.

CHAPTER 11: SINGLE CONNECTIONS

1. Christensen, "Julia and Emily," 34–35.

2. Debbie J. Christensen, personal correspondence.

3. Broderick, *My Parents Married on a Dare,* 125–26.

4. Ibid., 126.

5. Young, in *Journal of Discourses,* 4:297.

6. Hinckley, *Discourses of President Gordon B. Hinckley,* 1:62–63.

7. Hinckley, *Teachings of Gordon B. Hinckley,* 151.

8. *Hymns,* no. 309.

9. Romney, "Living Welfare Principles," 93.

10. Hinckley, "Except Ye Are One," 5.

CHAPTER 12: A SINGLE STANDARD

1. Tanner, "My Soul Delighteth in the Things of the Lord," 82.

2. Cook, "Live by Faith and Not by Fear," 72.

3. Samuelson, "Outward Expressions of the Inner Self," 13.

4. Ibid., 2.

5. Ibid., 3.

6. Pinborough, "Everything Good and Beautiful," 62.

7. Used by permission.

8. First Presidency letter, November 5, 1996, as quoted in Sorensen, "Doctrine of Temple Work," 62.

9. Nadauld, "Joy of Womanhood," 15.

10. Cox, "Spiritual Gems of Life," 5

11. Maxwell, "Reasons to Stay Pure," 42.

CHAPTER 13: EVERY SINGLE BLESSING FULFILLED

1. Karl G. Maeser, as quoted in Lee, *Stand Ye in Holy Places,* 117; see also Packer, "Stake Patriarch," 44.

2. Beck, "You Have a Noble Birthright," 106.

3. Woodruff, *Teachings of Presidents of the Church: Wilford Woodruff,* 110.

4. McConkie, *Doctrinal New Testament Commentary,* 3:391.

5. Benson, "In His Steps," 2.

6. Kingsley, "Welcome to Holland," as quoted in Jack, "Grounded, Settled, and Full of Hope," 20.

CHAPTER 14: WITH AN EYE SINGLE TO THE GLORY OF GOD

1. Faust, "Voice of the Spirit," 3.

2. Norman, institute class, September 20, 2007.

3. Cox, "Spiritual Gems of Life," 6.

4. Ibid.

5. "The Family," 102.

6. Faust, "From My Generation to Yours—with Love," 1–2.

7. Benson, "Born of God," 6.

SELECTED SOURCES

Books and Pamphlets

Broderick, Carlfred. *My Parents Married on a Dare: And Other Favorite Essays on Life.* Salt Lake City: Deseret Book, 1996.

For the Strength of Youth: Fulfilling Our Duty to God. Salt Lake City: The Church of Jesus Christ of Latter-day Saints, 2001.

Hafen, Bruce C. *The Broken Heart: Applying the Atonement to Life's Experiences.* Salt Lake City: Deseret Book, 1989.

Hinckley, Gordon B. *Discourses of President Gordon B. Hinckley, volume 1: 1995–1999.* Salt Lake City: Deseret Book, 2005.

———. *Teachings of Gordon B. Hinckley.* Salt Lake City: Deseret Book, 1997.

Holland, Jeffrey R., and Patricia T. Holland. *On Earth As It Is in Heaven.* Salt Lake City: Deseret Book, 1989.

Hymns of The Church of Jesus Christ of Latter-day Saints. Salt Lake City: The Church of Jesus Christ of Latter-day Saints, 1985.

Journal of Discourses. 26 vols. London: Latter-day Saints' Book Depot, 1854–86.

Kimball, Spencer W. *Faith Precedes the Miracle.* Salt Lake City: Deseret Book, 1972.

———. *Teachings of Presidents of the Church: Spencer W. Kimball.* Salt Lake City: The Church of Jesus Christ of Latter-day Saints, 2006.

———. *The Teachings of Spencer W. Kimball.* Edited by Edward L. Kimball. Salt Lake City: Bookcraft, 1982.

Lee, Harold B. *Stand Ye in Holy Places: Selected Sermons and Writings of President Harold B. Lee.* Salt Lake City: Deseret Book, 1974.

McConkie, Bruce R. *Doctrinal New Testament Commentary.* 3 vols. Salt Lake City: Bookcraft, 1965–73.

Mother Teresa of Calcutta. *My Life for the Poor.* Edited by Jose Luis Gonzalez-Balado and Janet N. Playfoot. San Francisco: Harper and Row, 1985.

Oaks, Dallin H. *With Full Purpose of Heart.* Salt Lake City: Deseret Book, 2002.

Penn, Mark J., and E. Kinney Zalesne. *Microtrends: The Small Forces behind Tomorrow's Big Changes.* New York: Twelve, 2007.

Perry, Anne. *The Face of a Stranger.* New York: Fawcett Books, 1990.

Preach My Gospel. Salt Lake City: The Church of Jesus Christ of Latter-day Saints, 2004.

Putnam, Robert D. *Bowling Alone: The Collapse and Revival of American Community.* New York: Simon & Schuster, 2000.

Schlessinger, Dr. Laura C. *The Proper Care and Feeding of Husbands.* New York: HarperCollins, 2004.

Smith, Joseph. *Teachings of Presidents of the Church: Joseph Smith.* Salt Lake City: The Church of Jesus Christ of Latter-day Saints, 2007.

Taylor, John. *Teachings of Presidents of the Church: John Taylor.* Salt Lake City: The Church of Jesus Christ of Latter-day Saints, 2001.

Telushkin, Joseph. *Jewish Literacy.* New York: William Morrow, 1991.

Thayne, Emma Lou. *As for Me and My House.* Salt Lake City: Bookcraft, 1989.

Woodruff, Wilford. *Teachings of Presidents of the Church: Wilford Woodruff.* Salt Lake City: The Church of Jesus Christ of Latter-day Saints, 2004.

Worldwide Leadership Training Meeting: Building Up a Righteous Posterity, February 9, 2008. Salt Lake City: The Church of Jesus Christ of Latter-day Saints, 2008.

ADDRESSES, ARTICLES, AND ONLINE RESOURCES

Andersen, Neil L. "Hold Fast to the Words of the Prophets." CES Fireside for Young Adults. Brigham Young University, Provo, Utah, March 4, 2007. Available at lds.org/broadcast/ces/cesfrsdanderson02154000.pdf

Ashton, Marvin J. "One for the Money." *Ensign,* September 2007, 36.

Ballard, M. Russell. "Great Shall Be the Peace of Thy Children." *Ensign,* April 1994, 59.

Beck, Julie B. "A 'Mother Heart.'" *Ensign,* May 2004, 75.

———. "You Have a Noble Birthright." *Ensign,* May 2006, 106.

———. Remarks at training meeting for wives of General Authorities, October 2007.

Bednar, David A. "Quick to Observe." *Ensign,* December 2006, 30.

Benson, Ezra Taft. "Born of God." *Ensign,* November 1985, 5.

———. "What I Hope You Will Teach Your Children about the Temple." *Ensign,* August 1985, 6.

———. "In His Steps." *Ensign,* September 1988, 2.

Christensen, Debbie J. "Julia and Emily: Sisters in Zion." *Ensign,* June 2004, 34.

Chu, Kathy. "'Til Debt Do Us Part." Gannett News Service. Available at blog.moschettilaw.com/2006/06/til_debt_do_us_part.html

Clegg, Gayle M. "The Finished Story." *Ensign,* May 2004, 14.

Cook, Quentin L. "Live by Faith and Not by Fear." *Ensign,* November 2007, 70.

Cox, Jordan J. "The Spiritual Gems of Life." Devotional address at Brigham Young University, Provo, Utah, January 17, 2006. Available at speeches.byu.edu/?act= viewitem&id=1514&tid=7

Crucy, Thierry. "Cécile Pelous: Love and Friendship in India," *Liahona,* March 1992, 8.

"Dating Statistics." Available at www.pickupdate.com/info/dating-statistics.html

Dew, Sheri. "Awake, Arise, and Come unto Christ." Address at BYU Women's Conference, Provo, Utah, May 2008. Available at ce.byu.edu/cw/womensconference/ archive/2008/pdf/sheriDew2008.pdf

Eyring, Henry B. "Education for Real Life." *Ensign,* October 2002, 14.

"The Family: A Proclamation to the World." *Ensign,* November 1995, 102.

Faust, James E. "Married or Single: Look beyond Yourself." *Ensign,* March 1980, 35.

———. "Power of the Priesthood." *Ensign,* May 1997, 41.

———. "Voice of the Spirit." *Ensign,* June 2006, 2.

———. "Welcoming Every Single One." *Ensign,* August 2007, 4.

Faust, Ruth W. "From My Generation to Yours—with Love." Address at luncheon for wives of General Authorities, October 4, 2007. Unpublished transcript.

Griffith, Thomas B. "The Very Root of Christian Doctrine." Devotional address at Brigham Young University, Provo, Utah, March 14, 2006. Available at speeches. byu.edu/?act=viewitem&id=1533

Grossman, Lev. "Grow Up? Not So Fast." *Time,* January 24, 2005.

Hinckley, Gordon B. "Converts and Young Men." *Ensign,* May 1997, 47.

———. "The Dawning of a Brighter Day." *Ensign,* May 2004, 81.

———. "Except Ye Are One." *Ensign,* November 1983, 5.

———. "'Fear Not to Do Good.'" *Ensign,* January 2000, 2.

———. "Forget Yourself." Fireside address at Brigham Young University, Provo, Utah, March 6, 1977. Available at speeches.byu.edu/?act=viewitem&id=812

———. "The Perpetual Education Fund." *Ensign,* May 2001, 51.

———. "Watch the Switches in Your Life." *Ensign,* January 1973, 91.

———. "What Are People Asking about Us?" *Ensign,* November 1998, 70.

Holland, Jeffrey R. "The Atonement." Devotional address at seminar for new mission presidents, Missionary Training Center, Provo, Utah, June 26, 2007. Unpublished transcript.

———. "This, the Greatest of All Dispensations." *Ensign,* July 2007, 53.

Hunter, Howard W. "A More Excellent Way." *Ensign,* May 1992, 61.

Jenkins, Carri P. "Cécile Pelous: Rubbing Away the Hurt." *BYU Today,* July 1992, 26.

Kingsley, Emily Perl. "Welcome to Holland." Quoted in Elaine L. Jack, "Grounded, Settled, and Full of Hope," *Ensign,* March 1996, 18.

"Karl G. Maeser Honored as BYU Founder 2007." Available at http://alumni.byu.edu/Sections/NewsAndEvents/homecoming/founder2007.cfm

Lee, Harold B. "A Sure Trumpet Sound: Quotations from President Lee." *Ensign,* February 1974, 77.

Lockhart, Barbara Day. "One Being Is As Precious in His Sight as the Other." Devotional address at Brigham Young University, Provo, Utah, May 12, 1992. Available at speeches.byu.edu/?act=viewitem&id=632&tid=7

Maxwell, Neal A. "Reasons to Stay Pure." *New Era,* March 2003, 42.

McConkie, Bruce R. "Agency or Inspiration?" *New Era,* January 1975.

———. "Agency or Inspiration—Which?" Devotional address at Brigham Young University. Provo, Utah, February 27, 1973. Available at speeches.byu.edu/ index.php?act=viewitem&id=616

Monson, Thomas S. "The Mighty Strength of the Relief Society." *Ensign,* November 1997, 94.

———. "Three Goals to Guide You." *Ensign,* November 2007, 118.

———. "Whom Shall I Marry?" *New Era,* October 2004, 4.

Nadauld, Margaret D. "The Joy of Womanhood." *Ensign,* November 2000, 14.

Oaks, Dallin H. Address in stake conference broadcast for northern Utah stakes, October 28, 2007.

———. "Be Not Deceived." *Ensign,* November 2004, 43.

———. "Dating versus Hanging Out." *Ensign,* June 2006, 10.

———. "Divorce." *Ensign,* May 2007, 70.

———. "The Student Body and the President." Devotional address at Brigham Young University, Provo, Utah, September 9, 1975. Available at speeches.byu.edu/ reader/reader.php?id=6076&x=21&y=4

Packer, Boyd K. "The Choice." *Ensign,* November 1980, 20.

———. "The Play and the Plan." CES Fireside address at Kirkland

Washington Stake conference, Kirkland, Washington, May 7, 1995. Unpublished transcript.

———. "The Stake Patriarch." *Ensign,* November 2002, 42.

Perry, L. Tom. "Called to Serve." *Ensign,* May 1991, 39.

Peterson, Karen S. "College Women Find the Non-Dating Game Confusing." *USA Today,* January/February 2001, on Norval Glenn and Elizabeth Marquardt, *Hooking Up, Hanging Out, and Hoping for Mr. Right: College Women on Dating and Mating Today* (Institute for American Values, 2001). Available at www.americanvalues.org/html/a-college_women.html

Pinborough, Jan. "Everything Good and Beautiful." *Ensign,* March 2003, 62.

"Portraits: In True Fashion." *Ensign,* September 1991, 66.

Romney, Marion G. "Living Welfare Principles." *Ensign,* November 1981, 92.

———. "Principles of Temporal Salvation." *Ensign,* April 1981, 2.

Samuelson, Cecil O. "Family, Education, and Careers." Address to College of Physical and Mathematical Sciences, Brigham Young University, Provo, Utah, March 17, 2005. Available at cpms.byu.edu/speeches/family-education-careers

———. "Outward Expressions of the Inner Self." Devotional address given at Brigham Young University, Provo, Utah, January 13, 2004. Available at speeches.byu.edu/ ?act=viewitem&id=992

Scott, R. Lloyd. "Glad Season of Hope and Caring." *Church News,* December 8, 2007, 3.

Scott, Richard G. "Learning to Recognize Answers to Prayer." *Ensign,* November 1989, 30.

Simmons, Dennis E. "But If Not . . ." *Ensign,* May 2004, 73.

Smith, Veon G. "Warning Signs of Infidelity." *Ensign,* January 1975, 58.

Sorensen, David E. "The Doctrine of Temple Work." *Ensign,* October 2003, 56.

Staheli, Donald L. "Obedience—Life's Great Challenge." *Ensign,* May 1998, 81.

Tanner, Susan W. "Daughters of Heavenly Father." *Ensign,* May 2007, 106.

———. "My Soul Delighteth in the Things of the Lord." *Ensign,* May 2008, 81.

Zwick, W. Craig. "Ponder, Pray, Perform, Persevere." *New Era,* May 2007, 40.

INDEX